AF673784

fl.

Selections from the Mahābhārata

Re-affirming Gītā's Call for the Good of All

OTHER BOOKS BY THE SAME AUTHOR

1. The Social Role of the Gītā: How and Why
2. The Social Message of the Gita Symbolized as Lokasaṁgraha
3. तुलसी रामायण... जगमंगल-परायण
   (Tulasī-Rāmāyaṇa: Jagmangal-Parāyaṇa)
4. मानस एवं गीता... लोकमंगल-गुञ्जिता
   (Mānas Evam Gītā: Lokmangal-Guñjita)
5. लोकसंग्रहसन्देशः
   (Lokasaṁgrahasandesh)
6. The Gītā and Tulasī-Rāmāyaṇa: Their Common Call for the Good of All

Selections from the Mahābhārata

Re-affirming Gītā's Call for the Good of All

SATYA P. AGARWAL
Ph.D. (UC, Berkeley)
Center for South Asia Studies
University of California
Berkeley, California,
U.S.A.

Publishers:
URMILA AGARWAL
11293, Ridermark Row, Columbia,
Maryland 21044 U.S.A.

First Edition: 2002

© SATYA P. AGARWAL
All Rights Reserved

ISBN: 81-208-1874-1

Distributors:

URMILA AGARWAL
C-157 Anand Vihar
Delhi 110 092

MOTILAL BANARSIDASS
41 U.A. Bungalow Road, Jawahar Nagar
Delhi 110 007 (India)

PRINTED IN INDIA
BY JAINENDRA PRAKASH JAIN AT SHRI JAINENDRA PRESS,
A-45 NARAINA, PHASE-I, NEW DELHI 110 028

To

All Karmayogins
of the world
who are determined
to work together
for a terror-free society

Contents

Preface

During the last ten years, my wife and I have been fortunate to receive immense love and affection from scholars as well as general readers and others, in whose minds we have become closely associated with the task of spreading the social message of the Gītā and Tulsī-Rāmāyaṇa. In this pleasant task, we have got full support from friends, relations and professional colleagues—turning the whole thing into a collective karma-yoga, voluntarily undertaken for the good of the society. Even our grandchildren, some of whom may be too young to understand fully the difference between a 'message' and a 'social message', have displayed warm appreciation of the valuable contribution of this extended family in the field of 'good books'. Moreover, the appreciation of the teenage grandchildren (named Isha and Kiran) was accompanied with a 'demand' that I should tell them a new 'Indian story' everyday. I was glad to fulfill this affectionate demand because this gave me an opportunity to go through the entire Mahābhārata systematically. From this collaborative buddhi-yoga, which was joyfully practised week after week, emerged an inspiring collection of Mahābhārata-stories—and they in turn (after due selection and editorial touch-up) became the nucleus of the present book.

But the Mahābhārata has a vast, ocean-like coverage, as is clear from its own declaration—

yannehāsti na kutracit

i.e. whatever is not found in this book, you will not be able to find anywhere else.

So what approach did we adopt to arrive at the selections contained in the present book? In brief, we utilized our expertise in mathematical statistics and social aspects of religion, to devise a three-stage procedure.

At the first stage, we classified the Mahābhārata into two broad categories, viz. (i) accounts or tales of the long conflict between the Pāṇḍavas and the Kauravas, and (ii) dialogues or talks on issues of dharma (i.e. principles and practices that hold the society together). Contrary to the popular impression that tales of conflict constitute the bulk of the Mahābhārata, we found that more than half of this epic is devoted to talks on issues of dharma. Since our emphasis is on the socio-religious message of the epic, we summarized the tales of conflict in a section of Part I of this book, and devoted the rest of the book to talks on issues of dharma.

At the second stage, we took as the starting point, that part of the Mahābhārata which consists of dialogues or talks on issues of dharma. After a thorough study we found that, out of a total of eighteen Parvans in the epic, we needed to look closely into eight, attaching special importance to Śānti-Parva and Vana-Parva (the other six Parvans being Udyoga-Parva, Anuśāsana-Parva, Ādi-Parva, Strī-Parva, Aśvamedha-Parva, and Mahāprasthānika-Parva). From these eight Parvans, we selected eighteen topics—keeping in mind the close association of the number 'eighteen' with the Mahābhārata as well as the Gītā. Regarding the total number of verses to be included in these eighteen selections (or topics or chapters), we found that the number '700' fitted neatly into our scheme, because this enabled us to give in this book, what we felt to be most important, and it had the additional advantage of providing to Part II of this book a Gītā-like appearance (since the Gītā itself has 700 verses divided into eighteen chapters). In other words, we feel that the socio-religious message of the Mahābhārata is broadly contained in the 700 verses which have been selected from eight different Parvans and which are distributed over eighteen chapters (numbered 2 to 19 in this book), forming Part II.

The third (and the final) stage of selection of verses was needed to fulfill two objectives. First, a linkage between the message of the Mahābhārata and that of the Gītā was to be established so as to highlight the Gītā-supportive role of the epic—this being the implication of Mahatma Gandhi's statement that "In this great work (i.e. Mahābhārata), the Gītā is the crown." Secondly, just as the message of the Gītā has been summarized by us (in our earlier publications) in terms of a fairly small number of verses (viz. less than one hundred), why not do the same thing in regard to the Mahābhārata?

This two-fold objective underlying the final stage of selection of the Mahābhārata-verses was accomplished by us by recalling (from our earlier writings) the ten-point summarization of the Gītā's message (also called 'framework'). The foundation of this framework is the commonly accepted statement that "the good of all" is the single most important criterion of excellence of any socio-spiritual (or socio-religious) approach to life's problems, particularly in the context of the conflict-ridden society of today. More specifically, we took as the reference-provider, the ten-point framework already formulated by us for the Gītā's message (and summarized again in chapter 20 of this book), and then selected those of the Mahābhārata-verses (keeping their total number below one hundred) which expressed the same or similar ideas. The concluding chapter of Part III of this book thus presents the Mahābhārata-verses finally selected from Parts I and II, which re-affirm and support (in a summary form) the Gītā's call for the good of all. On the issue of language, we felt that it would be useful to give the verses in their originality, i.e. in Sanskrit (accompanied with their simple meaning in English).

We hope those readers who do not find their favourite verses included in our selection will appreciate why this happened. In other words, we do not mean to say that verses not occurring here are not important—we only want to say that we had to draw a line so as to be able to fulfill a limited objective without letting the size of this book become too big.

Finally, we should mention that we found it convenient to use the Gītā Press edition of the Mahābhārata as the basic text. We feel that even if we had used the Critical Edition (brought out by V. S. Sukthankar and others), the main results of our study would have remained intact.

SATYA P. AGARWAL

Acknowledgements

The importance of feeling indebted to all those who help us is an essential part of the message of the Gītā as well as the Mahābhārata, the latter providing the most explicit statement on this subject, viz.

ṛṇavantaḥ sadā martyāḥ

i.e. All human beings should realize that they are always indebted to society.

Therefore I want to express my indebtedness and gratitude to all those who gave me the capability, advice and help, needed to produce this book. Moreover, I feel that such help and encouragement came to me throughout my life, both directly and indirectly, and not only during the last ten years which seem to relate more closely to the Mahābhārata project.

To begin with what I received at the earliest, how can I forget that I learnt the Gītā from my father and Tulasī-Rāmāyaṇa from my mother—and my sense of parental worship becomes deeper and deeper when I find that my informal education at home is spearheading my researches into newer aspects of 'lokasaṁgraha' all the time. Such realisation lies at the back of the rather inclusive approach that I adopt here.

Shri Hanuman Prasad Poddar, editor of Gītā Press, Gorakhpur, who was a close friend of my father, introduced me to various scholarly writings on the Gītā and other scriptures. Similar guidance was given to me by my elder brothers, cousin brother, and teachers of Hindi and Sanskrit.

Although my study of scriptures went on, during my stay at Berkeley from 1948 onward, practical examples of karmayoga on a modest scale, under Indian conditions, were provided by my father-in-law, Shri Dwarka Prasad Mital (who was a freedom-fighter with

Mahatma Gandhi), and my uncle-in-law, Shri Dilip Singh Mital (who worked with Vinoba Bhave).

After my retirement from the United Nations, the Indian community in Cairo, Egypt, led by Dr. R.S.S. Sarma and Dr. M. Sivamurthy, who organized so many socio-religious activities, enabled me, during 1988-89, to share my views on the Gītā and the Mānas, on a weekly basis, with members of an active Study Group.

During July-August 1990, I and my wife Urmila had an excellent opportunity to hold discussions on 'lokasaṁgraha' with Gītā-scholars in Canada, of whom special mention should be made of Prof. K. Sivaraman, Prof. Arvind Sharma, Prof. J.G. Arapura, Prof. V. Subramaniam, and Prof. K. Mishra (then visiting from Banaras Hindu University). In June 1991, we had the privilege of talking about 'lokasaṁgraha' with Swami Chinmayananda. In January 1992, we can never forget how Swami Ranganathananda, under medical advice to take rest, asked us to come and see him, to consult about 'lokasaṁgraha'. Dr. V. Madhusudan Reddy and Dr. Karan Singh provided an insight into Sri Aurobindo's interpretation of 'lokasaṁgraha'. Shri Shivananda reviewed for us what he had written on the Gītā and the Mānas in Hindi.

From February 1992, the renewal of my old ties with the University of California, Berkeley, enabled me to start giving a concrete shape to my ideas on 'lokasaṁgraha'. Prof. Robert P. Goldman, Chairman, and Dr. Steven M. Poulos, Vice-Chairman, Center for South Asia Studies, obtained for me a new University-linked identity, namely, as an honorary Research Associate. At the technical level, Dr. Barend A. van Nooten and Dr. Linda Hess of the Berkeley campus, and Swami Aparananda of the Berkeley-based Ramakrishna Mission, provided several sessions of useful discussion on 'lokasaṁgraha'. My first book in the present series entitled "The Social Role of Gītā: How and Why" came out in August, 1993.

In November 1994, the Governor of the State of Maryland, William Donald Schaefer, encouraged me by conferring upon me the Governor's Citation, and by recognizing my writings as an act of social service. Prof. M.V. Mathur presented me this Citation on behalf of the Governor, and added his own words of appreciation and encouragement.

On July 10, 1995, the President of India, Dr. Shankar Dayal Sharma, honoured me at the Rashtrapati Bhawan, New Delhi, for my second book entitled 'The Social Message of the Gītā: Symbolized as Lokasaṁgraha'. Shri T. N. Chaturvedi, M.P. also expressed admiration for my contribution.

In October 1996, Prof. Satish C. Goyal announced that my third book entitled "Tulasī-Rāmāyaṇa: Jagmangal-Parayaṇa" has won the Kunti Goyal International Award. The book-release ceremony was performed on January 31, 1997 at the Rashtrapati Bhawan, New Delhi, and the President of India, Dr. Shankar Dayal Sharma spoke words of praise. On August 10, 1997, the Mānas Sangam, Kanpur (under the leadership of Dr. Badri Narayan Tiwari) conferred on me a special Hindi Literary Award (marking 500 years of Tulasī's birth).

My fourth book, published in 1998, was entitled "Mānas Evam Gītā: Lokmangal-Gunjitā", and this was followed, in 1999, by the fifth book entitled "Lokasaṁgraha-Sandeśaḥ". Honouring these two books, Dr. Bhu Dev Sharma, Dr. Ram Prakash Agarwal and Shri Satya D. Gupta, acting on behalf of the International Conference on Tulasīdās and His Works (held at Florida International University), conferred upon me the International Tulasī Award in November 1999.

During 1999-2000, special words of encouragement and blessings were spoken to me by Dr. Natwerlal S. Jani, who was himself a great scholar and social worker. As a mark of my gratefulness to Dr. Jani (who left us for heaven), I dedicated to him my sixth book entitled "The Gītā and Tulasī-Rāmāyaṇa: Their Common Call for the Good of All." Other scholars and/or activists who gave valuable support included Dr. B. P. Shah, Prof. Ram Das Lamb, Acharya Sohanlal Ramrang, Sri Lallan Prasad Vyas, Dr. M.K. Gautam, Dr. Usha Shukla, Dr. Piyush Agarwal, Dr. Jagdish Rustagi, Shri Ravi Maharaj, Shri Satya Narayan Maharaj, Shri Baldeo O. Girwarr, Shri Rajendra Arun, Prof. Radhey Shyam Dwivedi, Shri P. C. Gupta, Prof. Usha Gupta, Prof. Rajnikant M. Pancholi, Shri Parvesh Swani, Pandit Padmaraj Joshi, and Dr. Sham Narula.

The years 2000-2001 have brought forth an intensification of lokasaṁgraha-related activities. My sixth book (referred to above) was greeted by Acharya Gopal Shastri (on a visit from Banaras) as a significant contribution to lokasaṁgraha literature, and he appealed to local temples and cultural associations to join hands in spreading that message for the good of the society. The Vedic Havan

Sabha of Bowie, MD responded to this appeal, and inspired further by Kedar and Santosh Sharma and Rakshpal Aggarwal, they included in their monthly functions, a series of brief talks by me on the lokasaṁgraha-message of the scriptures. Dr. Gopal Shrestha, Achyut Shrestha, and other members of the Nepali community invited me to give the same message (adjusted to time, place and society) at the Pashupatinath-Buddha temple and also at the annual convention of the Association of Nepalese in the Americas. The Shrestha brothers also made available to me Mahābhārata-related literature of great value for my research. Organizers of the religious activities at Mangal Mandir, including Dr. Kalpana Patel, Pankaj Desai and Surendra Daulat, gave me an opportunity to talk about the social message of the Gītā. To all these and other Karmayogins belonging to the local community, I want to express my gratitude.

Three other organizations of Washington D.C. - Maryland region expressed interest in lokasaṁgraha and wanted me to address their gatherings on this subject. The first one was the Spiritual Unfoldment Society of the World Bank, organized by Nandita Tannan. The second one was the Montgomery Study Circle, conducted by R. Narasimhan, in collaboration with Shiva-Vishnu Temple. The third one was a library-based seminar on social reform, convened by Dr. Pramud Rawat, which attracted a large audience. It was a wonderful experience to talk in detail about a Gītā-based reform movement (started by Rammohan Roy for Women's empowerment), and to receive warm appreciation from activists and scholars, including the famous Hindi poet, Shri Gulab Khandelwal, who was a special invitee to the seminar. I am highly grateful to all of these individuals and organizations.

I am glad to recall that valuable support and encouragement to my Mahābhārata-project was given in early 2001, by Dr. Steven Poulus (referred to earlier), Prof. Vasudha Dalmia, Chair, South and Southeast Asian Studies, Berkeley, Suzanne McMohan, South Asia specialist at UC Library, and Prof. Linda Hess of Stanford University (also referred to earlier). Bay Area Cultural Organisations of California), led by Leela Mathur, Anjana Gupta, Poonam Moonat, and Matra Mashruwalla, added a grass-root dimension to that support. To all these and other scholars/activists of that region, I want to give my heartfelt thanks.

Within my own family or svajanam, in the language of the Gītā, my wife Urmila's role as an active research partner has already been indicated in the above paragraphs. Over and above that, she provided not only constant companionship and encouragement but also very valuable feedback, based on her contacts with temple groups and cultural associations. Technical and moral support came from all the members of the family, viz. Nishkam, Kokila, Seema, David, Isha, Kiran, Priya and Maya. Close relatives who rendered valuable help, include Shri Harish Kashyap, Shrimati Nirmala Gupta, Renu Mital, Dr. K.M. Mital, Shri M.M. Agarwal, Savita and Anil Agarwal, Shri Arya Bhushan, Dr. K.V. Mital, Shri S.V. Mital, and Abhay Bhushan. To all of them as well as to many others who rendered help but whose names are not specifically mentioned (in order to keep this list short), I express my sincere thankfulness.

Finally, how can I write a book on Mahābhārata without referring to the terrorist attacks that took place in USA on 11th September 2001, and in India on 13th December 2001, because a Mahabharata-like situation of good versus evil has again been created by these attacks? Besides filling me with indescribable shock, the new situation made me imagine how Vyāsa must have felt at the misdeeds of the Kauravas when he wrote the Mahābhārata. My prayers for peace to the departed souls and for strength to their families, are accompanied with a firm conviction that all the Karmayogins of the world will work together in the spirit of the Gītā, to bring about a terror-free society. I also feel grateful to those whose sacrifice and strong determination will pull the world out of this crisis—they inspired me to redouble my effort and to complete this book fast, as a small contribution to the cause of 'lokasaṁgraha'.

Before closing, I must clarify that views expressed in this book are my own and not of the Center for South Asia Studies with whom I am associated as a Visiting Scholar.

Gītā Jayanti
26 December 2001 SATYA P. AGARWAL

Part One

BACKGROUND AND PLAN OF THIS STUDY

CHAPTER 1

A Brief Outline of the Mahābhārata Text and Plan of this Study

1.1. The Mahābhārata text, which is the longest literary composition of the ancient world, has been studied by scholars from various perspectives. We view it essentially as a mixture of two main components, viz. (i) accounts or tales of the long conflict between the Pāṇḍavas and the Kauravas, and (ii) dialogues or talks on issues of dharma (principles and practices that hold the society together). The two components (i.e. the tales and the talks, for short) display a variable pattern of inter-relationship—sometimes occurring separately but, in other places, getting intermixed. Our plan in this book (which will be specifically stated later) is to derive a socio-religious message from the Mahābhārata, based mainly on the dialogues (talks) but also utilizing selected portions from the tales of the basic conflict narrated in the epic. Our approach is broadly similar to Mahatma Gandhi's, as summarized by him in the statement, "The author of the Mahābhārata has used them (i.e. the various characters) to drive home his religious theme."[1]

1.2. Before we start looking at the two components (i.e. the tales and the talks), we want to draw attention to the fact that the Mahābhārata is divided into eighteen parts (called 'Parva'). The Sanskrit titles of the Parva's and important indicators of their contents are listed below :

1. Ādi-Parva (i.e. Origins of both the Pāṇḍavas and the Kauravas, and also of the conflict between them).

2. Sabhā-Parva (i.e. Assemblies where gambling took place).
3. Vana-Parva (i.e. Pāṇḍavas' stay in the woods. This Parva contains Vyādha-Gītā).
4. Virāṭa-Parva (i.e. Pāṇḍavas' stay in disguise at King Virāṭa's court).
5. Udyoga-Parva (i.e. Preparations for war).
6. Bhīṣma-Parva (i.e. Ten days of war when Bhīṣma led the Kauravas. This Parva contains Bhagavad-Gītā).
7. Droṇa-Parva (i.e. Five days of war when Droṇa led the Kauravas).
8. Karṇa-Parva (i.e. Two days of war when Karṇa led the Kauravas).
9. Śalya-Parva (i.e. One day of war when Śalya led the Kauravas).
10. Sauptika-Parva (i.e. Assault by night).
11. Strī-Parva (i.e. Grief-stricken widows).
12. Śānti-Parva (i.e. Dialogues between Bhīṣma and Yudhiṣṭhira on socio-religious issues. This Parva contains nine more Gītās).
13. Anuśāsana-Parva (i.e. Continuation of Śānti-Parva).
14. Aśvamedha-Parva (i.e. Performance of yajña by Yudhiṣṭhira. This Parva contains Anu-Gītā and Kāma-Gītā).
15. Āśramavāsika-Parva (i.e. Dhṛtarāṣṭra's last days in the forest).
16. Mausala-Parva (i.e. Self-destruction by Yādavas).
17. Mahāprasthānika-Parva (i.e. Pāṇḍavas' walk towards heaven).
18. Svargārohaṇa-Parva (i.e. Pāṇḍavas' arrival in heaven).

Tales of Conflict

1.3. Tales of conflict between the Pāṇḍavas and the Kauravas begin in Ādi-Parva (i.e. Parva No.1). Parties to the conflict are cousins, viz. five Pāṇḍava brothers (headed by Yudhiṣṭhira) on one side, and one hundred Kaurava brothers (headed by Duryodhana), on the other side. Jealousy on the part of Duryodhana, because of the superior skills of the Pāṇḍavas, was an important factor underlying the conflict. They had a common teacher, Droṇa by name, and Ādi-Parva has an interesting story (summarized below) which explains how Droṇa conducted a skill-test (in the use of bow and arrow) and declared Arjuna (Pāṇḍava No.3 by age) to be the best of all.

> "One day, Droṇa, desirous of testing the comparative skill of all his pupils, collected them in one place. The would-be target

was the head of an artificial bird, placed on the top of a tree. Droṇa began with Yudhiṣṭhira, 'Aim at the target and tell me whether you see the tree, myself and others also'. Yudhiṣṭhira replied, 'Yes, I see the bird, the tree, yourself, and others.' Droṇa then asked Duryodhana, and others (one by one) and they all gave the same answer as Yudhiṣṭhira. Finally, it was Arjuna's turn and he replied, 'I see the bird only, and nothing else.' Droṇa said, 'Describe the bird', and Arjuna replied, 'I can't, because I see only its head.' Droṇa then explained to all of his pupils that Arjuna was the best of them because of his pin-pointed concentration."[2]

1.4. After the death of Pāṇḍu (i.e. father of the five Pāṇḍavas), all the cousins (i.e. the Pāṇḍavas and the Kauravas) lived together in Hastināpur, the capital city, under the care of the blind king Dhṛtarāṣṭra (who was Pāṇḍu's brother). Duryodhana realized that, although his own skill in the use of mace was comparable to that of Bhīma (Pāṇḍava No.2 by age), the latter was far superior in boxing, weight-lifting, etc. Duryodhana's jealousy gave way to criminality and he started hatching a plot to put an end to Bhīma's life :

tato balamatikhyātaṁ
dhārtarāṣṭraḥ pratāpavān
bhīmasenasya tajjñātvā
duṣṭabhāvamadarśayat (I.127.25)

Simple Meaning—Then Duryodhana, himself quite powerful, but seeing that Bhīma displayed far greater might, began to show hostility towards him.

Ādi-Parva says that Vyāsa (who was like grandfather to the Pāṇḍavas as well as the Kauravas), predicted that unrighteous acts of the Kauravas will bring disaster to all :

vyāso mātaramabravīt....
kurūṇāmanayāccāpi
pṛthivī na bhaviṣyati (I.127. 5,8)

Simple Meaning—Vyāsa told his mother, "Because of the unjust attitude of the Kauravas, the whole world will face calamity."

Duryodhana's plot to kill Bhīma by poisoning him and throwing him into water did not succeed, but Yudhiṣṭhira (anxious to avoid open hostility) advised Bhīma not to tell any one about this incident :

tato yudhiṣṭhiro rājā
bhīmamāha vaco'rthavat
tūṣṇīṁ bhava na te jalpyaṁ
idaṁ kāryaṁ kathancana (I.128.34)

Simple Meaning—Then King Yudhiṣṭhira advised Bhīma, "Observe silence on this point—don't tell any one about what they did against you."

1.5. Mention should be made of the attempts made by Bhīṣma and Vidura to protect the Pāṇḍava brothers from the evil designs of Duryodhana. Bhīsma was the oldest (male) member of the royal family—he was called 'pitāmaha' (grandfather). He was known for his knowledge of dharma and he expressed his opinion fearlessly, to king Dhṛtarāṣṭra and to others as well. Vidura was Advisor to Dhṛtarāṣṭra—the latter seeking his advice on all important matters, but not always accepting it. Vidura played a crucial role in saving the lives of the Pāṇḍava brothers and their mother Kuntī, because otherwise they would have been burnt to death in an inflammable house (this was the last plot of Duryodhana described in Ādi-Parva). Vidura secretly told Yudhiṣṭhira about the plot and the way the Pāṇḍavas could escape into the woods. As a result, Duryodhana remained (for some time) under the wrong impression that the Pāṇḍavas have perished, while the five brothers and their mother secretly moved on, disguised as brahmins.

1.6. Two important achievements of the Pāṇḍavas relate to this period of their life. The first one was their putting an end to the terror that a demon (named Vaka) had caused to the society—the demon had thought of himself as the strongest being but Bhīma was able to kill him, inspired by his mother's advice :

etāvāneva puruṣaḥ
kṛtaṁ yasmin na naśyati (I.161.14)

Simple Meaning—He alone should be called a man who does good to society, recognizing that society has done good to him.

The second achievement of the Pāṇḍavas was the winning of Draupadī as a bride—this was due to Arjuna's unique performance as an archer. When mother Kuntī was told by the Pāṇḍavas, 'We have obtained alms today' (without giving any hint that this was Draupadī), the mother said, 'All five of you share the alms.' Thus Draupadī became the common wife of the five Pāṇḍava brothers.

1.7. When the latest news about the Pāṇḍavas reached Hastināpur, Dhṛtarāṣṭra invited them and it appeared that the Kauravas and the Pāṇḍavas could co-exist peacefully, the former at Hastināpur and the latter at the newly constructed (second) capital at Indraprastha. After some time, the Pāṇḍavas, with the help of Lord Kṛṣṇa, put an end to the cruel rule of Jarāsandha in Magadha who had planned to put to death a large number of subordinate kings. Gradually, the Pāṇḍavas extended their sovereignty and were in a position to declare themselves as the most powerful rulers on earth. Duryodhana too was invited to the grand celebrations, but the newly aroused jealousy in the minds of the Kauravas proved to be a turning point in the Mahābhārata story.

1.8. Duryodhana sought the help of his uncle, Śakuni who was an expert in gambling and who had no scruples to playing unfair games in order to ruin his opponent. The Pāṇḍava chief, Yudhiṣṭhira, who was an embodiment (or son) of Dharma, somehow yielded to the temptation of gambling, and agreed to play. Since Śakuni's wickedness was widely known, we wonder why Yudhiṣṭhira became such a silly victim and lost everything—the kingdom, his brothers, his own self, and finally, Draupadī too. At this point, Karṇa (who was ignorant about his biological parents but was brought up by a charioteer) made the most unrighteous suggestion to Duryodhana that Draupadī should be brought to the assembly hall as a slave. Duryodhana's younger brother, Duḥśāsana committed the crime of dragging Draupadī to the hall, and he even tried to pull off her dress, but the Almighty God listened to Draupadī's prayers and frustrated Duḥśāsana's criminal attempt (by providing, as if by magic, an inexhaustible length to Draupadī's dress). The incredibly vulgar scene triggered off by Duryodhana, with the support of the wicked trio (Śakuni, Karṇa and Duḥśāsana) finally came to an end when king Dhṛtarāṣṭra ordered the restoration of freedom to Draupadī. Even the kingdom of Yudhiṣṭhira was given back to him by Dhṛtarāṣṭra, but the Pāṇḍavas lost the kingdom again through a second game of unfair gambling, the punishment this time being that they were doomed to live in the woods for twelve years and thereafter spend one year in disguise (without being recognized).

This marks the end of Parva No.2 in the Mahābhārata, and the feelings of Janamejaya (the great grandson of Arjuna) at this point of story-listening are summarized in the following verse :

evaṁ dyūtajitāḥ pārthāḥ
kopitāśca durātmabhiḥ
dhārtarāṣṭraiḥ sahāmātyair
nikṛtyā dvijasattama
śrāvitāḥ paruṣā vācaḥ
sṛjadbhirvairamuttamam (III.1.1-2)

Simple Meaning—O Vaiśampāyana, so far you have told me that Duryodhana and his associates (who were evil-minded) deceitfully defeated my ancestors at gambling—who then became enraged. Also, that the use of harsh language by the Kauravas brought about fierce animosity between the two parties.

1.9. Since this section of the epic is devoted to tales of conflict between the Pāṇḍavas and the Kauravas, we skip the next thirteen years (the events of which are narrated in the Mahābhārata Parvas No. 3 and 4, and which contain relatively minor skirmishes). Parva No.5 describes how Vidura and Lord Kṛṣṇa tried their best to avert war. However, Duryodhana refused to do anything that could be called a just settlement of the dispute and therefore the great war became inevitable. Parva No.6 begins by giving a picturesque description of the two huge armies facing each other at Kurukṣetra, waiting for final orders to start fighting. At this critical juncture, Arjuna became confused as to whether he should fight against Bhīṣma and Droṇa (who were supporting Duryodhana). Lord Kṛṣṇa's advice to Arjuna is called 'Bhagavad-Gītā (or Gītā for short). Kṛṣṇa was helping Arjuna as his charioteer—giving advice but not directly participating in the fight. After listening to the Gītā, Arjuna agreed to do his duty as a supporter of Yudhiṣṭhira (who was fighting for a right cause), and the great war began.

1.10. Number eighteen is the most significant number, for the Gītā as well as the Mahābhārata. The Gītā has eighteen chapters (and the Mahābhārata's eighteen Parva's are already listed in para 1.2). The Mahābhārata war lasted eighteen days. Total participants in the war numbered eighteen akṣauhiṇī's (army divisions), of whom the Pāṇḍavas had only seven while the Kauravas had eleven. The Nārāyaṇīya Dharma section of the Mahābhārata (ref. chapter 13 of this book) has eighteen chapters while the Anu-Gītā section (ref. chapter 18 of this book) has thirty-six chapters (i.e. eighteen plus eighteen).

1.11. The commander-in-chief of the Pāṇḍava forces was Dṛṣṭdyumna, who was Draupadī's brother. On the Kaurava side, Bhīṣma led the forces for the first ten days, and after his fall (not death), Droṇa was the leader for five days, and after his death, Karṇa was the leader for two days, and after his death, Śalya was the leader for one day (which was the last day of the war).

1.12. We shall briefly refer to only a few points relating to the war. Bhīṣma, the grandfather, was practically invincible, so how did he fall? He himself told the Pāṇḍavas (whose cause he supported, although unable to leave the Kauravas physically) that he will not fight against Śikhaṇḍī (who was a woman by birth but later had a change of sex). So Arjuna placed Śikhaṇḍī in the front and, using him as a means to dissuade Bhīṣma from fighting, Arjuna shot arrows to bring Bhīṣma down. However, Bhīṣma had yogic powers to determine the time of his own death (which occurred later at the end of Parva No.13).

1.13. Droṇa's death too had to be brought about by a special device, based on the knowledge that he will stop fighting if he heard of his son's death. His son's name was Aśvatthāmā, so an elephant having the same name was killed by the Pāṇḍavas, and Yudhiṣṭhira announced 'Aśvatthāmā is dead' (adding in a low voice that it was an elephant). Droṇa believed that Yudhiṣṭhira always speaks the truth, so he stopped fighting and was killed. About the punishment that Yudhiṣṭhira received for telling a lie, K.M. Ganguli (who translated the Mahābhārata into English) wrote, 'Before this, Yudhiṣṭhira's car had stayed at a height of four fingers' breadth from the surface of the earth. After, however, he had said that untruth, his car touched the earth.'[3]

1.14. Parva's No.7 (Droṇa-Parva) also contains a heart-rending account of how the young son of Arjuna (Abhimanyu by name) was killed by the Kauravas. Abhimanyu's importance lies not only in the supreme heroism that he displayed, but also in the fact that his (posthumous) son (Parīkṣita by name) ultimately succeeded Yudhiṣṭhira on the throne. The Mahābhārata says that even birds lamented over the passing away of Abhimanyu, by crying out, 'Alas, this one lies on the field, slain, while fighting singly, by six mighty warriors of the Kaurava army, headed by Droṇa and Karṇa.'[4]

1.15. The complicated story of Karṇa's life and death is told in the Mahābhārata, piece by piece, in a very moving style. He was born to Kuntī (mother of the Pāṇḍavas) before her marriage, so she abandoned him as an infant. A charioteer brought Karṇa up, who (i.e. Karṇa) proved to be a great archer, comparable to Arjuna. Karṇa did not know about his biological parents. Duryodhana (anxious to have Karṇa on his side) conferred a big title on him, and they became close friends too. Just before the commencement of the war preparations, Lord Kṛṣṇa told Karṇa about his close biological relationship with the Pāṇḍavas, and appealed to him to change sides, but Karṇa refused to do so. On the seventeenth day of the war, when Karṇa was fighting against Arjuna, the wheel of Karṇa's chariot got stuck in mud. Karṇa argued, 'It is against dharma to hit me under these circumstances,' but Lord Kṛṣṇa told him that an appeal to dharma can not be made by Karṇa who had himself committed so many unrighteous acts. So Karṇa lost his life at the hands of Arjuna.

1.16. The eighteenth (and the last) day of the war brought Duryodhana and Bhīma face to face, fighting with mace. The only way to kill Duryodhana was to hit him on his thigh—but that was against the normal rules of the war. The Mahābhārata condones Bhīma's breaking of the rule at this time because Duryodhana had himself broken the legal and moral codes so many times. The insult done to Draupadī by the wicked Kauravas was avenged by Bhīma.

1.17. After the last day of fighting was over, (i.e. when the Kauravas had been defeated), a terrible massacre of most of the surviving members of the Pāṇḍava forces was carried out at night by Droṇa's son (and his associates). The Mahābhārata says that the five Pāṇḍava brothers remained safe, because they were protected by Lord Kṛṣṇa :

> *yatrāmucyanta te pārthāḥ*
> *pañca kṛṣṇabalāśrayāt* (I.2.301)

Simple Meaning—The five Pāṇḍava brothers escaped unhurt (from this massacre) because they were under the protective care of Lord Kṛṣṇa.

Details of this massacre are given in Parva No.10. As a result, although the Pāṇḍavas won the war, there was not a single surviving member of their next generation who could succeed Yudhiṣṭhira on the throne. Arjuna's grandson, Parīkṣita, who was born later (reference para 1.14), gradually grew up to take charge. The tragic chain of events, described in great detail by the Mahābhārata, prompted Mahatma Gandhi to draw the following conclusion :

> "The author of the Mahābhārata has not established the necessity of physical warfare; on the contrary he has proved its futility. He has made the victors shed tears of sorrow and repentance, and has left them nothing but a legacy of miseries.
> .... In this great work the Gītā is the crown. Its second chapter, instead of teaching the rules of physical warfare, tells us how a perfected man is to be known. In the characteristics of the perfected man of the Gītā, I do not see any to correspond to physical warfare. Its whole design is inconsistent with the rules of conduct governing the relations between warring parties... But if the Gītā believed in ahiṁsā (non-violence)... why did the author take a war-like illustration? When the Gītā was written, although people believed in ahīṁsā, wars were not only not taboo, but nobody observed the contradiction between them and ahiṁsā."[5]

Talks on Issues of Dharma

1.18. Now we look at the talks on issues of dharma, that constitute an equally (or even more) important part of the Mahābhārata. In fact, from the viewpoint of the number of pages, more than half of the Mahābhārata is devoted to such talks or dialogues. The following seven Parva's are particularly relevant for identifying dialogues on issues of dharma (other than Bhagavad-Gītā which occurs in Bhīṣma-Parva) :

(a) Vana-Parva
(b) Udyoga-Parva
(c) Śānti-Parva
(d) Anuśāsana-Parva
(e) Aśvamedha-Parva

(f) Mahāprasthānika-Parva
(g) Svargārohaṇa-Parva

1.19. The Parva-Saṁgraha section of Ādi - Parva (which provides an advance indication of the main topics of each Parva) refers to Vana - Parva as 'mahat' :

ataḥ paraṁ tritīyaṁ tu
jñeyamāraṇyakaṁ mahat (I.2.143)

Simple Meaning—The third Parva (i.e. Vana - Parva) is fit to be called 'great'.

Vana - Parva is great, not only because it is the second longest Parva (the longest being Śānti - Parva), but also because three Ṛṣis (Brihadaśva, Lomaśa and Mārkaṇḍeya) narrate to Yudhiṣṭhira in this Parva a large number of religious stories. Furthermore, the famous dialogue betwen Yudhiṣṭhira and Yakṣa (who was Dharmarāja in disguise), which was told by Vaiśampāyana, is also included in Vana-Parva. We list below seven important stories that were narrated by the three Ṛṣis and Vaiśampāyana :

(i) Nala and Damayantī
(ii) Dadhīci
(iii) Vyādha-Gītā (preceded by a housewife's advice)
(iv) Rāmāyaṇa
(v) Sāvitrī
(vi) Śivi
(vii) Yakṣa-Yudhiṣṭhira dialogue

Out of these, we shall present (ii), (iii), (v), (vi) and (vii) in some detail in chapters three to six (combining (ii) and (vi) together in chapter three).

1.20. Udyoga-Parva, at the very start, provides a good example where preparation for war goes hand-in-hand with dialogues of the two parties with Lord Kṛṣṇa—the dialogues bringing out the difference between spirituality and materialism. In order to gather support for their respective causes, both Arjuna and Duryodhana went to Dvārakā, the capital city of Kṛṣṇa's Kingdom. Duryodhana arrived there first. He was admitted to the room where Kṛṣṇa was taking a nap. There were two chairs for visitors, one near His head and the other near His feet. Duryodhana, out of arrogance, occupied the chair near Kṛṣṇa's head. Shortly thereafter, Arjuna arrived, and, out of respect for Kṛṣṇa, he was glad to occupy the chair near His feet.

When Kṛṣṇa got up, He first saw Arjuna and started talking with him. Duryodhana intervened and said that he was the first to arrive there. Aftert listening to both of them, Kṛṣṇa said, "I want to help both of you. I shall divide into two parts whatever I have. In part one, I include myself, alone without any army, and with my further declaration that I will not fight. In part two, I include my army, ready to fight. Out of these two options, tell me, Arjuna, what is your preference?"

Arjuna replied immediately, "Kṛṣṇa, I choose you. Whether you fight or not, I want you."

Duryodhana felt happy and said, "I am fully satisfied with the second option, i.e. the army, ready to fight."

1.21. After Duryodhana had left with the army, Lord Kṛṣṇa spoke to Arjuna, "It seems that you did not think properly while making your choice. Since I will not fight, what use shall I be to you? Perhaps you ought to have chosen the army instead."

Arjuna smiled and said, " I have thought out the entire strategy. You will not fight, but you can still be my charioteer."

And the Mahābhārata describes how Lord Kṛṣṇa played a crucial role for ensuring Arjuna's victory. In fact, the Gītā shows that Arjuna not only placed the reins of his horses in Lord Kṛṣṇa's hands, but he also became His disciple, in thought, word and deed.

The message that we get from the above for our present discussion is that Duryodhana's preference for the army, even at the cost of losing Lord Kṛṣṇa, gave a clear indication, in advance, that he was following the path of self-destruction.

1.22. When Dhṛtarāṣṭra got the news that Lord Kṛṣṇa will support the Pāṇḍavas, he became so worried that he could not even sleep. He then sought the advice of Vidura who was not only his advisor but also Dharma's incarnation. Vidura's advice given to Dhṛtarāṣṭra in Udyoga - Parva is called 'Vidura - Nīti' (i.e. advice based on morality and justice). Chapter seven of this book is devoted to Vidura-Nīti. Advance intimation of this is given in the Parva-Saṁgraha section of Ādi-Parva in the following verses :

śrutvā ca pāṇḍavān yatra
vāsudevapurogamān

prajāgaraḥ samprajajñe
dhṛtarāṣṭrasya cintayā
viduro yatra vākyāni
vicitrāṇi hitāni ca
śrāvayāmāsa rājānaṁ
dhṛtarāṣṭraṁ manīṣiṇaṁ (I.2.227-8)

Simple Meaning—When Dhṛtarāṣṭra heard about Lord Kṛṣṇa's assurance of support to the Pāṇḍavas, he spent a sleepless night, full of anxiety. It was on that occasion that Vidura spoke words of widsom, which were intended to do good to the king (i.e. Dhṛtarāṣṭra).

1.23. Immediately after listening to Vidura-Nīti, Dhṛtarāṣṭra expressed a desire for a continuation of similar conversation on dharma. Vidura suggested the name of Ṛṣi Sanat-Sujāta who was the immortal son of Brahmā, and who, even after attaining the status of a Ṛṣi, continued to look very young. The Parva-Saṁgraha section of Ādi-Parva says that the dialogue between Dhṛtarāṣṭra and this Ṛṣi, narrated in Udyoga-Parva, was based on the highest spiritual knowledge :

tathā sanatsujātena
yatrādhyātmamanuttamaṁ
manastāpānvito rājā
śrāvitaḥ śokalālasaḥ (I.2.229)

Simple Meaning—Ṛṣi Sanat-Sujāta recited to the anxious and sorrowing monarch the excellent truths of Vedantic philosophy.

We shall summarize Sanat-Sujāta's teachings in chapter eight.

1.24. One more section of Udyoga-Parva deserves to be mentioned at this point—and this relates to Lord Kṛṣṇa's speech at the Kaurava assembly because He tried to persuade Dhṛtarāṣṭra to control the unrighteousness of Duryodhana. The Mahābhārata attaches much importance to this speech, as reflected in the reference thereto in the Parva-Saṁgraha section of Ādi-Parva :

yatra kṛṣṇo dayāpannaḥ
sandhimicchan mahāmatiḥ
svayamāgācchamaṁ kartuṁ
nagaraṁ nāgasāvhayaṁ
pratyākhyānaṁ ca kṛṣṇasya

rājñā duryodhanena vai
śamārthe yācamānasya
pakṣayorubhayorhitaṁ (I.2.231-2)

Simple Meaning—Moved by compassion and a strong desire for peace, Kṛṣṇa went personally to the Kaurava capital, Hastināpur, to try to avert war. Although Kṛṣṇa's ideas were for the benefit of both the parties, Duryodhana opposed them.

We shall present Kṛṣṇa's plea in chapter nine.

1.25. Śānti-Parva is the longest Parva in the Mahābhārata, accounting for nearly one-fifth of the entire epic. This Parva has three distinct parts :

(a) Rāja-dharma i.e. dharma of the kings
(b) Āpad-dharma i.e. dharma adjusted to difficult circumstances
(c) Mokṣa-dharma i.e. dharma leading to mokṣa or salvation.

Such a comprehensive coverage of dharma is achieved through a long dialogue between Bhīṣma and Yudhiṣṭhira. As we mentioned in para 1.12, Bhīṣma fell down on the battlefield on the tenth day of the war, but he did not die because he had the yogic power to determine the time of his passing away. After the war was over, although Yudhiṣṭhira became king, he felt unhappy that so many lives of near and dear ones were lost. Lord Kṛṣṇa tried to console him and then suggested that, since Bhīṣma (the grandfather who had immense knowledge) was still alive, Yudhiṣṭhira should respectfully go to him and hear his words of wisdom on all aspects of dharma :

sa hi bhūtaṁ bhaviṣyacca
bhavacca bharatarṣabha
vetti dharmavidāṁ śreṣṭhaṁ
tamasmi manasā gataḥ ....
tad yudhiṣṭhira gāṅgeyaṁ
bhīṣmaṁ bhīmaparākramaṁ
abhigamyopasaṃgṛhya
pṛccha yat te manogataṁ (XII.46,19,21)

Simple Meaning—Kṛṣṇa said to Yudhiṣṭhira, 'I have been thinking of Bhīṣma, who knows dharma, who has knowledge of past, present and future, and who can be called 'śreṣṭha' (guide to others as in Gītā III.21). I suggest that you call on him, respectfully, and seek his advice on all the questions that arise in your mind.'

1.26. While answering Yudhiṣṭhira's questions—which fall under three broad categories mentioned in the preceding paragraph—Bhīṣma adopted a style of illustrating most of his replies with the help of a story. In this way, there are as many as seventy-five stories in Śānti-Parva. Probably the most famous of these stories (from the socio-religious point of view) is based on the dialogue between Tulādhāra (a person engaged in trade) and Jājali (a brahmin). Another important story is related to Nārāyaṇīya dharma. Out of the remaining stories, as many as nine convey a message which bears resemblance to a part of the teachings of Bhagavad-Gītā—these stories are often referred to as Gītās. Selections from these and some other stories will be presented in chapters eleven to fifteen of this book. As an indicator of the importance attached to each of the three divisions of Śānti-Parva, we quote below four verses (two of them partly) from the Parva-Saṁgraha section of Ādi-Parva :

śāntiparvaṇi dharmāsca vyākhyātāḥ śāratalpikāḥ
rājabhirveditavyāste samyajjñānabubhutsubhiḥ
āpaddharmāśca tatraiva kālahetupradarśinaḥ
yān buddhvā puruṣaḥ samyak sarvajñatvamavāpnuyāt
mokṣadharmāśca kathitā vicitrā bahuvistarāḥ
dvādaśaṁ parva nirdiṣṭametat prājñajanapriyam
(I.2.326-9)

Simple Meaning—It is in Śānti-Parva that Bhīṣma, speaking from his bed of arrows, explained various aspects of dharma, including dharma of kings, dharma adjusted to difficult circumstances, and dharma leading to mokṣa or salvation. Because of this, Śānti-Parva (which is Parva No.12) is dear to kings as well as to those who look for guidance to face emergencies, and above all, it is the favorite Parva of the wise.

1.27. Anuśāsana-Parva is a continuation of Śānti-Parva, i.e. of the dialogue between Bhīṣma and Yudhiṣṭhira, and the general style of Bhīṣma's reply (viz. making use of a story) is also maintained. However, this Parva is considerably shorter than Śānti-Parva, and the coverage of topics too is not so wide. Whereas Śānti-Parva deals with rāja-dharma, āpad-dharma and mokṣa-dharma, Anuśāsana-Parva pays most of its attention to practical applications of dharma. For instance, the topic of dāna (meaning charity or sharing) is discussed in detail. Bhīṣma says that five types of motives that underlie dāna should be kept in view :

dharmādarthād bhayāt kāmāt
kāruṇyāditi bhārata
dānaṁ pañcavidhaṁ jñeyaṁ
kāraṇairyairnibodha tat (XIII.138.6)

Simple Meaning—Dāna (giving) could be motivated by five considerations, viz. dharma (duty), artha (monetary gain), bhaya (fear), kāma (psychological satisfaction), and kāruṇya (pity).

Furthermore, Bhīṣma's approach to dāna takes into account not only money or commodities, but also non-material things like sympathy and assurance of fearlessness :

sāntvadaṁ sarvabhūtānāṁ
sarvaśokair vimucyate .... (XIII.57.21)

abhayaṁ sarvabhūtebhyo
vyasane cāpyanugrahaḥ
yaccābhilaṣitaṁ dadyāt
tṛṣitāyābhiyācate
dattaṁ manyeta yad datvā
tad dānaṁ śreṣṭhamucyate (XIII.59.3-4)

Simple Meaning—One who shows sympathy towards all beings, never feels unhappy.... Best forms of dāna (giving) are—to assure every one that they need have no fear, to help those who are in need, to make available the desired thing, to quench the thirst of others. Above all, there should be no expectation of any return (from those whom you help).

1.28. It will be interesting to see how Bhīṣma made use of a story or another teacher to give wise advice to Yudhiṣṭhira. One of the questions which Yudhiṣṭhira asked Bhīṣma was :

kena vṛttena rājendra
vartamānā narā bhuvi
prāpnuvantyuttamaṁ svargaṁ
kathaṁ ca narakaṁ nṛpa (XIII.111.2)

Simple Meaning—O pitāmaha (grandfather), by what conduct does one attain to heaven, and by what conduct does one sink into hell?

Bhīṣma replied that the best person to answer your question is Bṛhaspati, the guru of the gods. Then Bṛhaspati arrived there and started talking with Yudhiṣṭhira. The question-answer session with Bṛhaspati went on till Yudhiṣṭhira put his last question of that session :

ahiṁsā vaidikaṁ karma
dhyānamindriyasaṁyamaḥ
tapo'tha guruśuśrūṣā
kiṁ śreyaḥ puruṣaṁ prati (XIII.113.1)

Simple Meaning—Which one of the following six virtues contributes the most to one's good—ahiṁsā (non-violence), Vedic Karma, dhyāna (meditation), saṁyama (self-discipline), tapas (austerity), and guru-sevā (respectful service to guru or teacher)?

Bṛhaspati's reply is contained in nine verses and thereafter he went back to Indra-loka. We give below a part of what Bṛhaspati told Yudhiṣṭhira :

ahiṁsāpāśrayaṁ dharmaṁ yaḥ sādhayati vai naraḥ
trīn doṣān sarvabhūteṣu nidhāya puruṣaḥ sadā
kāmakrodhau ca saṁyamya tataḥ siddhimavāpnute ...
na tat parasya saṁdadhyāt pratikūlaṁ yadātmanaḥ
eṣa samkṣepato dharmaḥ kāmādanyaḥ pravartate
pratyākhyāne ca dāne ca sukhaduḥkhe priyāpriye
ātmaupamyena puruṣaḥ pramāṇamadhigacchati
(XIII.113, 3-4, 8-9)

Simple Meaning—Ahiṁsā is the most important of all the virtues. One who is guided by ahiṁsā, is able to overcome all the vices (like lust, anger, greed, arrogance, etc.) and therefore achieves success. As a practical application of ahiṁsā, one should not do to others what one would consider disagreeable if others do it to him (or her). This is the essence of dharma in brief. Whatever is contrary to this is the result of selfishness. Another expression for denoting such conduct is ātmaupamya i.e. seeing the same ātman in all, and therefore realizing that, just as we like happiness, pleasant things, etc. and dislike unhappiness, unpleasant things, etc., others will behave similarly.

1.29. We notice that ahiṁsā (non-violence) figured prominently in Yudhiṣṭhira's dialogue with Bṛhaspati. In fact, Anuśāsana-Parva devotes a good deal of attention to ahiṁsā, and two important points brought out in this Parva deserve special mention here. First, Bhīṣma told Yudhiṣṭhira a story how a brahmin won over a rākṣasa (monster) by ahīṁsā. Such stories occurring in Buddhist literature are well-known, but this Mahābhārata story seems to have remained practically unknown, partly because the brahmin's name is not specified by Bhīṣma. So we shall reproduce this story in chapter sixteen. The second important point made by Bhīṣma in the context of ahiṁsā is his opinion (supported by Ṛṣis) that the practice of ahiṁsā should be extended so as to include vegetarianism. We shall summarize such views of Bhīṣma in chapter seventeen.

1.30. The Parva-Saṁgraha section of Ādi-Parva says that Anuśāsana-Parva describes Bhīṣma's journey to heaven after he had taught Yudhiṣṭhira about several important aspects of dharma, including the need to adjust dharma according to changes in time and place :

rahasyaṁ caiva dharmāṇāṁ
deśakālopasaṁhitaṁ
etat subahuvṛttāntam
uttamaṁ cānuśāsanaṁ
bhīsmasyātraiva samprāptiḥ
svargasya parikīrtitā (I.2.335-6)

Simple Meaning—Anuśāsana-Parva (that follows Śānti-Parva) includes Bhīṣma's advice on practical aspects of dharma which need to take into account the changing needs of place and time. This Parva also describes how Bhīṣma ascended to heaven.

1.31. One of the adjustment problems that Yudhiṣṭhira raised in Anuśāsana-Parva was related to Yajña—he really wanted that the traditional definition of yajña should be modified so that it may become suitable for all, rich as well as the poor :

na te śakyā daridreṇa
yajñāḥ prāptuṁ pitāmaha

bahūpakaraṇā yajñā
nānāsambhāravistarāḥ (XIII.107.2)

Simple Meaning—O grandfather, yajña requires so many costly commodities, etc. and is thus beyond the reach of poor people.

1.32. Aśvamedha-Parva has been accorded, by Gītā-lovers, a special place in the Mahābhārata, next only to Bhīsma-Parva (which can be called the focal point of the epic because it contains Bhagavad-Gītā). While Bhagavad-Gītā contains the teaching given directly (and for the first time in the epic) by Lord Kṛṣṇa to Arjuna, we have Anu-Gītā in Aśvamedha-Parva where, too, Lord Kṛṣṇa gives the teaching to Arjuna directly (but for the second time in the epic). B.A. Van Nooten clarifies this point in the following words :

> "Before Kṛṣṇa returns to his own country, Dvārakā, he repeats to Arjuna a discourse on morality, the structure of the universe, and so on, called the Anu-Gītā "Later Song"—later, that is, relative to the Bhagavad-Gītā."[6]

The fact that the Mahābhārata itself views Lord Kṛṣṇa as the center-piece of the epic is brought out in the opening chapter of Ādi-Parva, and the following verse from that chapter should be enough to summarize that view :

bhagavān vāsudevaśca
kīrtyate'tra sanātanaḥ
sa hi satyamṛtaṁ caiva
pavitraṁ puṇyameva ca (I.1.256)

Simple Meaning—In this holy book (Mahābhārata), glories of Lord Kṛṣṇa have been sung—He is true and just, pure and holy.

1.33. An obvious question relating to Anu-Gītā is, 'Why was it considered necessary?' Aśvamedha-Parva answers this question by stating that it was Arjuna who took the initiative and who requested Kṛṣṇa to give the teaching again because he did not fully remember what he had heard earlier :

yat tad bhagavatā proktaṁ
purā keśava sauhṛdāt
tat sarvaṁ puruṣavyāghra
naṣṭaṁ me bhraṣṭacetasaḥ

mama kautūhalaṁ tvasti
teṣvartheṣu punaḥ punaḥ
bhavāṁstu dvārakāṁ gantā
nacirādiva mādhava (XIV.16.6-7)

Simple Meaning—Arjuna said, 'O Kesava, what you as the Lord said unto me at that time, because of your affection for me, has all been forgotten by me—and for this I only blame myself, in the sense that I lost my mental concentration. O Mādhava, again and again, my desire becomes prominent, to listen to what you had told me earlier—and I am expressing that desire to you now, because you will soon be leaving for Dvārakā.

1.34. Because of the special attention that Anu-Gītā deserves, we shall summarize its contents in chapter eighteen of this book. Here we shall indicate only four of the main points which support the characterization of Anu-Gītā as a direct follow-up of Bhagavad-Gītā :

(i) Verse III.20 of Bhagavad-Gītā mentions Janaka as an ideal karmayogin but no explanation is indicated therein. Anu-Gītā contains twnety-five verses about Janaka which clarify how he was an ideal Karmayogin engaged in doing good to all.

(ii) Verse XVIII.20 of Bhagavad-Gītā gives the social message of unity in diversity. Anu-Gītā repeats this message although the linguistic expressions used are different.

(iii) Verse III.11 of Bhagavad-Gītā glorifies 'paraspara-bhāva' i.e. an attitude of mutual co-operation and help. Anu-Gītā has four verses giving the same message (and using the same words too).

(iv) Verses XVI.1-3 of Bhagavad-Gītā list virtues that constitute 'daivī-sampat' (divine qualities). Anu-Gītā too has a section resembling these verses of Bhagavad-Gītā. (Please see chapter eighteen for details).

1.35. Before moving on to the last two Parva's of the Mahābhārata, we want to refer briefly to two more sections of Aśvamedha-Parva :

(i) This Parva has a small section which contains one more Gītā, called 'Kāma-Gītā'. There are only eleven verses in that Gītā, and we shall write about it in chapter eighteen of this book (i.e. along with Anu-Gītā).

(ii) Towards the end of Aśvamedha-Parva, there is a section containing an interesting story of a mongoose, the message of the story being that even a small help given by a poor person is more praiseworthy than a big one given by a king. This can be linked with Yudhiṣṭhira's suggestion (referred to in para 1.31) that religious practices (including yajña) should be equally suitable for all the people, rich or poor. We shall write about the mongoose story in chapter twenty-one of this book.

1.36. Mahāprasthānika-Parva, although the shortest of all the Parva's in size, has two important dialogues, viz. (i) between Yudhiṣṭhira and Bhīma and (ii) between Yudhiṣṭhira, on the one hand, and Indra and Dharmarāja, on the other. The occasion for both the dialogues was 'the great departure', i.e. the final journey on foot, to high mountains leading to heaven's entrance, by the five Pāṇḍava brothers and Draupadi, after having installed Parīkṣita on the throne. With a view to testing Yudhiṣṭhira's adherence to the subtle principles of righteousness, Dharmarāja assumed the form of a dog who became the seventh member of the walking team.

1.37. Shortly before Yudhiṣṭhira and the dog approached the entrance to heaven, Draupadī fell down, and thereafter Sahadeva, Nakula, and Arjuna fell down too, in that order, and finally Bhīma also fell down. Each time, Bhīma asked Yudhiṣṭhira why the particular person fell, and Yudhiṣṭhira gave him a reply. Such exchange of words between the two brothers occurred five times. This is the first of the two dialogues narrated in Mahāprasthānika-Parva. Yudhiṣṭhira's replies help us understand what dharma is, or rather what adharma (violation of dharma) is. But it is through the second dialogue that Dharmarāja tested Yudhiṣṭhira himself. In the end, Yudhiṣṭhira was declared to be a truly righteous person, because he refused to enter heaven without the dog who had walked behind him. Because of the important role that both these dialogues play in explaining dharma, we shall present them in chapter nineteen.

1.38. Finally, it is in Svargārohaṇa-Parva that Dharmarāja tested Yudhiṣṭhira for the third time in the epic. As a part of the testing procedure, an illusion (māyā) was created by Indra, because of which Yudhiṣṭhira did not find his brothers and Draupadī in heaven. The celestial messenger then took Yudhiṣṭhira to an illusory hell. Yudhiṣṭhira was pained to see his near and dear ones there, the more so when they cried out :

bho bho dharmaja rājarṣe
puṇyābhijana pāṇḍava
anugrahārthamasmākaṁ
tiṣṭha tāvanmuhūrtakaṁ ....
santiṣṭhaṣva mahābāho
muhūrtamapi bhārata
tvayi tiṣṭhati kauravya
yātanāsmān na bādhate (XVIII.2.32,35)

Simple Meaning—'O righteous king, please stay here for a while, out of compassion for us. Prior to your arrival here, we were experiencing pain, but your presence takes away that pain.'

Yudhiṣṭhira then decided that he would rather stay in hell with his brothers and wife, and not go to heaven at all, by himself :

na hyahaṁ tatra yāsyāmi
sthito'smīti nivedyatāṁ
matsaṁśrayādime dūtāḥ
sukhino bhrātaro hi me (XVIII.2.52)

Simple Meaning—Yudhiṣṭhira told the celestial messenger, 'Please tell Indra that I do not want to return to heaven. I prefer to stay in hell because my presence here takes away the pain of my near and dear ones and makes them happy.'

At that point, Dharmarāja came to Yudhiṣṭhira (i.e. the former's son) and told him that all this was just an illusion, created for testing his priorities. Since Yudhiṣṭhira did not want to leave his near and dear ones (even for the sake of heaven), he was declared to have proved his righteousness. Before closing this account of 'talks on issues of dharma', we reproduce four of the verses, addressed by Dharmarāja to Yudhiṣṭhira, in the last Parva of the Mahābhārata :

eṣā tṛtīyā jijñāsā tava rājan kṛtā mayā
na śakyase cālayituṁ svabhāvāt pārtha hetutaḥ
pūrvaṁ parīkṣito hi tvaṁ praśnād dvaitavane mayā
araṇīsahitasyārthe tacca nistīrṇavānasi

sodaryeṣu vinaṣṭeṣu draupadyā tatra bhārata
śvarūpadhāriṇā tatra punastvaṁ me parīkṣitaḥ ...
na ca te bhrātaraḥ pārtha narakārhā viśāmpate
māyaiṣā devarājena mahendreṇa prayojitā
(XVIII.3.32-34, 36)

Simple Meaning— 'O Yudhiṣṭhira, this is the third occasion that I have tested you. Dharma is natural to you and nothing can sway you away from it. Long ago, the first time that I tested you, I assumed the form of yakṣa, but you answered all my questions properly. For the second test, I assumed the form of a dog, and although you lost your brothers and Draupadī, you did not abandon me ... Your near and dear ones deserve to live in heaven, not in hell, and the vision that you had about their suffering in hell was only an illusion created by Indra (to help me test you—and this was the final test which you have passed).'

Purpose, Plan and Scope of this Study

1.39. In the light of the beckground depicted above, we can specifically state the purpose, plan and scope of this study. Our purpose is to identify those verses of the Mahābhārata which support Bhagavad-Gītā's call for the good of all—this we regard as the essence of dharma. In this sense, the present study is a follow-up of our books on Bhagavad-Gītā (or Gītā for short) which look primarily at the socio-religious message of that well-known scripture. Since we have listed (in our earlier publications) ten points as constituting a framework concretizing the Gītā's call for the good of all, our task in the present study can be said to have a relatively limited scope. In other words, guided by a ten-point yardstick (which we shall reproduce in chapter twenty of this book for ready reference), we plan to select relevant verses of the Mahābhārata, and then make a point-by-point presentation of the same. Indications have been given in the earlier parts of this chapter as to which sections of the Mahābhārata, being particularly supportive to the Gītā, will be selected (fully or partly) for inclusion in this book. As far as we know, no other study of the Mahābhārata has so far been conducted in such detail from this (Gītā-supportive) perspective.

1.40. We are aware of the debate among scholars as to which version of the Mahābhārata should be used as the basic text.

Personally, since Śrī Hanuman Prasad Poddar, former Editor of Gītā Press, Gorakhpur was a close family friend, we have used the Gītā Press edition of the Mahābhārata published in six volumes in the 1980's. We do want to make it clear, however, that our non-utilization of the Critical Edition (brought out by V.S. Sukthankar and others)[7] should not be interpreted, in any way, to indicate lack of appreciation or respect for it.

1.41. Structurally, this book is divided into three parts. Part one, entitled 'Background and Plan of this Study', has only one chapter (i.e. the present one) containing a brief outline of the Mahābhārata-text and a statement of what we plan to select therefrom and why. Part two, entitled 'Mahābhārata-selections (other than Bhagavad-Gītā)', has eighteen chapters (as if to remind us of the importance attached to the number eighteen by the Gītā as well as the Mahābhārata). Selected portions of the Mahābhārata that are presented here are the main sources which provide the specific verses needed for the last chapter of this book. Part three entitled 'Gītā's call for the Good of all and Mahābhārata's support to it', has two chapters. The first of these two chapters is based on our own books on the Gītā, the main idea being to list ten points of the Gītā's call for the good of all. The second of these two chapters (which is also the last chapter of this book) summarizes as well as illustrates by verses, point-by-point, how the Mahābhārata supports Gītā's ten-point call for the good of all.

PART TWO

MAHĀBHĀRATA-SELECTIONS (OTHER THAN BHAGAVAD-GĪTĀ)

Chapter 2

Śakuntalā, Nahuṣa and Yayāti—Three of the Famous Ancestors of the Pāṇḍavas

2.1. We have identified Śakuntalā as the most famous ancestor of the Pāṇḍavas whose story has been told in Ādi-Parva (i.e. Parva No.1). She was the daughter of Ṛṣi Viśvāmitra, her mother being Menakā, an Apsarā (heavenly nymph). But Śakuntalā was brought up by Ṛṣi Kaṇva who found her, as an infant, on the banks of the river Mālinī. Kaṇva gave her the name 'Śakuntalā' because she was protected by Śakunta-birds, as he himself tells in the Mahābhārata :

nirjane tu vane yasmāc
chakuṁtaiḥ parivāritā
śakuntaleti nāmāsyāḥ
kṛtaṁ cāpi tato mayā (I.72.16)

Simple Meaning—Ṛṣi Kaṇva says, 'In a forest, away from human habitation, I found this baby who was protected by Śakunta-birds, therefore I gave her the name 'Śakuntalā'.

2.2. Ādi-Parva describes how king Duṣyanta, during the course of a hunting expedition, visited the āśrama (hermitage) of Ṛṣi Kaṇva. The Ṛṣi was not there at that time. The king fell in love with Śakuntalā, so he proposed to her that they should get married according to 'Gandharva form' (i.e. mutual consent).

But Śakuntalā placed a condition :

yadi dharmapathastveṣa yadi cātmā prabhurmama
pradāne pauravaśreṣṭha śṛṇu me samayaṁ prabho
satyaṁ me pratijānīhi yathā vakṣyāmyahaṁ rahaḥ
mayi jāyeta yaḥ putraḥ sa bhavet tvadanantaraḥ
yuvarājo mahārāja satyametad bravīmi te
yadyetadevaṁ duṣyanta astu me saṅgamastvayā
(I.73.15-17)

Simple Meaning—Śakuntalā said, 'O King Duṣyanta, if the Gandharva form of marriage (i.e. mutual consent of grown up persons), as proposed by you, is in accordance with dharma, then I give my consent, but I want to put one condition. Although there is no other witness here, you have to give me your word that you accept my condition, viz. that if I give birth to a son, then he will succeed you on the throne. I am speaking from my heart, and if you too declare your firm acceptance of my condition, then we can get married.'

2.3. Duṣyanta accepted Śakuntalā's condition, stayed with her at the āśrama for a while, and then returned to his kingdom. Ṛṣi Kaṇva gave his blessings to Śakuntalā and continued to look after her as also the son to whom she gave birth. In fact, the little boy spent the first six years of his life in Kaṇva's āśrama. Ādi-Parva says that the name 'Sarva-damana' (meaning one who could control all animals) was given to him :

astvayaṁ sarvadamanaḥ
sarvaṁ hi damayatyasau
sa sarvadamano nāma
kumāraḥ samapadyata (I.74.8)

Simple Meaning—Residents of the āśrama said, 'We have seen that this little boy can control all animals, therefore we feel that 'Sarvadamana' will be an appropriate name for him.' So Śakuntalā's son became known by this name.

2.4. Śakuntalā's greatness was particularly brought to light when she and her six-year old son went to King Duṣyanta and, seeing that the king pretended not to remember his visit to Kaṇva's āśrama, she had to plead forcefully for the truth to be honored. B.A. van Nooten says,

"Śakuntalā, looking the king straight in the face, burst forth in an impassioned speech, one of the finest in the epic."[1]

We can get a glimpse of the lofty statements made by Śakuntalā from the verses reproduced here (and also in the next paragraph) :

yathā matsaṅgame pūrvaṁ yaḥ kṛtaḥ samayastvayā
taṁ smarasva mahābhāga kaṇvāśramapadaṁ prati ...
jānannapi mahārāja kasmādevaṁ prabhāṣase
na jānāmīti niḥśankaṁ yathānyaḥ prākṛto janaḥ
atra te hṛdayaṁ veda satyasyaivānṛtasya ca
kalyāṇaṁ vada sākṣyeṇa mā'tmānamavamanyathāḥ
(I.74.18, 25-6)

Simple Meaning—Śakuntalā said to Duṣyanta, 'O best of men, remember the promise that you made when we got together in the āśrama of Ṛṣi Kaṇva .... O king, although you know the truth very well, why do you talk in this manner, saying like any commoner 'I do not know'. In this matter, I know, it is your heart that is witness to its truth or falsehood. Speak from your heart and that will be to your good—please do not degrade yourself.'

2.5. Śakuntalā wanted the king to recognize that his own high status depended so much on his wife :

ardhaṁ bhāryā manuṣyasya
bhāryā śreṣṭhatamaḥ sakhā
bhāryā mūlaṁ trivargasya
bhāryā mūlaṁ tariṣyataḥ ....
kāntāreṣvapi viśrāmo
janasyādhvanikasya vai
yaḥ sadāraḥ sa viśvāsyas
tasmād dārāḥ parā gatiḥ (I.74.41,44)

Simple Meaning—Śakuntalā continued, 'A wife is half the man, the wife is the best friend, the wife is the root of threefold morality—dharma (duty), artha (wealth) and kāma (pleasure), the wife provides the best support for the journey to the other world .... Even in the wilderness, to the traveller his wife brings security, he who has a wife is trusted by everyone, therefore, a wife is the best goal.'

2.6. Ādi-Parva says that Śakuntala's statements received incontrovertible support from a heavenly voice which convinced the king as well as all others who were present there at that critical juncture :

vāguvāca hi duṣyantaṁ ....
satyamāha śakuntalā ....
māvamaṁsthāḥ śakuntalāṁ ....
bhartavyo'yaṁ tvayā yasmād
asmākaṁ vacanādapi
tasmād bhavatvayaṁ nāmnā
bharato nāma te sutaḥ (I.74.109-115)

Simple Meaning—The heavenly voice spoke to Duṣyanta, Śakuntalā's statements are true, therefore do not show disrespect to her. Following our advice, you will provide 'bharaṇam' (support and protection) to this boy (who is your son), so he will be known as 'Bharata'.

2.7. Duṣyanta bestowed full honors on Śakuntalā and showered paternal affection on the little boy who was given a new name 'Bharata' as advised by the heavenly voice. The king told Śakuntalā that he had never forgotten her—he had only wanted the common people to hear the full story through the heavenly voice so that they too are convinced about the legitimacy of their son :

kṛto lokaparokṣo'yaṁ
sambandho vai tvayā saha
tasmādetanmayā devi
tvacchuddhyarthaṁ vicāritam (I.74.122)

Simple Meaning—Duṣyanta said to Śakuntalā, 'O Devi (respectable lady like a goddess), this plan was devised by me so that the purity of our relationship may become known to all—otherwise they might have remained in the dark because no one else was present when we got married.'[2]

2.8. The qualities which Bharata had acquired at Ṛṣi Kaṇva's āśrama, were further developed under the parental care of Śakuntalā and Duṣyanta. In due course of time, Bharata succeeded Duṣyanta as a king but surpassed him—and all other ancient rulers too—so much so that the Sanskrit name of India, viz. 'Bhārata-varṣa' is derived from him. Śakuntalā has been duly recognized as the mother who contributed so much to the building up of Bharata's character. We should also mention that, on the basis of this story of the Mahābhārata, Kālidāsa wrote his play 'abhijñānaśākuntalam' which, when translated into non-Indian languages, brought universal acclaim, not only to Kālidāsa but also to the entire Sanskrit literature.[3]

2.9. Next the story of Nahuṣa who was a famous king, several generations prior to Bharata. The story of Nahuṣa's rise, fall and ultimate redemption is told in the Mahābhārata, little by little, in five Parva's (viz. Ādi, Vana, Udyoga, Śānti, and Anuśāsana). After Indra had killed the mighty asura (i.e. demon named Vritra), he (i.e. Indra) went into hiding, to escape possible revenge (or punishment for having killed a brahmin). Then the devas (gods) and the Ṛṣis, uniting together, made Nahuṣa the king of the three worlds. This represented the great rise of Nahuṣa. However, it did not last very long, and his own mistake brought about his fall. Nahuṣa insulted Ṛṣis and they cursed him and turned him into a snake. Subsequently, out of compassion, they said that the righteous Yudhiṣṭhira will release him from the curse. In this way, Nahuṣa finally attained salvation.[4]

2.10. We have identified Nahuṣa as a famous ancestor of the Pāṇḍavas, not because of his brief elevation to the position of Indra, but because of the words of wisdom that he spoke after having been converted into a snake. According to his own confession, made to Yudhiṣṭhira in Vana-Parva, high position had made him arrogant—and this is one of the lessons that he taught to those who might become mad due to power and prosperity :

> *suprajñamapi cecchūramṛddhir mohayate naraṁ*
> *vartamānaḥ sukhe sarvo muhyatīti matirmama*
> *so'hamaiśvaryamohena madāviṣṭo yudhiṣṭhira*
> *patitaḥ pratisambuddhastvāṁ tu sambodhayāmyaham*
> (III.181.30-1)

Simple Meaning—Nahuṣa (in the form of a snake) spoke to Yudhiṣṭhira, 'Power and prosperity have an intoxicating impact on men—even on those who are considered wise and balanced. In fact, in my opinion, every one engrossed in materialistic enjoyment loses mental balance. In my own case, high position made me arrogant, and I realised this only after I fell down from that position. Having gone through this experience, I am saying these words of caution (almost like a warning)—and although I am talking to you, my message is for all those who need such a warning.'

2.11. Other words of wisdom that Nahuṣa spoke, were contained in the replies that he gave to Yudhiṣṭhira's questions on dharma.

We reproduce below only three verses (two of them partly) which glorify ahiṁsā (non-violence), truthful and pleasant speech, and help given to good causes—and play down the role of jāti (caste) and kula (family) :

pātre dattvā priyāṇyuktvā
satyamuktvā ca bhārata
ahiṁsānirataḥ svargaṁ
gacchediti matirmama ....
satyaṁ damastapo dānaṁ
ahiṁsā dharmanityatā
sādhakāni sadā puṁsāṁ
na jātirna kulaṁ nṛpa (III.181.2, 42-3)

Simple Meaning—Nahuṣa (in the form of a snake) spoke to Yudhiṣṭhira, 'In my opinion, four virtues help attain heaven—to help the right person, to say what is pleasant, to say what is true, and continued practice of ahiṁsā (non-violence).... Caste and family have no role in attaining a state of spiritual perfection—that state can be reached with the help of six virtues—truth, self-discipline, austerity, giving or sharing, non-violence, and steadfastness in the practice of dharma (duty).'

2.12. The third and the last of the famous ancestors of the Pāṇḍavas, whose story we shall present now, was Yayāti (son of Nahuṣa). His (i.e. Yayāti's) experiences—which are a mixture of joy and sorrow spread over a wide span of time—are described mainly in Ādi-Parva. He was a great king, devoted to the welfare of his subjects. His first wife was Devayānī, daughter of Śukrācārya who was the guru of the asuras (demons). But Yayāti lacked self-discipline and he took a second wife, Śarmiṣṭhā, without the approval of the first wife. This enraged Devayānī and her father—and the latter pronounced a curse on Yayāti :

nanvahaṁ pratyavekṣyaste
madadhīno'si pārthiva
mithyācārasya dharmeṣu
cauryaṁ bhavati nāhuṣa (I.83.36)

Simple Meaning—Śukrācārya spoke to Yayāti, 'O king, you took a wrong step without my approval, thinking as if you are independent—but you are not. You have not followed the right dharma, and therefore you have to reap the consequences.'

As a result of the curse, Yayāti suddenly lost his youth and became prematurely old. Subsequently, out of compassion, Śukrācārya modified the curse and indicated a possible—but strange—way for Yayāti to attain youth again :

nāhaṁ mṛṣā bravīmyetaj
jarāṁ prāpto'si bhūmipa
jarāṁ tvetāṁ tvamanyasmin
saṁkrāmaya yadīcchasi (I.83.39)

Simple Meaning—Śukrācārya spoke to Yayāti again, 'O king, I never tell a lie. My curse has brought old age prematurely to you. However, I now suggest a possible way out. If you want, you can exchange your old age with the youth of some one else.'

Yayāti felt encouraged because he believed that at least one of his five sons would agree to transfer his youth to the father (i.e. Yayāti), and take upon himself the old age of the father. So it came as a rude shock to Yayāti when the eldest son—and thereafter the next three sons—said 'No' to the father[5]. Luckily for him, the youngest son, Pūru, said 'Yes' :

jarayāhaṁ praticchanno
vayorūpadharastava
yauvanaṁ bhavate dattvā
cariṣyāmi yatha'ttha mām (I.84.32)

Simple Meaning—Pūru said to Yayāti, 'Respected father, I shall take upon myself your age and appearance (i.e. I shall become old). I shall give my youth to you (i.e. you will be young again). After this exchange, I shall do whatever you advise me to do.'

2.13. Ādi-Parva says that Yayāti, having regained youth, enjoyed life for a long time. However, one day, wisdom dawned upon him and he gave back the youth to Pūru and himself retired to the woods as an old man. He spoke words of wisdom—based on his own disillusionment—and Yayāti is famous mainly for such teachings (Two verses are given below but several more will be mentioned in connection with the next phase of his life) :

na jātu kāmaḥ kāmānāṁ
upabhogena śāmyati

haviṣā kṛṣṇavartmeva
bhūya evābhivardhate ....
tasmādenāmahaṁ tyaktvā
brahmaṇyādhāya mānasaṁ
nirdvandvo nirmamo bhūtvā
cariṣyāmi mṛgaiḥ saha (I.85.12,16)

Simple Meaning—Yayāti spoke to Pūru, 'Desires for sense objects are always unending—the more you enjoy, the more you want to enjoy. Just as by pouring ghee on fire, you can not extinguish fire, similarly by satisfying your desires, you can not achieve the end of desires .... Therefore, I shall withdraw myself from sense objects and concentrate all my attention on God. I shall go beyond the pairs of opposites (like pain and pleasure, heat and cold), I shall go beyond the sense of 'I' and 'mine', and I shall live in the woods, playing with the animals.'

2.14. While living in the woods, Yayāti followed dharma appropriate to his old age, and, as a reward for good deeds, he was declared fit to live in Indra-loka (heaven). The unusual nature of experiences—with alternate periods of rise and fall—came to Yayāti again. First, a glimpse into his rise. As an indicator of the high status accorded to Yayāti by Indra, the latter wanted to hear the teachings that he (i.e. Yayāti) had imparted to Pūru—and we reproduce below two of the verses that Yayāti had spoken to Pūru (and which Yayāti recalled for the benefit of Indra) :

ākruśyamāno nākrośenmanyureva titikṣataḥ
ākroṣṭāraṁ nirdahati sukṛtaṁ cāsya vindati ....
na hīdṛśaṁ saṁvananaṁ tṛṣu lokeṣu vidyate
dayā maitrī ca bhūteṣu dānaṁ ca madhurā ca vāk
(I.87.7,12)

Simple Meaning—Even if wronged (through abuse, etc.), one should not do wrong in return. In that case, the wrong-doer's feeling of guilt burns his own self—and his virtues too (if any) are transferred to the person who does not do wrong in return .... Four virtues are most effective and they receive glorification in the three worlds—and these virtues are : compassion towards all, friendliness for all, willingness to share what one has, and sweet words on all occasions.

2.15. Next, about Yayāti's fall. Because of an unfortunate lapse in conduct, he showed disrespect to some members of Indra-loka, and this prompted Indra to terminate his (i.e. Yayāti's) stay in heaven :

yadāvamaṁsthāḥ sadṛśaḥ śreyasaśca
alpīyasaścāviditaprabhāvaḥ
tasmāllokāstvantavantastaveme
kṣīṇe puṇye patitāsyadya rājan (I.88.3)

Simple Meaning—Indra said to Yayāti, 'O king, you have shown disrespect to several people (including those who are equal to you or superior to you or inferior to you), without appreciating their merits, therefore your virtues have been exhausted, and you must fall down from heaven.'

2.16. Finally, about Yayāti's re-entry into heaven. While Yayāti was gradually falling down from Indra-loka, his daughter Mādhavī, and her four sons (i.e. Yayāti's grandsons) came to his rescue. They heard words of wisdom (some of which are reproduced below) and ultimately helped Yayāti in being re-elevated to heaven :

tapaśca dānaṁ ca śamo damaśca
hrīrārjavaṁ sarvabhūtānukampā
svargasya lokasya vadanti santo
dvārāṇi saptaiva mahānti puṁsām
naśyanti mānena tamo'bhibhūtāḥ
puṁsaḥ sadaiveti vadanti santaḥ (I.90.22)

Simple Meaning—Yayāti gave the teaching to Aṣṭaka (who was one of his grandsons), 'Wise people say that there are seven gates through which admission may be gained into heaven. These are—tapas (austerity), dānam (charity or sharing), śamaḥ (calmness of mind), damaḥ (control our senses), hrī (modesty), ārjava (uprightness), and compassion (anukampā) towards all beings. Wise people further say that, just as gates become inaccessible due to darkness, similarly gates to heaven are lost due to vanity.'

tad vai nṛśaṁsaṁ tadasatyamāhur
yaḥ sevate'dharmamanarthabuddhiḥ (I.92.5)

Simple Meaning—Yayāti continued his teaching to Aṣṭaka, 'A person whose thinking is perverted, follows the path of unrighteousness—such conduct is false and cruel.'

In conclusion, Yayāti told Aṣṭaka (who was a king at that time) that he (i.e. Yayāti) sang the praises of virtues, not merely from a theoretical angle, but by recalling the example of King Śivi :

dānaṁ tapaḥ satyamathāpi dharmo
hrīḥ śrīḥ kṣamā saumyamatho vidhitsā
rājannetānyaprameyāṇi rājñaḥ
śiveḥ sthitānyapratimasya buddhyā (I.93. 19)

Simple Meaning—Yayāti concluded his address to Aṣṭaka by saying, 'O king, in my opinion, King Śivi provides the best example of one who has the right attitude to dharma and who possesses more virtues than others—for example, he not only has the seven virtues that constitute the seven gates to heaven, but he also has two additional virtues, viz. forgiveness, and desire to stick to the right path under all circumstances.'

This appreciative statement of Yayāti about the virtues of King Śivi set in motion the process by which he (i.e. Yayāti) was re-elevated to heaven. For purposes of picking up appropriate selections for this book, we too received from this a helpful suggestion that the story of Śivi must receive due attention—and we accomplish this in the next chapter.

CHAPTER 3

Glorification of Sacrifices Made by Śivi and Dadhīci

3.1. In the closing verse of the preceding chapter (that was reproduced from Ādi-Parva), Yayāti sang praises of Śivi. The full story of Śivi's sacrifice (which was made for others—not for selfish gain) is narrated by Ṛṣi Mārkaṇḍeya to Yudhiṣṭhira in Vana-Parva. More specifically, King Śivi offered to give his own flesh to save the life of a pigeon. Although Śivi's story is exemplary for selfless workers, it is not an isolated event for the Mahābhārata. In fact, Vana-Parva itself contains one more story glorifying selfless sacrifice—that story relates to Ṛṣi Dadhīci's giving up his own life to enable the gods to overpower the cruelest of the demons. Ṛṣi Lomaśa narrated this story to Yudhiṣṭhira. Here we present both these stories—one after the other—because they both glorify unique acts of sacrifice voluntarily done for the good of others.

3.2. We begin with the story of Śivi. The closing part of this story reveals (but we want to bring it forward to clarify the underlying purpose) that the whole thing was part of a test, viz., that Indra and Agni wanted to see whether King Śivi would really put his own life at risk in order to save the life of a bird. For this purpose, Indra assumed the form of a hawk while Agni assumed the form of a pigeon. Because of its importance, we present practically the entire story as narrated by Ṛṣi Mārkaṇḍeya to Yudhiṣṭhira in Vana-Parva. A notable linguistic feature of this story is that it is written partly in prose and partly in poetry :

3.3. *atha kapoto rājño divyāsanāsīnasyotsaṅgaṁ nyapatat*
(III. 197.3)

Simple Meaning—One day, when King Śivi was seated on the royal seat, a pigeon fell down, on the lap of the king.

atha purohito rājānamabravīt prāṇarakṣārthaṁ
śyenād bhīto bhavantaṁ prāṇārthī prapadyate
(III. 197.4)

Simple Meaning—The royal priest, addressing the king, said, 'O Sovereign, this pigeon is afraid that a hawk wants to eat it up, and therefore, hoping to save its own life, it is seeking protection from you (i.e. from a compassionate King).'

vasu dadātu antavān pārthivo'sya niṣkṛtiṁ
kuryād ghoraṁ kapotasya nipātamāhuḥ (III. 197.5)

Simple Meaning—The priest continued, 'Wise people say that the falling of a pigeon upon one's body is indicative of a great danger. I suggest that, with a view to averting the likely risk to your life, you give charity.'

3.4. *atha kapoto rājānamabravīt prāṇarakṣārthaṁ*
śyenād bhīto bhavantaṁ prāṇārthī prapadye
aṅgairaṅgāni prāpyārthī munirbhūtvā
prāṇāṁstvāṁ prapadye (III. 197.6)

Simple Meaning—Immediately after the priest had spoken, the pigeon also addressed the king and said, 'O Sovereign, afraid of the hawk and desirous of saving my life, I have come to you for protection. In fact, I am not a pigeon, I am a Muni (spiritual aspirant). Having assumed the form of a pigeon, I have come here and I pray, 'Please protect my life.'

svādhyāyena karśitaṁ brahmacāriṇaṁ māṁ
viddhi tapasā damena yuktamācāryasya
apratikūlabhāṣiṇam evaṁ yuktamapāpaṁ māṁ viddhi
(III. 197.7)

Simple Meaning—The pigeon continued, 'Please treat me as a genuine student of the Vedas, as one who has led the Brahmacarya mode of life, that is, one who has observed the discipline and stayed away from enjoyments. I have practiced virtues like tapas (austerity) and damaḥ (control over senses). I have never spoken anything that may be disagreeable to my teacher. I have never committed any sin.'

gadāmi vedān vicinomi chandaḥ
sarve veda akṣaraśo me adhītāḥ
na sādhu dānaṁ śrotriyasya pradānaṁ
mā prādāh śyenāya na kapoto'smi (I. 197.8)

Simple Meaning—The pigeon, concluding his statement addressed to King Śivi, pleaded for protection, by saying, 'O monarch, I am not a pigeon. Please treat me as a learned brahmin because I recite the Vedas, I know their prosody—indeed, I have studied all the Vedas letter by letter. I pray to you not to hand me over to the hawk—he is hungry and he will eat me up. Giving me to the hawk can not be considered 'dānam' (i.e. sharing) of the right type.'

3.5. *atha śyeno rājānamabravīt*
paryāyeṇa vasatirvā bhaveṣu
sarge jātaḥ pūrvamasmāt kapotāt
tvamādadāno' tha kapotamenaṁ
mā tvaṁ rājan vighnakartā bhavethāḥ (III. 197.9-10)

Simple Meaning—The hawk, arguing his own case, addressed the king by saying, 'O monarch, living creatures pass through the process of being reborn in different species, in an unknown order, and so it might be that, in a former birth, this pigeon could have been your father. Maybe that is why you are now protecting this pigeon. However, I urge you not to put an obstacle in the way of my getting the food of my choice—and that will be the case if you do not let me eat this pigeon.'

3.6. Rājovāca:
kenedṛṣī jātu parā hi dṛṣṭā
vāgucyamānā śakunena saṁskṛtā
yāṁ vai kapoto vadate yāṁ ca śyena
ubhau viditvā kathamastu sādhu (III. 197.11)

Simple Meaning—Thus addressed by the pigeon and the hawk, King Śivi spoke in wonderment, 'Has anyone, prior to this day, seen birds speak so beautifully in the refined language of man ? I wonder how, after listening to the pigeon and the hawk, a proper course of action can be devised.'

nāsya varṣaṁ varṣati varṣakāle
nāsya bījaṁ rohati kāla uptaṁ
bhītaṁ prapannaṁ yo hi dadāti śatrave
na trāṇaṁ labhet trāṇamicchan sa kāle (III. 197.12)

Simple Meaning—While the king was wondering what course of action would be proper, it occurred to him that one option (viz. to hand over the pigeon to the hawk) was definitely improper—and this verse explains why it is so. The king said, 'He that gives up a frightened creature seeking protection, can not hope to get protection when he himself needs it—even clouds do not provide adequate rain for him, nor do the seeds, though planted in the field, grow for him.'

ukṣāṇaṁ paktvā saha odanena
asmāt kapotāt prati te nayantu
yasmin deśe ramase'tīva śyena
tatra māṁsaṁ śivayaste vahantu (III. 197.15)

Simple Meaning—Having decided that he will not hand over the pigeon to the hawk, the king made an offer to provide some other food to the hawk. The king said, 'O hawk, please agree to spare the life of this pigeon, because my people will make available to you food of your choice. I shall also let you live in any place that you like—and plenty of food will be supplied to you there.'

3.7. Śyena uvāca:

nokṣāṇaṁ rājan prārthayeyaṁ na cānyad
asmānmāṁsamadhikaṁ vā kapotāt
devairdattaḥ so'dya mamaiṣa bhakṣas
tanme dadasva śakunānāmabhāvāt (III. 197.16)

Simple Meaning—The hawk replied, 'O king, I do not want any other food—I just want to eat this pigeon. It has been given to me by the gods. Therefore, please hand over this pigeon to me as my food for today.'

3.8. Rājovāca:

tyaje prāṇān naiva dadyāṃ kapotaṁ
saumyo hyayaṁ kiṁ na jānāsi śyena
yathā kleśaṁ mā kuruṣveha saumya
nāhaṁ kapotamarpayiṣye kathancit (III. 197.18)

Simple Meaning—The king replied, 'O hawk, I am willing to give up my own life but I will not give this pigeon to you. Don't you know how innocent and pretty this pigeon is. In fact, I see the same qualities in you too. I advise you not to take the trouble of pressing this point any further because I will not hand over this pigeon to you under any circumstances.'

3.9. Śyena uvāca:
ūrordakṣiṇādutkṛtya svapiśitaṁ tāvad rājan
yāvanmāṁsaṁ kapotena samam tathā tasmāt
sādhu trātaḥ kapotaḥ praśaṁseyuśca śivayaḥ
kṛtaṁ ca priyaṁ syānmameti (III. 197.20)

Simple Meaning—The hawk replied, 'O king, this pigeon can be saved if you give me an equivalent amount of your own flesh, taking it from your right thigh. Such action on your part will be admired by all the people, and it will satisfy my needs too.'

3.10. *atha sa dakṣiṇādūrorutkṛtya svamāṁsapeśiṁ*
tulayā' dhārayat gurutara eva kapota āsīt (III. 197.21)

Simple Meaning—The king accepted the hawk's conditional offer and cut off a piece of flesh from his own right thigh as may be equal to the weight of the pigeon. However, the flesh of the king weighted less than the pigeon.

punaranyamuccakarta gurutara eva kapotaḥ
evaṁ sarvaṁ samadhikṛtya śarīraṁ tulāyāṁ
āropayāmāsa tat tathāpi gurutara eva
kapota āsīt (III. 197.22)

Simple Meaning—In an attempt to equalize with the weight of the pigeon, the king cut off more of his own flesh—from all parts of his body—but the flesh of the king still weighed less than the pigeon.

atha rājā svayameva tulāmāruroha na ca
vyalīkamāsīd rājña etad vṛttāntaṁ dṛṣṭvā
trāta ityuktvā prālīyata śyeno'tha rājā
abravīt (III. 197.23)

Simple Meaning—Finally, the king himself ascended the scale (i.e. he offered his entire body to equalise with the weight of the pigeon). The king did this happily, with no trace of pain or grief. At this point, the hawk announced, 'The pigeon has been saved'. Then the hawk disappeared (i.e. was no longer visible). The king then spoke to the pigeon.

kapotaṁ vidyuḥ śivayastvāṁ kapota
pṛcchāmi te śakune ko nu śyenaḥ
nānīśvara īdṛśaṁ jātu kuryād
etaṁ praśnaṁ bhagavan me vicakṣva (III. 197.24)

Simple Meaning—'O pigeon, all the people thought that you are a pigeon. I now ask you, who was this hawk ? It seems that none else, other than God, can do what the hawk did. Please give me a clear answer.'

3.11. Kapota uvāca:
vaiśvānaro' haṁ jvalano dhūmaketur
athaiva śyeno vajrahastaḥ śacīpatiḥ
sādhu jñātuṁ tvāmṛṣabhaṁ sauratheya
nau jijñāsayā tvatsakāśaṁ prapannau (III. 197.25)

Simple Meaning—The pigeon replied, 'O king, I shall clarify everything. I look like a pigeon but, in reality, I am Agni (who assumed this form). The hawk was Indra. Both of us came here to test you. You have passed the test—you are really great.'

3.12. Next, the story of Ṛṣi Dadhīci which is perhaps even more touching than that of Śivi, from three considerations. First, the events of Dadhīci-story represented a real-life situation, and did not form part of a drama (or test) engineered by Indra. (of course, Śivi did not know it was a drama). Secondly, whereas King Śivi was asked to give only his flesh, Ṛṣi Dadhīci was asked to give his life (In the end, Śivi too offered his life voluntarily). Thirdly, the cause for which the sacrifice was made was bigger (i.e. affecting more people) in the case of Dadhīci, as compared to Śivi. These observations of ours should not be interpreted as an undervaluation of Śivi's sacrifice—he has been rightly called 'really great' in the preceding paragraph.

3.13. Because of its importance, we shall present the Dadhīci-story also in some detail, following the narration of Ṛṣi Lomaśa in Vana-Parva. The opening verse introduces the cruel demons, whose defeat was possible only through the strength of Dadhīci's sacrifice :

āsan kṛtayuge ghorā dānavā yuddhadurmadāḥ
kālakeyā iti khyātā gaṇāḥ paramadāruṇāḥ (III. 100.3)

Simple Meaning—In Satya-yuga (i.e. long ago), there was a large group of cruel demons, known as Kālakeyas, who were practically invincible.

te tu vṛtraṁ samāśritya nānāpraharaṇodyatāḥ
samantāt paryadhāvanta mahendrapramukhān surān
(III. 100.4)

Simple Meaning—Under the leadership of Vṛtrāsura, these demons, equipped with deadly weapons, attacked the gods (whose chief was Indra) from all directions.

3.14. *tato vṛtravadhe yatnamakurvamstridaśāḥ purā*
purandaraṁ puraskṛtya brahmāṇamupatasthire
(III. 100.5)

Simple Meaning—All the gods put together their efforts, with a view to overpowering Vṛtrāsura. Realizing that they did not have adequate means to achieve success, the gods (with Indra as their leader) went to Brahmā, seeking advice.

3.15. *kṛtāñjalīmstu tān sarvān*
parameṣṭhītyuvāca ha
viditaṁ me surāḥ sarvaṁ
yad vaḥ kāryaṁ cikīrṣitam (III. 100.6)

Simple Meaning—All the gods stood before Brahmā with folded hands. Brahmā then told the gods, 'I know what you want, in relation to the problem that you are facing.'

tamupāyaṁ pravakṣyāmi
yathā vṛtraṁ vadhiṣyatha
dadhīca iti vikhyāto
mahānṛṣirudāradhīḥ (III. 100.7)

Simple Meaning—Brahmā continued, 'I shall show you the way which will enable you to kill Vṛtrāsura. You need the help of the great Ṛṣi (sage) Dadhīci, who is very kind and large-hearted.'

3.16. *taṁ gatvā sahitāḥ sarve*
varaṁ vai samprayācata
sa vo dāsyati dharmātmā
suprītenāntarātmanā (III. 100.8)

Simple Meaning—Brahmā went on, 'My advice is that all of you, firmly united, go to Ṛṣi Dadhīci and request him to grant you a boon. He is a pious soul, and he will gladly fulfil your wish.'

sa vācyaḥ sahitaiḥ sarvair
bhavadbhirjayakānkṣibhiḥ
svānyasthīni prayaccheti
trailokyasya hitāya vai (III. 100.9)

Simple Meaning—Brahmā specified the boon that the Gods should ask for, "When the Ṛṣi asks you how he could help, then all of you should make a joint request, viz. O great soul, for the good of the three worlds, we have to kill Vṛtrāsura, and to enable us to do that, kindly give us your bones.'

sa śarīraṁ samutsṛjya
svānyasthīni pradāsyati
tasyāsthibhirmahāghoraṁ
vajraṁ saṁskriyatāṁ dṛḍham (III. 100.10)

Simple Meaning—Brahmā concluded his advice to the gods with an assurance that Ṛṣi Dadhīci will gladly give up his life to save the world, 'O gods, don't entertain the least doubt about the successful completion of the plan that I have told you. Ṛṣi Dadhīci is a great soul and he will gladly give you his bones, to enable you to make the most powerful weapon (which will be called 'vajra').'

3.17. *nārāyaṇaṁ puraskṛtya*
dadhīcasyāśramaṁ yayuḥ
sarasvatyāḥ pare pāre
nānādrumalatāvṛtam (III. 100.13)

Simple Meaning—The gods, acting on the advice of Brahmā, and led by Nārāyaṇa, went to the āśrama (hermitage) of Ṛṣi Dadhīci, which was located on the banks of the river Saraswati and which presented a peaceful sight with plenty of trees and creepers.

mahiṣaiśca varāhaiśca
sṛmaraiścamarairapi
tatra tatrānucaritaṁ
śārdūlabhayavarjitaiḥ (III. 100.15)

Simple Meaning—Since Ṛṣi Dadhīci had achieved spiritual perfection based on the highest level of 'ahiṁsā' (non-violence), even the animals of his āśrama had given up violence. Therefore, buffaloes, boars, deer and other living creatures wandered there at pleasure, without any fear from tigers.

3.18. *tasya pādau surā rājan*
abhivādya praṇamya ca
ayācanta varaṁ sarve
yathoktaṁ parameṣṭhinā (III. 100.20)

Simple Meaning—Ṛṣi Lomaśa, narrating this story to King Yudhiṣṭhira said, 'O King, the gods paid full respects to Ṛṣi Dadhīci (saluting his feet and bowing unto him) and then begged of him the boon (i.e. asked for his bones)—exactly as Brahmā had advised them to do.'

3.19. *tato dadhīcaḥ paramapratītaḥ*
surottamāṁstānidamabhyuvāca
karomi yad vo hitamadya devāḥ
svaṁ cāpi dehaṁ svayamutsṛjāmi (III. 100.21)

Simple Meaning—Ṛṣi Dadhīci felt happy that he would be able to contribute to the good of the worlds. So he said to the gods, 'What is to the good of all of you will be done by me immediately, i.e. I shall give up my body voluntarily.'

sa evamuktvā dvipadāṁ variṣṭhaḥ
prāṇān vaśī svān sahasotsasarja
tataḥ surāste jagṛhuḥ parāsor
asthīni tasyātha yathopadeśam (III. 100.22)

Simple Meaning— Ṛṣi Dadhīci—the foremost of men, the great Yogin, having said so to the gods, suddenly renounced his life. Thereafter, the gods, acting on the advice of Brahmā, took the bones of the Ṛṣi (to make the special weapon 'vajra' which put an end to the cruelty of the demon Vṛtrāsura).[1]

3.20. Before concluding this section, we want to mention that the Dadhīci-story is retold in Śānti-Parva, although the narration there is rather brief. We reproduce here only the following lines from that narration (which is in prose) :

atha dadhīcastathaivāvimanāḥ
sukhaduḥkhasamo mahāyogī ātmānaṁ
samādhāya śarīraparityāgaṁ cakāra (XII. 342.40)

Simple Meaning— Ṛṣi Dadhīci was a great Yogin, even-minded towards joys and sorrows, and constantly experiencing bliss. He concentrated his ātman into Paramātman, and cast off his body (for the good of the three worlds).

CHAPTER 4

Vyādha-Gītā—How a Butcher Taught a Brahmin

4.1. The story of a butcher teaching a brahmin is one of the most popular narrations in the Mahābhārata. It occurs in Vana-Parva (i.e. Parva No.3) and is told to Yudhiṣṭhira by Ṛṣi Mārkaṇḍeya. In fact, the full story has three characters, viz. a brahmin, a housewife and a butcher. Briefly, the story starts when a brahmin with yogic power, feels disturbed due to a bird dropping dirt on his head. Then, merely by his angry looks, the bird falls down dead. This incident fills the brahmin with arrogance. With this feeling, he goes to a house, begging for food, but the housewife (nursing her sick husband) says, 'Please wait'. The brahmin expresses anger, at which the housewife says, 'I am not a bird'. The brahmin is amazed and asks her how she came to know about the bird. The housewife says, 'A butcher in Mithilā will answer your question'. So the brahmin goes to see the butcher (Vyādha in Sanskrit), and listens to Vyādha-Gītā (i.e. teachings of the butcher)—and even puts into practice what he learns from this visit.

4.2. With this background, we present selected verses from Vana-Parva which tell the story as well as summarize the teachings given by Vyādha to the brahmin. The brahmin's name is Kauśika, but the names of other characters is not specified in the Mahābhārata. The opening verses introduce the brahmin as a learned person (but the weak point of his character, viz. arrogance, is brought out gradually as the story goes on) :

kaścid dvijātipravaro
vedādhyāyī tapodhanaḥ

tapasvī dharmaśīlasca
kauśiko nāma bhārata (III. 206.1)

Simple Meaning—Ṛṣi Mārkaṇḍeya tells the story to Yudhiṣṭhira, 'O descendent of Bharata, there was a learned brahmin, Kauśika by name, who was known because of his Vedic studies, austerities, etc.'

sāṅgopaniṣado vedān
adhīte dvijasattamaḥ
sa vṛkṣamūle kasmiṁścid
vedānuccārayan sthitaḥ (III. 206.2)

Simple Meaning— That learned brahmin used to spend a good deal of time, studying the Vedas, the Upaniṣads, etc. One day, he sat under a tree with the intention of reciting the Vedas.

4.3. *upariṣṭācca vṛkṣasya*
balākā sannyalīyata
tayā purīṣamutsṛṣṭaṁ
brāhmaṇasya tadopari (III. 206.3)

Simple Meaning— It so happened that a bird, which was resting on the branches of the same tree, disturbed the brahmin by dropping dirt on his head.

tāmavekṣya tataḥ kruddhaḥ
samapadhyāyata dvijaḥ
bhṛśaṁ krodhābhibhūtena
balākā sā nirīkṣitā (III. 206.4)

Simple Meaning— Such a behavior on the part of the bird aroused the anger of the brahmin. He threw angry looks at the bird, as if he cursed her.

apadhyāta ca vipreṇa
nyapatad dharaṇītale
balākāṁ patitāṁ dṛṣṭvā ....
grāmaṁ bhaikṣyāya saṁśritaḥ (III. 206.5,7)

Simple Meaning— Because of the angry looks of the brahmin, the bird fell down dead. The brahmin noted that the bird had been punished for its misbehavior. Shortly thereafter, the brahmin went to the nearby village begging for food.

4.4. *praviṣṭastat kulaṁ yatra*
pūrvaṁ caritavāṁstu saḥ
dehīti yācamāno'sau
tiṣṭhetyuktaḥ striyā tataḥ (III. 206.8)

Simple Meaning— The brahmin stood in front of a house where he had begged earlier too. He announced his arrival and said, 'Please give me food'. He then heard the housewife's reply, 'Please wait'.

kurvatī patiśuśrūṣāṁ
sasmārātha śubhekṣaṇā ....
bhikṣāmādāya viprāya
nirjagāma yaśasvinī (III. 206.16-17)

Simple Meaning— The housewife had to look after her sick husband (and this took some time). Then she realized that a brahmin was waiting at the door, and desirous of helping him too, she came to the door with food.

Brāhmaṇa uvāca:
kimidaṁ bhavati tvaṁ māṁ
tiṣṭhetyuktvā varāṅgane
uparodhaṁ kṛtavatī
na visarjitavatsyasi (III. 206. 18)

Simple Meaning— The brahmin spoke angrily to the housewife, 'O lady, what sort of behavior is this ? Either you should have given me food immediately, or you should have asked me to go to the next house. Why did you say, 'Please wait'—and then kept me waiting for such a long time ?'

4.5. Stryuvāca:
nāhaṁ balākā viprarṣe
tyaja krodhaṁ tapodhana ....
balākā hi tvayā dagdhā
roṣāt tad viditaṁ mayā
krodhaḥ śatruḥ śarīrastho
manuṣyāṇāṁ dvijottama (III. 206. 23,32)

Simple Meaning— The housewife replied, 'O learned brahmin, please don't be angry (because I had to pay urgent attention to my sick husband). I know that your angry looks burnt a bird to death—but I am not a bird. Moreover, anger is not good for you—it is a man's great enemy.'

na tu tattvena bhagavān
dharmaṁ vetsīti me matiḥ
yadi vipra na jānīṣe
dharmaṁ paramakaṁ dvija
dharmavyādhaṁ tataḥ pṛccha
gatvā tu mithilāṁ purīm (III. 206. 43,44)

Simple Meaning— The housewife (after explaining the cause of delay for which she was sorry), concluded with some words of advice to the brahmin, 'O scholar, although you have studied the Vedas, it seems to me that you have not understood the essence of dharma. With a view to helping you in this matter, I suggest that you go to Mithilā and see 'dharmavyādha' (i.e. the righteous butcher)—he will answer all your questions about dharma.'

4.6. *tato jagāma mithilāṁ*
janakena surakṣitāṁ
dharmasetusamākīrṇāṁ
yajñotsavavatīṁ śubhām (III. 207.6)

Simple Meaning— The brahmin accepted the housewife's advice and went to Mithilā, the capital city of the famous King Janaka, which was also a center for dharma-related activities and discussions.

dharmavyādhamapṛcchacca
sa cāsya kathito dvijaiḥ
apaśyat tatra gatvā taṁ
sūnāmadhye vyavasthitam (III. 207.10)

Simple Meaning— Having arrived in Mithilā, the brahmin asked the people there about Dharmavyādha and they showed him the way to the meat-store where this famous butcher sold meat.

4.7. Vyādha uvāca:
ekapatnyā yadukto'si
gaccha tvaṁ mithilāmiti
jānāmyetadahaṁ sarvaṁ
yadarthaṁ tavamihāgataḥ (III. 207.14)

Simple Meaning— The butcher welcomed the brahmin and added, 'O learned guest, I know that you have been advised by the housewife to come here and discuss with me issues of dharma.'

śrutvā ca tasya tad vākyaṁ
sa vipro bhṛśavismitaḥ
dvitīyamidamāścaryaṁ
ityacintayata dvijaḥ (III. 207.15)

Simple Meaning— The brahmin was amazed to hear these words of the butcher. He had earlier felt the same way when the housewife spoke about the bird, and he now said to himself, 'This is the second surprise that I have experienced.'

4.8. *agratastu dvijam kṛtvā*
sa jagāma gṛhaṁ prati ....
tataḥ sukhopaviṣṭastaṁ
vyādhaṁ vacanamabravīt (III. 207.17, 18)

Simple Meaning— The butcher took the brahmin to his (i.e. the butcher's) house and again spoke words of welcome. When the brahmin had occupied a comfortable seat in the house, he asked the butcher why, after having acquired so much knowledge about dharma, he still sold meat.

Vyādha uvāca:
kulocitamidaṁ karma
pitṛpaitāmahaṁ paraṁ
vartamānasya me dharme
sve manyuṁ mā kṛthā dvija (III. 207.20)

Simple Meaning— The butcher said, 'O learned brahmin, my family has been engaged in this occupation (of selling meat) since many generations, so I have felt that this work is suitable for me too, and is not contrary to dharma. Please do not think that I am doing anything improper.'

vidhātrā vihitaṁ pūrvaṁ
karma svamanupālayan
prayatnācca gurū vṛddhav
śuśrūṣe 'haṁ dvijottama (III.207.21)

Simple Meaning— The butcher added, 'Although for purposes of earning a living, I carry on my hereditary occupation, I devote a good deal of my time to look after my parents who are quite old now.'

pareṇa hi hatān brahman varāhamahiṣānahaṁ
na svayaṁ hanmi viprarṣe vikrīṇāmi sadā tvahaṁ
na bhakṣayāmi māṁsāni .... (III.207.32,33)

Simple Meaning— The butcher clarified that selling of meat did not imply that he himself killed animals or ate meat, 'O kind-hearted soul, I only sell the meat of those animals which have been killed by others, i.e. I myself do not kill any animal. Furthermore, I do not eat meat (i.e. I am a vegetarian).'

4.9. Brāhmaṇa uvāca:
śiṣṭācāraṁ kathamahaṁ
vidyāmiti narottama (III.207.60)

Simple Meaning— The brahmin said, 'O best among men, I want to learn from you about right conduct.'

Vyādha uvāca:
kāmakrodhau vaśe kṛtvā
dambhaṁ lobhamanārjavaṁ
dharmamityeva santuṣṭās
te śiṣṭāḥ śiṣtasammatāḥ (III.207.63)

Simple Meaning— The butcher said, 'Right conduct is achieved through a co-ordinated effort in two directions, viz. keeping under control the vices (the most harmful vices being selfishness, anger, vanity, greed and crookedness), and promoting virtues (the most helpful virtues being those that hold the society together). Such an approach leads to right conduct and is maintained even after attaining the state of perfection.'

ahiṁsā satyavacanaṁ sarvabhūtahitaṁ paraṁ ....
yad bhūtahitamatyantaṁ
tat satyamiti dhāraṇā (III. 207.74 and 209.4)

Simple Meaning— Ahiṁsā (non-violence) and Satya (truth) are the two main pillars of dharma through which the highest good of all can be achieved. In fact, a decision on what is true (under difficult circumstances) should be made by sticking to that course of action which leads to the highest good of beings.

sarvabhūtadayāvanto
ahiṁsāniratāḥ sadā ....

nyāyopetā guṇopetāḥ
sarvalokahitaiṣiṇaḥ (III. 207.84, 86)

Simple Meaning— A visible characteristic of those who are devoted to ahiṁsā is that they have compassion towards all beings and their conduct is lawful and just. Moreover, the essence of all the virtues that these people have, is the desire to do good to all.

4.10. Brāhmaṇa uvāca:

pativratāyāḥ satyāyāḥ
śīlāḍhyāyā yatavrata
saṁsmṛtya vākyaṁ dharmajña
guṇavānasi me mataḥ (III. 215.4)

Simple Meaning— The brahmin said, 'I am convinced that you not only know dharma but you also put it into practice. I recall that the housewife, who advised me to come here and who herself is so virtuous, had such a high opinion about the virtues that you possess. (I have also been wonder-struck by the way both of you come to know of things as if by divine sight).'

Vyādha uvāca:

yat tadā tvaṁ dvijaśreṣtha
tayokto māṁ prati prabho
dṛṣtameva tayā samyag
ekapatnyā na saṁśayaḥ (III. 215.5)

Simple Meaning— The butcher said, 'O learned brahmin, I am glad that you appreciate the spiritual attainment of the virtuous housewife—she really has divine sight and she told you in advance about me and my practice of dharma.'

tvadanugrahabuddhyā tu
vipraitad darśitaṁ mayā
vākyaṁ ca śṛṇu me tāta
yat te vakṣye hitaṁ dvija (III. 215.6)

Simple Meaning— The butcher went on, 'I have told you all this because I am favorably inclined towards you. I hope you will continue listening to me because I shall say what will do good to you (i.e. please don't take it as a criticism).'

4.11. *tvayā vinikṛtā mātā*
pitā ca dvijasattama

anisṛṣṭo'si niṣkrānto
gṛhāt tābhyāmanindita
vedoccāraṇakāryārthaṁ
ayuktaṁ tat tvayā kṛtaṁ
tava śokena vṛddhau tau
andhībhūtau tapasvinau (III.215.7-8)

Simple Meaning— The butcher said to the brahmin, 'O Vedic scholar, I want you to realize that you did not attach due importance to the wishes of your parents—in fact, you left home (for the purpose of learning the Vedas) without their permission. This was an improper act on your part because, due to the grief and shock caused by your absence, your old parents became blind.'

tau prasādayituṁ gaccha
mā tvāṁ dharmo'tyagādayaṁ
tapasvī tvaṁ mahātmā ca
dharme ca nirataḥ sadā (III. 215.9)

Simple Meaning— The butcher added words of advice, 'O learned brahmin, please go home for the pleasure of your parents. Don't think that this will make you less righteous—you are a great soul, devoted to austerity and dharma—and your return to your parents will not have any adverse impact on your virtues.'

sarvametadapārthaṁ te
kṣipraṁ tau samprasādaya
śraddadhasva mama brahman
nānyathā kartumarhasi
gamyatāmadya viprarṣe
śreyaste kathayāmyaham (III. 215.10)

Simple Meaning— The butcher concluded with an assurance that his advice will definitely do good to the brahmin, 'O great scholar, please have faith in what I say. You left home for study and austerity, but this path led you nowhere because you neglected your obligations to your parents. Now is the time for you to regain what you have lost. Please return to your parents and look after them. This—and nothing else—is the proper way for you, to achieve what is good for you.'

4.12. Brāhmaṇa uvāca:

patamāno'dya narake
bhavatāsmi samuddhṛtaḥ
bhavitavyamathaivaṁ ca
yad dṛṣṭo'si mayānagha (III. 215.16)

Simple Meaning— The brahmin said, 'O pure soul, I was falling into hell, but you have saved me. I am lucky that I came here and saw you. Now I am going to do exactly as you have advised me'.

rājā yayātirdauhitraiḥ
patitastārito yathā
sadbhiḥ puruṣaśārdūla
tathāhaṁ bhavatā dvijaḥ (III. 215.17)

Simple Meaning— The brahmin recalled the old story of King Yayāti's fall and re-entry into heaven (summarized by us in para 2.16), and spoke to the butcher, 'O pious well-wisher, just as Yayāti's grandsons saved him when he was falling down from heaven (and re-elevated him), similarly, you have saved me and shown me the way by which I can re-acquire the virtues associated with a brahmin.'

mātāpitṛbhyāṁ śuśrūṣāṁ
kariṣye vacanāt tava
nākṛtātmā vedayati
dharmādharmaviniścayam (III. 215.18)

Simple Meaning— The brahmin declared his acceptance of the advice given by the butcher, 'O great soul, I shall follow your advice and serve my parents. I am now convinced that purity of heart and gratefulness are necessary for acquiring the ability to distinguish between dharma and adharma (i.e. between right and wrong).'

4.13. *durjñeyaḥ śāśvato dharmaḥ*
śūdrayonau hi vartate
na tvāṁ śūdramahaṁ manye
bhavitavyaṁ hi kāraṇam (III. 215.19)

Simple Meaning— Although the main purpose of the brahmin's visit to Mithilā was achieved, a curiosity of his still remained to be cleared—and so he said to the butcher, 'O pure soul, I do not consider you as a śūdra (a person of low caste) but this is how the society views you. I wonder how, in spite of being a śūdra, you understand dharma fully, even those aspects which are difficult to know. There must be some special reason why this combination of śūdrahood and knowledge of dharma is found in you.'

Vyādha uvāca:
ahaṁ hi brāhmaṇaḥ pūrvaṁ
āsaṁ dvijavarātmajaḥ ....
ātmadoṣakṛtairbrahman
avasthāmāptavānimām (III. 215.22-23)

Simple Meaning— The butcher said, 'O learned brahmin, I too was a brahmin in my earlier life, possessing knowledge of the Vedas, etc. This downfall of mine (from a brahmin to a śūdra) is the result of my own fault'.

4.14. The butcher then narrated a story of his previous birth—how he mistakenly killed a Ṛṣi, for which he apologized and asked for forgiveness. We omit details of this story, but pick up the thread from the point when the Ṛṣi softened his curse and mixed therewith his blessing :

Ṛṣiruvāca:
śūdrayonyāṁ vartamāno
dharmajño hi bhaviṣyasi
mātāpitrośca śuśrūṣāṁ
kariṣyasi na saṁśayaḥ
tayā śuśrūṣayā siddhiṁ
mahattvaṁ samavāpsyasi (III. 216.4-5)

Simple Meaning— The Ṛṣi said, 'Although you will be born in a śūdra family, you will acquire full knowledge of dharma and you will have the virtue of looking after your parents—and such service of the parents will lead you to spiritual perfection.'

4.15. Brāhmaṇa uvāca:
sāmpratаṁ ca mato me'si brāhmaṇo nātra saṁśayaḥ
brāhmaṇaḥ patanīyeṣu vartamāno vikarmasu
dāmbhiko duṣkṛtaḥ prāyaḥ śūdreṇa sadṛśo bhavet
yastu śūdro dame satye dharme ca satatotthitaḥ
taṁ brāhmaṇamahaṁ manye vṛttena hi bhaved dvijaḥ
(III. 216.13-14)

Simple Meaning— The butcher's story (of previous birth) set at rest the curiosity of the brahmin, who then spoke words of wisdom, 'O pure soul, in my opinion, you are a brahmin, and there is no doubt about that, because good conduct is the main determinant of brahminhood. Even if one is a brahmin by birth, he is like a śūdra if he is engaged in unrighteous activities and is down with vices. On the other hand, even if one is a śūdra by birth, he is, in my opinion, a brahmin if he has virtues (like purity, self-discipline, truth, etc.) and if he is trying all the time for his spiritual upliftment.'

4.16. We conclude this summary of Vyādha-Gītā by reproducing two lines which show how the brahmin and the butcher bade farewell to each other :

āpṛcche tvāṁ svasti te'stu
dharmastvāṁ parirakṣatu ....
bāḍhamityeva taṁ vyādhaḥ
kṛtāñjaliruvāca ha (III. 216.31-32)

Simple Meaning— The brahmin finally said, 'O pious soul, I now seek your permission to go. I wish you the best and I pray that dharma may always protect you'. The butcher, with folded hands, reciprocated the parting wish, and said, 'Very well, O learned brahmin, best wishes and prayers from me to you too'.

As an indicator of the importance of Vyādha-Gītā, we may mention that Swami Vivekananda included a summary of it in "karma-yoga" which is one of his most famous books based mainly on Bhagavad-Gītā.[1]

CHAPTER 5

Story of Aśvapati and Sāvitrī

5.1. The story of King Aśvapati and his daughter Sāvitrī was narrated to Yudhiṣṭhira by Ṛṣi Mārkaṇḍeya in Vana-Parva. For the women of India, Sāvitrī has since become a famous name whose strength of character was recognized even by Yama, the god of death. However, in this short presentation, we want to include, along with Sāvitrī, her father Aśvapati also because he was a spiritually perfect Karmayogin, devoted to the good of all, as the following verses of the Mahābhārata show :

āsīnmadreṣu dharmātmā rājā paramadhārmikaḥ
brahmaṇyaśca mahātma ca satyasandho jitendriyaḥ
yajvā dānapatirdakṣaḥ paurajānapadapriyaḥ
pārthivo'śvapatirnāma sarvabhūtahite rataḥ
kṣamāvānanapatyaśca satyavāg vijitendriyaḥ

(III. 293.5-7)

Simple Meaning— Once upon a time, long ago, Aśvapati was the king of Madra-deśa. His devotion to dharma was perfect. He was a great soul, adhering to truth, and self-disciplined. He honored learned people, performed yajñas, shared his wealth with others, and was a strong believer in karma-yoga. He was always engaged in doing good to all the people, urban as well as rural, and they in turn loved him. In spite of all the virtues, his happiness was incomplete because he had no children. (We should hasten to add that this problem was solved when Sāvitrī was born).

5.2. Vidyut Aklujkar, in his article entitled 'Sāvitrī : Old and New' says that Sri Aurobindo, in his English epic 'Savitri' has attached much importance to her father also :

> "Out of the Mahābhārata myth of about 700 verses, Aurobindo has created what is perhaps the largest epic in Modern English, of about 24,000 lines and 17 cantos.... Apart from the symbolic interpretation that changes the impact of his new epic, Aurobindo has introduced many significant changes in the story. Aurobindo's Aśvapatī (Aswapathy in his spelling) is an active seeker of truth, a yogin, "the leader of the human race on its evolutionary march", whose journey into the occult worlds occupies more than one-third of the epic."[1]

5.3. Now the famous story of Sāvitrī in brief. As we mentioned in para 5.1, King Aśvapati, while advancing in age, had only one reason for being unhappy—he had no child. He performed penance for eighteen years in the hope of obtaining a son. Goddess Sāvitrī appeared before the king and said that, by the grace of Brahmā, he will be blessed with a daughter of great effulgence (tejas) who will bring even greater bliss to him than any son could have done. Ṛṣi Mārkaṇḍeya told Yudhiṣṭhira why the daughter was called 'Sāvitrī' :

sāvitryā prītayā dattā
sāvitryā hutayā hyapi
sāvitrītyeva nāmāsyās
cakrurviprāstathā pitā (III. 293.24)

Simple Meaning—The daughter was given to Aśvapati by goddess Sāvitrī, who was pleased by the chanting of gāyatrī-mantra, therefore the father (Aśvapati) as well as the brahmin-priests gave the name 'Sāvitrī' to the daughter.

5.4. Sāvitrī grew up, unsurpassed in beauty, wisdom and virtue. However, awed by her radiance, no one came forward to seek her hand. So her father sent her off to find a match for herself :

Rājovāca:
putri pradānakālaste
na ca kaścid vṛṇoti māṁ
svayamanviccha bhartāraṁ
guṇaiḥ sadṛśamātmanaḥ (III. 293.32)

Simple Meaning—King Aśvapati said to his daughter Sāvitrī, 'My dear daughter, this is the right time when you should get married. However, awed by your radiance, no one has come forward to seek your hand. Therefore, you yourself have to find a suitable match (i.e. one who is as qualified as you are).'

prārthitaḥ puruṣo yaśca sa nivedyastvayā mama
vimṛśyāhaṁ pradāsyāmi varaya tvaṁ yathepsitam
(III. 293.33)

Simple Meaning—The king clarified what he had in his mind, 'When you have found a suitable match, tell me about that young man so that, after due consideration, I shall finalize your marriage with him. But you have to choose one whom you like.'

5.5. Sāvitrī travelled to various places and finally succeeded in finding a suitable match for herself. When she returned to her father to make the announcement, Ṛṣi Nārada also happened to be there. Sāvitrī said , in front of all, 'I have identified Satyavān as my husband-to-be. His father Dyumatsena used to be a king, but suddenly he became blind, so a neighboring ruler deprived Dyumatsena of his kingdom. He now lives in the woods, with his wife and son (i.e. Satyavān).'

5.6. Ṛṣi Nārada (who could read the future also) said that Satyavān has all the qualities to match Sāvitrī's, but his life's span will come to an end after one year :

Nārada uvāca:
sa dāntaḥ sa mṛduḥ śūraḥ
sa satyaḥ saṁyatendriyaḥ
sa maitraḥ so'nasūyaśca
sa hrīmān dyutimāṁśca saḥ (III. 294.19)

Simple Meaning--Ṛṣi Nārada listed the various qualities of Satyavān, for example, he said, 'Satyavān is great in self-discipline, he is brave but mild, truthful as well as avoiding extremes. He is friendly towards all, he does not find faults of others, he has a great personality but he does not show it off.'

eko doṣo'sti nānyo'sya
so'dyaprabhṛti satyavān
saṁvatsareṇa kṣīṇāyur
dehanyāsaṁ kariṣyati (III. 294.23)

Simple Meaning—After listing the qualities of Satyavān, Ṛṣi Nārada pointed out one serious problem, 'O king, I see only one problem, viz. that Satyavān's life span will come to an end after one year from today and he will give up this body.'

5.7. However, Sāvitrī's firm determination was not shaken, and she announced again :

sakṛdaṁśo nipatati
sakṛt kanyā pradīyate
sakṛdāha dadānīti
trīṇyetāni sakṛt sukṛt (III. 294.26)

Simple Meaning—Sāvitrī said, 'O my respected father, I believe in the old saying that there are three things in life which take place only once (i.e. decisions relating to them are made only once) and these three things are—division of property among brothers, giving away of one's daughter in marriage and use of the words 'I give' while making a donation.'

After making a general statement, Sāvitrī made a categorical announcement of her determination not to change her mind about marriage with Satyavān.

dīrghāyurathavālpāyuḥ
saguṇo nirguṇo'pi vā
sakṛd vṛto mayā bhartā
na dvitīyaṁ vṛṇomyaham (III. 294.27)

Simple Meaning—Sāvitrī's final words were, 'As I already said, I have identified Satyavān as my husband-to-be. That decision of mine is final, and is not subject to change, whether he will have a long life or a short life, and whether he has qualities or does not have qualities—under no circumstances am I going to choose another husband.'

5.8. Aśvapati travelled with Sāvitrī to the woods where Satyavān and his parents lived, to perform a simple marriage ceremony. Satyavān's father, Dyumatsen, while welcoming Sāvitrī as his daughter-in-law, wondered how she will adjust to life in the woods, but Sāvitrī's enthusiastic acceptance of her new role set every one's mind at rest :

gate pitari sarvāṇi
sannyasyābharaṇāni sā

jagṛhe valkalānyeva
vastraṁ kāṣāyameva ca (III. 295.18)

Simple Meaning—After the marriage ceremony (of Sāvitrī and Satyavān), Aśvapati returned to his kingdom. When her father had departed, Sāvitrī put off all her ornaments, and clad herself in barks and red-colored clothes appropriate to life in the woods.

paricārairguṇaiścaiva
praśrayeṇa damena ca
sarvakāmakriyābhiśca
sarveṣāṁ tuṣṭimādadhe (III. 295.19)

Simple Meaning—Sāvitrī earned everyone's pleasure and appreciation, because of her selfless service, good qualities, tenderness, self-denial, and performance of acts suited to everyone's needs and desires.

5.9. *śvaśrūṁ śarīrasatkāraiḥ*
sarvairācchādanādibhiḥ
śvaśuraṁ devasatkārair
vācaḥ saṁyamanena ca (III. 295.20)

Simple Meaning—Sāvitrī gratified her mother-in-law by attending to her person and by offering her suitable clothes and ornaments. Similarly, she gratified her father-in-law by worshipping him as a god and by using words that reflected her self-discipline.

tathaiva priyavādena
naipuṇena śamena ca
rahaścaivopacāreṇa
bhartāraṁ paryatoṣayat (III. 295.21)

Simple Meaning—Sāvitrī pleased her husband by her sweet words, her skill in every kind of work, the evenness of her temper, and by indications of her love in private. (It is significant that Sāvitrī viewed her duties from a balanced perspective, and gave priority to the needs of her parents-in-law, and then attended to her husband too).

5.10. *evaṁ tatrāśrame teṣāṁ*
tadā nivasatāṁ satāṁ
kālastapasyatāṁ kaścid
apākrāmata bhārata (III. 295.22)

Simple Meaning—Ṛṣi Mārkaṇḍeya said to Yudhiṣṭhira, 'O descendant of Bharata, encouraged by the sweet behavior of Sāvitrī, the family intensified their spiritual practices and spent their time in that nice atmosphere (where other pious dwellers of the woods also lived).'

sāvitryā glāyamānāyās
tiṣṭhantyāstu divāniśaṁ
nāradena yaduktaṁ tad
vākyaṁ manasi vartate (III. 295.23)

Simple Meaning—Ṛṣi Mārkaṇḍeya added, 'Although, outwardly, everything appeared to be moving on nicely, there was no peace in the mind of Sāvitrī, because she was the only one in that group who knew what Ṛṣi Nārada had predicted about Satyavān's life—she recalled those words day and night and sorrow filled her heart.'

5.11. Finally, the fateful day arrived when, according to Nārada's forecast, Satyavān's life was destined to come to an end (although no one else, other than Sāvitrī, knew about it). Sāvitrī did not want her husband to go alone to another part of the woods on that day, so she got permission from her parents-in-law and acompanied Satyavān :

ubhābhyāmabhyanujñātā
sā jagāma yaśasvinī
saha bhartrā hasantīva
hṛdayena vidūyatā (III. 296.29)

Simple Meaning—Sāvitrī obtained permission from both (i.e. her mother-in-law and father-in-law) to go with Satyavān to another part of the forest. Outwardly, she was smiling as she walked with her husband, but she was extremely sad at heart (as if burning with fire of grief).

anuvrajantī bhartāraṁ
jagāma mṛdugāminī
dvidheva hṛdayaṁ kṛtvā
taṁ ca kālamavekṣatī (III. 296.33)

Simple Meaning—Ṛṣi Mārkaṇḍeya draws attention to Sāvitrī's capacity to face the approaching crisis—it was as if she divided her heart into two parts, using one part to walk with Satyavān (without giving him any hint of what she was afraid of), and using the other to wait for the arrival of the messenger of death.

5.12. Satyavān suddenly felt pain all over his body, and unable to walk or stand any longer, he lay down on the ground, as if fast asleep :

Satyavānuvāca:
vyāyāmena mamānena
jātā śirasi vedanā
angāni caiva sāvitrī
hṛdayaṁ dūyatīva ca
asvasthamiva cātmānaṁ
lakṣaye mitabhāṣiṇi (III. 297.3-4)

Simple Meaning—Satyavān said to Sāvitrī, 'O dear, it seems that the hard work involved in cutting wood has caused me headache and pain all over my body. I also have a burning sensation in my heart. In fact, I am feeling quite unwell.'

sūlairiva śiro viddhaṁ
idaṁ saṁlakṣayāmyahaṁ
tat svaptumicche kalyāṇi
na sthātuṁ śaktirasti me (III. 297.5)

Simple Meaning—Satyavān continued, 'O Sāvitrī, I feel as if my head is being pierced with numerous darts. O my well-wisher, I want to sleep because I don't have any strength to stand.'

5.13. Sāvitrī saw Yama (the god of death) and entered into conversation with him. When Yama started going back (with Satyavān's life), Sāvitrī followed him. She was able to do so because of the strength of her character. Yama was impressed, so he offered to grant her a boon (other than Satyavān's life)—advising her at the same time that she should not follow him (i.e. Yama) any longer :

Yama uvāca:
nivarta tuṣto'smi tvānayā girā
svarākṣaravyanjanahetuyuktayā
varaṁ vṛṇīṣveha vināsya jīvitaṁ
dadāni te sarvamanindite varam (III. 297.26)

Simple Meaning—Yama said to Sāvitrī, 'O faultless lady, please do not follow me any more. I am highly pleased with the way you have spoken to me—you have expressed wonderful ideas in faultless speech. Ask for a boon, I shall grant you any boon other than the life of Satyavān.'

5.14. Sāvitrī's first wish was that her father-in-law should regain his eye-sight :

Sāvitryuvāca:
cyutaḥ svarājyād vanavāsamāśrito
vinaṣṭacakṣuḥ śvaśuro mamāśrame
sa labdhacakṣurbalavān bhavennṛpas
tava prasādājjvalanārkasannibhaḥ (III. 297.27)

Simple Meaning—Sāvitrī said to Yama, 'O kind-hearted god, the favor that I seek from you is for the restoration of my father-in-law's eyesight—having lost his kingdom as well as eye-sight, he is leading a life of retirement in the woods. I pray that by your grace, he may get back his eye-sight and he may be strong and effulgent like the fire and the sun.' (We want to remark that Sāvitrī's sense of priorities is an indicator of her wisdom).

5.15. Yama granted the first boon, but Sāvitrī kept following him. When asked by Yama why she did not want to go back, Sāvitrī said :

satāṁ sannivaset samāgame (III. 297.30)

i.e. that one should live in the company of good people. Yama was pleased with this statement and he offered to grant her a second boon (other than Satyavān's life) :

Yama uvāca:
mano'nukūlaṁ budhabuddhivardhanaṁ
tvayā yaduktaṁ vacanaṁ hitāśrayaṁ
vinā punaḥ satyavato'sya jīvitaṁ
varaṁ dvitīyaṁ varayasva bhāmini (III. 297.31)

Simple Meaning—Yama said to Sāvitrī, 'O wise lady, the statement that you have made is beneficial to all—I am pleased with this and it can enhance the wisdom of even the learned people—therefore I shall grant you a second boon (other than Satyavān's life).'

5.16. Sāvitrī's second wish was that her father-in-law should regain his kingdom and that his devotion to dharma should remain steadfast for ever :

Sāvitryuvāca:
hṛtaṁ purā me śvaśurasya dhīmataḥ
svameva rājyaṁ labhatāṁ sa pārthivaḥ
jahyāt svadharmaṁ na ca me guruṛyathā
dvitīyametad varayāmi te varam (III. 297.32)

Simple Meaning—Sāvitrī said to Yama, 'O generous god, the second favor that I seek from you is for the restoration of my father-in-law's kingdom. Although my father-in-law is wise, his kingdom was snatched away from him. I pray that by your grace, he may regain his kingdom, and that his devotion to dharma may remain steadfast for ever.'

5.17. Yama granted the second boon, but Sāvitrī still kept following him. When asked by Yama why she did not want to return, Sāvitrī said :

santastvevāpyamitreṣu dayām prāpteṣu kurvate
(III.297.36)

i.e. good people (like you) show compassion to even their foes when they seek their protection. Yama was pleased with this statement and he offered to grant her a third boon (other than Satyavān's life) :

Yama uvāca:
pipāsitasyeva bhaved yathā payas
tathā tvayā vākyamidaṁ samīritaṁ
vinā punaḥ satyavato'sya jīvitaṁ
varaṁ vṛṇīṣveha śubhe yadicchasi (III. 297.37)

Simple Meaning—Yama said to Sāvitrī, 'O good lady, as water gives relief to the thirsty soul, so do I feel pleasure by listening to your wise statement, therefore I shall grant you a third boon (other than Satyavān's life)—if you would like to ask for it.'

5.18. Sāvitrī's third wish was that her parents (to whom she was the only child) should have sons to carry forward the dharmic tradition of their family :

Sāvitryuvāca:
mamānapatyaḥ pṛthivīpatiḥ pitā
bhavet pituḥ putraśataṁ tathaurasaṁ

kulasya santānakaraṁ ca yad bhavet
tṛtīyametad varayāmi te varaṁ (III. 297.38)

Simple Meaning—Sāvitrī said to Yama, 'O merciful god, the third boon that I seek is that my parents (who have no sons) should have one hundred sons to carry forward the tradition of the family.'

5.19. Yama granted the third boon but Sāvitrī still kept following him. When asked by Yama why she did not want to go back, Sāvitrī said :

satsu viśeṣeṇa sarvaḥ praṇayamicchati (III. 297.42)

i.e. everyone (including me) wants to be particularly close to good people (like you). Yama was pleased with this statement and he offered to grant her a fourth boon (other than Satyavān's life) :

Yama uvāca:
udāhṛtaṁ te vacanaṁ yadangane
śubhe na tādṛk tvadṛte śrutaṁ mayā
anena tuṣṭo'smi vināsya jīvitaṁ
varaṁ caturthaṁ varayasva gaccha ca (III. 297.44)

Simple Meaning—Yama said to Sāvitrī, 'O exemplary lady, I have never heard from any one else such a nice statement as you have spoken. I am so pleased with you that I shall grant you a fourth boon (other than Satyavān's life)—and thereafter you should go back.'

5.20. Sāvitrī's fourth wish was that she and Satyavān should have one hundred sons to carry forward the dharmic tradition of this family :

Sāvitryuvāca:
mamātmajaṁ satyavatastathaurasaṁ
bhavedubhābhyāmiha yat kulodvahaṁ
śataṁ sutānāṁ balavīryaśālināṁ
idaṁ caturthaṁ varayāmi te varam (III. 297.45)

Simple Meaning—Sāvitrī said to Yama, 'O boon-granting god, the fourth boon that I look forward to receiving from you is, that I and Satyavān may have one hundred sons, possessed of strength and prowess and capable of carrying forward the dharmic tradition of this family.'

5.21. Yama granted the fourth boon and then advised Sāvitrī to return :

Yama uvāca:
śataṁ sutānāṁ balavīryaśālināṁ
bhaviṣyati prītikaraṁ tavābale
pariśramaste na bhavennṛpātmaje
nivarta dūraṁ hi pathastvamāgatāḥ (III. 297.46)

Simple Meaning—Yama said to Sāvitrī, 'O patient lady, I grant you this boon and you will have one hundred sons, possessed of strength and prowess, and a source of great delight to you. O princess, I now ask you to go back—you have already come too far and must be feeling tired.'

5.22. Sāvitrī pleaded that walking behind her husband did not cause any fatigue. She was grateful to have the opportunity of talking with a good person like Yama whose mission was to help others and thus to bear the burden of the world :

santaḥ parārthaṁ kurvāṇā
nāvekṣanti parasparaṁ ....
santo bhūmiṁ tapasā dharayanti (III. 297.48, 49)

Simple Meaning—Sāvitrī spoke words of wisdom, referring to the helpful nature of good people, 'Good persons do good to others without expecting any benefit for themselves in return .... through this type of spiritual practice, they are able to sustain the world.'

5.23. Yama was so pleased that he offered to grant Sāvitrī a special, fifth boon :

Yama uvāca:
yathā yathā bhāṣasi dharmasaṁhitaṁ
mano'nukūlaṁ supadaṁ mahārthavat
tathā tathā me tvayi bhaktiruttamā
varaṁ vṛṇīṣvāpratimaṁ pativrate (III. 297.51)

Simple Meaning—Yama said to Sāvitrī, 'O great lady spiritually devoted to husband, the more I hear your statements that contain the nectar of dharma, expressed in such sweet and appealing terms, the more affection I feel towards you. Therefore I shall grant you a special, fifth boon.'

5.24. Sāvitrī then pointed out to Yama that, since he has already blessed her (and Satyavān) with one hundred sons (to be born), the only way to have that blessing fulfilled would be to bring Satyavān back to life :

Sāvitryuvāca:
na te'pavargaḥ sukṛtād vinākṛtas
tathā yathānyeṣu vareṣu mānada
varaṁ vṛṇe jīvatu satyavānayaṁ
yathā mṛtā hyevamahaṁ patiṁ vinā (III. 297.52)

Simple Meaning—Sāvitrī said to Yama, 'O bestower of honors, the fourth boon that you granted to me was itself a special boon, because it can be fulfilled only when I live with my husband. In fact, without my husband, I am like a dead person. Therefore, the special boon that I now specifically seek is that Satyavān may come to life again.'

5.25. Yama accepted Sāvitrī's plea, and released Satyavān's life. Sāvitrī then returned and found that her husband was alive. Satyavān himself felt as if he woke up from a long sleep. Then both of them walked back home to see the mother and the father (the latter's eye-sight having been restored by Yama). Everyone felt happy and amazed when they heard from Sāvitrī the full story of her encounter with Yama.[2] Vidyut Aklujkar has summarized the virtues because of which Sāvitrī is recognized as a truly great woman :

"Sāvitrī knows about the impending death of her chosen mate, but in spite of that, she enters the union .... When Satyavān dies, Sāvitrī does not lament. Hers is only a calm, resolute confrontation with Death. She has the strength of character that is a natural outcome of a life of righteous observances, and although she is neither impolite nor aggressive, she never gives up. Like a calculating diplomat, she accepts whatever is offered to her and perseveres in the quest for more. In the end, when she returns, she has her mission fulfilled and has earned a perennial place in the list of great women."[3]

CHAPTER 6

Dialogue between Yakṣa and Yudhiṣṭhira

6.1. The dialogue between Yakṣa and Yudhiṣṭhira is one of the most important sections of the Mahābhārata. This dialogue occurs in Vana-Parva (i.e. Parva No.3) when the Pāṇḍavas had nearly completed their twelve years of stay in various woods. The narrator is Vaiśampāyana who told Janamejaya (i.e. son of Parīkṣita referred to in para 1.14) that Dharmarāja (i.e. the Lord of dharma) assumed the form of a Yakṣa, to see his son Yudhiṣṭhira (referred to in paras 1.8 and 1.38) and also to test whether he (i.e. Yudhiṣṭhira) can give appropriate answers to more than a hundred questions on various aspects of dharma. Yudhiṣṭhira came out successful in the test, and the incident that appeared to bring disaster to the Pāṇḍavas had a happy ending.

6.2. According to B.A. van Nooten "Yakṣas are originally spirits of trees and of bodies of water that are locally deified and later became identified with a class of gods of the Great Tradition. A Yakṣa has monstrous eyes, a great body, is as high as a palm tree, resembling the blazing sun, irresistible, looking like a mountain. Often they are benevolent and together with the Gandharvas form the retinue of the God of Wealth, Kubera." [1]

6.3. The setting for the dialogue between Yakṣa and Yudhiṣṭhira is provided by a deer who ran extremely fast and carried away with itself, as if by chance, a brahmin's fire-making sticks. The brahmin requested the Pāṇḍavas to get those sticks back from the deer, to enable him to perform his yajña. The Pāṇḍavas agreed to help but the deer ran too fast and then became invisible. Losing sight of the deer, the Pāṇḍavas, feeling tired, disappointed and thirsty, approached a banyan tree and sat down in its shade. Yudhiṣṭhira asked Nakula (one of the younger brothers) to climb the tree and look around, in a desperate attempt to find some water in that inhospitable surrounding. Nakula was able to spot a lake inhabited by cranes. However, as soon as Nakula stooped down to drink the water of the lake, he heard a voice from the sky, which was Yakṣa's warning :

Yakṣa uvāca:
mā tāta sāhasaṁ kārṣīr
mama pūrvaparigrahaḥ
praśnānuktvā tu mādreya
tataḥ piba harasva ca (III. 312.12)

Simple Meaning— Yakṣa said to Nakula (whose mother's name was Mādrī, i.e. the second wife of Pāṇḍu referred to in para 1.4), 'O son of Mādrī, do not commit the rash act of drinking water from this lake which has already been taken by me under my control. First answer my questions and then you may drink this water and also take away as much water as you want.'

However, Nakula ignored this warning and drank some water because he was extremely thirsty. Then, as if punished by Yakṣa for the disregard shown to his warning, Nakula dropped down dead. When Nakula did not return with water, Yudhiṣṭhira asked the other three brothers to go, one after the other, but they all met with the same fate. Finally Yudhiṣṭhira went himself and his long conversation with Yakṣa began.

6.4. After a preliminary exchange of words, Yakṣa introduced himself, and in reply thereto, Yudhiṣṭhira expressed his willingness to answer all the questions according to his prajñā (i.e. intellectual capacity) :

Yudhiṣṭhira uvāca:
na cāhaṁ kāmaye yakṣa tava pūrvaparigrahaṁ
kāmaṁ naitat praśaṁsanti santo hi puruṣāḥ sadā
yadātmanā svamātmānaṁ praśaṁse puruṣarṣabha
yathāprajñaṁ tu te praśnān prativakṣyāmi pṛccha mām
(III. 313.43-44)

Simple Meaning— Yudhiṣṭhira said to Yakṣa, 'I do not want anything which is already under your control. I also do not want to praise myself—in fact, self-praise is not approved by good people. Since you want to put questions to me, please go ahead—I shall answer all your questions according to my intellectual capacity.'

6.5. In all, Yakṣa put one hundred and twenty-four questions—these were put in a quick sequence and most of them were asked in groups of four at a time. Considering the significance attached to Yudhiṣṭhira's replies, by readers of the Mahābhārata, we present here practically the entire dialogue :

Yakṣa uvāca:
kiṁ svidādityamunnayati
ke ca tasyābhitaścarāḥ
kaścainamastaṁ nayati
kasmiṁśca pratitiṣṭhati (III. 313.45)

Simple Meaning—Yakṣa asked, 'What is it that makes the sun rise ? Who keeps him company ? Who causes him to set ? And in whom is he established ?'

Yudhiṣṭhira uvāca:
brahmādityamunnayati
devāstasyābhitaścarāḥ
dharmaścāstaṁ nayati ca
satye ca pratitiṣṭhati (III. 313.46)

Simple Meaning—Yudhiṣṭhira replied, 'Brahman makes the sun rise, gods keep him company, dharma causes him to set, and he is established in truth.'

6.6. Yakṣa uvāca:
kenasvicchrotriyo bhavati kenasvid vindate mahat
kenasvid dvitīyavān bhavati rājan kena ca buddhimān
(III. 313.47)

Simple Meaning—Yakṣa asked, 'By what does one become learned ? By what does one attain what is great ? How can one have a second person's company ? How can one acquire the right intellect ?'

Yudhiṣṭhira uvāca:
śrutena śrotriyo bhavati

tapasā vindate mahat
dhṛtyā dvitīyavān bhavati
buddhimān vṛddhasevayā (III. 313.48)

Simple Meaning—Yudhiṣṭhira replied, 'It is by the study of 'Śrutí' (i.e. Vedas and Upaniṣads) that a person becomes learned, it is by tapas (self-discipline) that one acquires what is great, it is by patience that a person can have a second person's company, and it is by serving old people that one acquires the right intellect.'

6.7. Yakṣa uvāca:

kiṁ brāhmaṇānāṁ devatvaṁ
kaśca dharmaḥ satāmiva
kaścaiṣāṁ mānuṣo bhāvaḥ
kimeṣāmasatāmiva (III. 313.49)

Simple Meaning—Yakṣa asked, 'What constitutes the divinity of the brahmins, what is their dharma like that of good people, what is their human attribute, and what practice of theirs is like that of unrighteous people ?'

Yudhiṣṭhira uvāca:

svādhyāya eṣāṁ devatvaṁ tapa eṣāṁ satāmiva
maraṇaṁ mānuṣo bhāvaḥ parivādo'satāmiva (III. 313.50)

Simple Meaning—Yudhiṣṭhira replied, 'Study of scriptures constitutes their divinity, their tapas (self-discipline) constitutes dharma like that of good people, their liability to death is their human attribute, and to speak ill of others is a practice like that of unrighteous people.'

6.8. Yakṣa uvāca:

kiṁ kṣatriyāṇāṁ devatvaṁ
kaśca dharmaḥ satāmiva
kaścaiṣāṁ mānuṣo bhāvaḥ
kimeṣāmasatāmiva (III. 313.51)

Simple Meaning—Yakṣa asked, 'What constitutes the divinity of the kṣatriyas, what is their dharma like that of good people, what is their human attribute, and what practice of theirs is like that of unrighteous people ?'

Yudhiṣṭhira uvāca:

iṣvastrameṣāṁ devatvaṁ

yajña eṣāṁ satāmiva
bhayaṁ vai mānuṣo bhāvaḥ
parityāgo'satāmiva (III. 313.52)

Simple Meaning—Yudhiṣṭhira replied, 'Arrows and weapons constitute their divinity, their yajña (sacrifice) constitutes dharma like that of good people, their liability to fear is their human attribute, and refusal of protection to those who seek their help is a practice like that of unrighteous people.'

6.9. Yakṣa uvāca:

kimekaṁ yajñiyaṁ sāma kimekaṁ yajñiyaṁ yajuḥ
kā caiṣāṁ vṛṇute yajñaṁ kāṁ yajño nātivartate
(III. 313.53)

Simple Meaning—Yakṣa asked, 'What is that which constitutes the equivalent of Sāma-Veda in a spiritual sacrifice, what is the equivalent of Yajur-Veda, what is the equivalent of Ṛg-Veda, and what is that which a spiritual sacrifice can not do without ?'

Yudhiṣṭhira uvāca:

prāṇo vai yajñiyaṁ sāma
mano vai yajñiyaṁ yajuḥ
ṛgekā vṛṇute yajñaṁ
tāṁ yajño nātivartate (III. 313.54)

Simple Meaning—Yudhiṣṭhira replied, 'Life is the equivalent of Sāma-Veda in a spiritual sacrifice, mind is the equivalent of Yajur-Veda, prayerfulness is the equivalent of Ṛg-Veda, and it is prayerfulness alone which a spiritual sacrifice can not do without.'

6.10. Yakṣa uvāca:

kiṁsvidāvapatāṁ śreṣṭhaṁ
kiṁsvinnivapatāṁ varaṁ
kiṁsvit pratiṣṭhamānānāṁ
kiṁsvit prasavatāṁ varaṁ (III. 313.55)

Simple Meaning—Yakṣa asked, 'What is most important to those who want to prepare land for cultivation, what is most important to those who want to sow, what is most important to those who are prosperous, and what is most important to those who bring forth children ?'

Yudhiṣṭhira uvāca:
varṣamāvapatām śreṣṭham bījaṁ nivapatāṁ varaṁ
gāvaḥ pratiṣṭhamānānāṁ putraḥ prasavatāṁ varaḥ
(III. 313.56)

Simple Meaning—Yudhiṣṭhira replied, 'Rain is most important to those who want to prepare land for cultivation, seed is most important to those who want to sow, cows are most important to those who are prosperous, and a son is most important to those who bring forth children.'

6.11. Yakṣa uvāca:
indriyārthānanubhavan
buddhimāṁllokapūjitaḥ
sammataḥ sarvabhūtānāṁ
ucchvasan ko na jīvati (III. 313.57)

Simple Meaning—Yakṣa asked, 'What person, in spite of enjoying all the objects of the senses, endued with intelligence, regarded by the world and liked by all the beings, though breathing, is still not really alive ?

Yudhiṣṭhira uvāca:
devatātithibhṛtyānāṁ
pitṛṇāmātmanaśca yaḥ
na nirvapati pañcānāṁ
ucchvasan na sa jīvati (III. 313.58)

Simple Meaning—Yudhiṣṭhira replied, 'That person who does not offer due shares to gods, guests, dependents, ancestors, and ātman (i.e. spiritual needs of one's own self), though breathing, is still not really alive.'

6.12. Yakṣa uvāca:
kiṁsvid gurutaraṁ bhūmeḥ kiṁsviduccataraṁ ca khāt
kiṁsvicchīghrataraṁ vāyoḥ kiṁsvid bahutaraṁ tṛṇāt
(III. 313.59)

Simple Meaning—Yakṣa asked, 'What is weightier than the earth itself, what is higher than the heavens, what is faster than the wind, and what is more numerous than grass ?'

Yudhiṣṭhira uvāca:
mātā gurutarā bhūmeḥ

khāt pitoccatarastathā
manaḥ śīghrataraṁ vātāc
cintā bahutarī tṛṇāt (III. 313.60)

Simple Meaning—Yudhiṣṭhira replied, 'The mother is weightier than the earth, the father is higher than the heavens, mind is faster than the wind, and our thoughts are more numerous than grass.'

6.13. Yakṣa uvāca:

kiṁsvit suptaṁ na nimiṣati
kiṁsvijjātaṁ na copati
kasyasviddhṛdayaṁ nāsti
kiṁsvid vegena vardhate (III. 313.61)

Simple Meaning—Yakṣa asked, 'What is that which does not close its eyes while asleep, what is that which does not move after birth, what is that which is without heart, and what is that which swells with its own impetus ?'

Yudhiṣṭhira uvāca:

matsyaḥ supto na nimiṣati
aṇḍaṁ jātaṁ na copati
aśmano hṛdayaṁ nāsti
nadī vegena vardhate (III. 313.62)

Simple Meaning—Yudhiṣṭhira replied, 'A fish does not close its eyes while asleep, an egg does not move after birth, a stone is without heart, and a river swells with its own impetus.'

6.14. Yakṣa uvāca:

kiṁsvit pravasato mitraṁ
kiṁsvinmitraṁ gṛhe sataḥ
āturasya ca kiṁ mitraṁ
kiṁsvinmitraṁ mariṣyataḥ (III. 313.63)

Simple Meaning—Yakṣa asked, 'Who is the friend of one travelling far away from home, who is the friend of one living in the home, who is the friend of a sick person, and who is the friend of one about to die ?'

Yudhiṣṭhira uvāca:

sārthaḥ pravasato mitraṁ
bhāryā mitraṁ gṛhe sataḥ

āturasya bhiṣanmitraṁ
dānaṁ mitraṁ mariṣyataḥ (III. 313.64)

Simple Meaning—Yudhiṣṭhira replied, 'The friend of one travelling far away from home is his companion, the friend of one living in the home is his wife, a doctor is the friend of a sick person, and charity is the friend of one about to die.'

6.15. Yakṣa uvāca:

ko'tithiḥ sarvabhūtānāṁ
kiṁsvid dharmaṁ sanātanaṁ
amṛtaṁ kiṁsvid rājendra
kiṁsvid sarvamidaṁ jagat (III. 313.65)

Simple Meaning—Yakṣa asked, 'Who is the guest of all beings, what is the dharma that has no specific beginning, what is nectar, and what constitutes this entire universe ?'

Yudhiṣṭhira uvāca:

atithiḥ sarvabhūtānāṁ
agniḥ somo gavāmṛtaṁ
sanātano'mṛto dharmo
vāyuḥ sarvamidaṁ jagat (III. 313.66)

Simple Meaning—Yudhiṣṭhira replied, 'Agni (i.e. god of fire) is the guest of all beings, dharma based on spiritual principles has no specific beginning, cow's milk is nectar, and this entire universe consists of air alone.'

6.16. Yakṣa uvāca:

kiṁsvideko vicarate
jātaḥ ko jāyate punaḥ
kiṁsviddhimasya bhaiṣajyaṁ
kiṁsvidāvapanaṃ mahat (III. 313.67)

Simple Meaning—Yakṣa asked, 'Who travels alone, who is born again and again, what is the remedy against cold, and what is the largest kṣetra (field) ?'

Yudhiṣṭhira uvāca:

sūrya eko vicarate
candramā jāyate punaḥ
agnirhimasya bhaiṣajyaṁ
bhūmirāvapanaṁ mahat (III. 313.68)

Simple Meaning—Yudhiṣṭhira replied, 'The sun travels alone, the moon is born again and again, fire is the remedy against cold, and the earth is the largest kṣetra (field).'

6.17. Yakṣa uvāca:

kiṁsvidekapadaṁ dharmyaṁ
kiṁsvidekapadaṁ yaśaḥ
kiṁsvidekapadaṁ svargyaṁ
kiṁsvidekapadaṁ sukham (III. 313.69)

Simple Meaning—Yakṣa asked, 'What is one main support of dharma, what is one main support of fame, what is one main support of heaven, and what is one main support of happiness ?'

Yudhiṣṭhira uvāca:

dākṣyamekapadaṁ dharmyam
dānamekapadaṁ yaśaḥ
satyamekapadaṁ svargyaṁ
śīlamekapadaṁ sukham (III. 313.70)

Simple Meaning—Yudhiṣṭhira replied, 'Skill in action is one main support of dharma, act of sharing is one main support of fame, truth is one main support of heaven, and good conduct is one main support of happiness.'

6.18. Yakṣa uvāca:

kiṁsvidātmā manuṣyasya
kiṁsvid daivakṛtaḥ sakhā
upajīvanaṁ kiṁsvidasya
kiṁsvidasya parāyaṇam (III. 313.71)

Simple Meaning—Yakṣa asked, 'What is the soul of man, who is the friend bestowed on man by the gods, what is the chief support of human existence, and what is it that binds human beings together ?'

Yudhiṣṭhira uvāca:

putra ātmā manuṣyasya
bhāryā daivakṛtaḥ sakhā
upajīvanaṁ ca parjanyo
dānamasya parāyaṇam (III. 313.72)

Simple Meaning—Yudhiṣṭhira replied, 'A son is the soul of man, the wife is the friend bestowed on man by the gods, clouds are the chief support of human existence, and acts of sharing bind human beings together.'

6.19. Yakṣa uvāca:

dhanyānāmuttamaṁ kiṁsvid
dhanānāṁ syāt kimuttamaṁ
lābhānāmuttamaṁ kiṁ syāt
sukhānāṁ syāt kimuttamam (III. 313.73)

Simple Meaning—Yakṣa asked, 'What is the best of all laudable things, what is the most valuable possession that one can have, what is the best of all gains, and what is it that gives the greatest happiness ?'

Yudhiṣṭhira uvāca:
dhanyānāmuttamaṁ dākṣyaṁ
dhanānāmuttamaṁ śrutaṁ
lābhānāṁ śreya ārogyaṁ
sukhānāṁ tuṣṭiruttamā (III. 313.74)

Simple Meaning—Yudhiṣṭhira replied, 'Skill in action is the best of all laudable things, knowledge of scriptures is the most valuable possession that one can have, health is the best of all gains, and contentment gives the greatest happiness.'

6.20. Yakṣa uvāca:

kaśca dharmaḥ paro loke
kaśca dharmaḥ sadāphalaḥ
kiṁ nayamya na śocanti
kaiśca sandhirna jīryate (III. 313.75)

Simple Meaning—Yakṣa asked, 'What is the highest dharma in the world, which dharmic practices do people use to obtain what they want, what is that which, if controlled, causes no regrets,and who are they whose friendship does not break ?'

Yudhiṣṭhira uvāca:
ānṛśaṁsyaṁ paro dharmas
trayīdharmaḥ sadāphalaḥ
mano yamya na śocanti
sandhiḥ sadbhirna jīryate (III. 313.76)

Simple Meaning—Yudhiṣṭhira replied, 'ānṛśaṃsya (i.e. absence of cruelty) is the highest dharma, people use dharmic practices referred to in the Vedas to obtain what they want, mind, if controlled, causes no regrets, and friendship with good people does not break.'

6.21. Yakṣa uvāca:

kiṁ nu hitvā priyo bhavati
kiṁ nu hitvā na śocati
kiṁ nu hitvārthavān bhavati
kiṁ nu hitvā sukhī bhavet (III.313.77)

Simple Meaning—Yakṣa asked, 'What is that which, if given up, endears you to others, what is that which, if given up, leads to no regrets, what is that which, if given up, makes you feel wealthy, and what is that which, if given up, makes you feel happy ?'

Yudhiṣṭhira uvāca:

mānaṁ hitvā priyo bhavati
krodhaṁ hitvā na śocati
kāmaṁ hitvārthavān bhavati
lokhaṁ hitvā sukhī bhavet (III. 313.78)

Simple Meaning—Yudhiṣṭhira replied, 'It is arrogance which, if given up, endears you to others, it is anger which, if given up, leads to no regrets, it is selfish desires which, if given up, makes you feel wealthy, and it is greed which, if given up, makes you feel happy.'

6.22. Yakṣa uvāca:

kimarthaṁ brāhmaṇe dānaṁ
kimarthaṁ naṭanartake
kimarthaṁ caiva bhṛtyeṣu
kimarthaṁ caiva rājasu (III. 313.79)

Simple Meaning—Yakṣa asked, 'What is the motive which prompts you to give money to brahmins, what is the motive which prompts you to give money to artists, what is the motive which prompts you to give money to dependents, and what is the motive which prompts you to give money to kings ?'

Yudhiṣṭhira uvāca:

dharmārthaṁ brāhmaṇe dānaṁ yaśo'rthaṁ naṭanartake
bhṛtyeṣu bharaṇārthaṁ vai bhayārthaṁ caiva rājasu
(III. 313.80)

Simple Meaning—Yudhiṣṭhira replied, 'Dharma is the motive which prompts you to give money to brahmins, fame is the motive which prompts you to give money to artists, providing support is the motive which prompts you to give money to dependents, and obtaining relief from fear is the motive which prompts you to give money to kings.'

6.23. Yakṣa uvāca:

kenasvidāvṛto lokaḥ
kenasvinna prakāśate
kena tyajati mitrāṇi
kena svargaṁ na gacchati (III. 313.81)

Simple Meaning—Yakṣa asked, 'With what is the world enveloped, why does its real nature not become known, for what are friends forsaken, and why do people fail to go to heaven ?'

Yudhiṣṭhira uvāca:

ajñānenāvṛto lokas
tamasā na prakāśate
lobhāt tyajati mitrāṇi
sangāt svargaṁ na gacchati (III. 313.82)

Simple Meaning—Yudhiṣṭhira replied, 'The world is enveloped with ignorance, its real nature does not become known because of tamas (unrighteousness), people forsake their friends due to greed, and they fail to go to heaven due to attachment.'

6.24. Yakṣa uvāca:

mṛtaḥ kathaṁ syāt puruṣah kathaṁ rāṣṭraṁ mṛtaṁ bhavet
śrāddhaṁ mṛtaṁ kathaṁ vā syāt kathaṁ yajño mṛto bhavet
(III. 313.83)

Simple Meaning—Yakṣa asked, 'Because of what may one be considered as dead, because of what may a kingdom be considered as dead, because of what may an ancestral worshipping ceremony be considered as dead, and because of what may a yajña (sacrifice) be considered as dead ?'

Yudhiṣṭhira uvāca:

mṛto daridraḥ puruṣo
mṛtaṁ rāṣṭramarājakaṁ
mṛtamaśrotriyaṁ śrāddhaṁ
mṛto yajñastvadakṣiṇaḥ (III. 313.84)

Simple Meaning—Yudhiṣṭhira replied, 'Because of poverty may one be considered as dead, because of anarchy may a kingdom be considered as dead, because of lack of learning of the priest may an ancestral worshipping ceremony be considered as dead, and because of lack of respect may a yajña (sacrifice) be considered as dead.'

6.25. Yakṣa uvāca:

kā dik kimudakaṁ proktaṁ
kimannaṁ kiṁ ca vai viṣaṁ
śrāddhasya kālamākhyāhi
tataḥ piba harasva ca (III. 313.85)

Simple Meaning—Yakṣa askded, 'Who shows the way, what has been spoken of as water by the Vedas, what has been spoken of as food, what is poison, and what is the proper time for performing an ancestral worshipping ceremony ? Then you may drink water and also take away as much as you like.'

Yudhiṣṭhira uvāca:

santo dig jalamākāśaṁ gaurannaṁ prārthanā viṣaṁ
śrāddhasya brāhmaṇaḥ kālaḥ kathaṁ vā yakṣa manyase
(III. 313.86)

Simple Meaning—Yudhiṣṭhira replied, 'Good people show the way, space has been spoken of as water by the Vedas, earth has been spoken of as food, to ask for something is poison, and the proper time for performing an ancestral worshipping ceremony depends on the availability of a learned priest. I wonder what your opinion is.'

6.26. Yakṣa uvāca:

tapaḥ kim lakṣaṇaṁ proktaṁ ko damaśca prakīrtitaḥ
kṣamā ca kā parā proktā kā ca hrīḥ parikīrtitā
(III. 313.87)

Simple Meaning—Yakṣa asked, 'What is tapas (self-discipline), what is the best type of restraint, what constitutes forgiveness, and what is the appropriate concept of shame ?'

Yudhiṣṭhira uvāca:

tapaḥ svadharmavartitvaṁ manaso damanaṁ damaḥ
kṣamā dvandvasahiṣṇutvaṁ hrīrakāryanivartanam
(III. 313.88)

Simple Meaning—Yudhiṣṭhira replied, 'Tapas is commitment to one's duty, restraint of the mind is the best type of restraint, forgiveness consists in enduring dualities, and the appropriate concept of shame is to stay away from all unworthy acts.'

6.27. Yakṣa uvāca:

kiṁ jñānaṁ procyate rājan
kaḥ śamaśca prakīrtitaḥ
dayā ca kā parā proktā
kiṁ cārjavamudāhṛtam (III. 313.89)

Simple Meaning—Yakṣa asked, 'What is knowledge, what is the best type of serenity, what constitutes compassion, and what is the appropriate concept of uprightness ?'

Yudhiṣṭhira uvāca:

jñānaṁ tattvārthasambodhaḥ
śamaścittapraśāntatā
dayā sarvasukhaiṣitvaṁ
ārjavaṁ samacittatā (III. 313.90)

Simple Meaning—Yudhiṣṭhira replied, 'Knowledge is the right understanding of the divine principle, tranquility of thoughts is the best type of serenity, compassion consists in wishing happiness of all, and even-mindedness is the appropriate concept of uprightness.'

6.28. Yakṣa uvāca:

kaḥ śatrurdurjayaḥ puṁsām
kaśca vyādhiranantakaḥ
kīdṛśaśca smṛtaḥ sādhur
asādhuḥ kīdṛśaḥ smṛtaḥ (III. 313.91)

Simple Meaning—Yakṣa asked, 'What enemy is difficult to conquer, what disease is endless, whom would you call a good man, and whom would you call a bad man ?'

Yudhiṣṭhira uvāca:

krodhaḥ sudurjayaḥ śatrur
lobho vyādhiranantakaḥ
sarvabhūtahitaḥ sādhur
asādhurnirdayaḥ smṛtaḥ (III.313.92)

Simple Meaning—Yudhiṣṭhira replied, 'Anger is the enemy that is difficult to conquer, greed is an endless disease, in my opinion, a good man is one who does good to all, and lack of compassion is the main characteristic of a bad man.'

6.29. Yakṣa uvāca:

ko mohaḥ procyate rājan
kaśca mānaḥ prakīrtitaḥ
kimālasyaṁ ca vijñeyaṁ
kaśca śokaḥ prakīrtitaḥ (III. 313.93)

Simple Meaning—Yakṣa asked, 'What is delusion, what is pride, what is laziness, and what is grief ?'

Yudhiṣṭhira uvāca:

moho hi dharmamūḍhatvaṁ
mānastvātmābhimānitā
dharmaniṣkriyatā'lasyaṁ
śokastvajñānamucyate (III. 313.94)

Simple Meaning—Yudhiṣṭhira replied, 'Delusion means being confused about one's duty, pride consists in self-recognition, laziness means not discharging one's duty, and grief is the sure outcome of ignorance.'

6.30. Yakṣa uvāca:

kiṁ sthairyamṛṣibhiḥ proktaṁ
kiṃ ca dhairyamudāhṛtaṁ
snānaṁ ca kiṁ paraṁ proktaṁ
dānaṁ ca kimihocyate (III. 313.95)

Simple Meaning—Yakṣa asked, 'What type of steadiness do the Ṛṣi's admire, what form does one's patience take, what is the concept of cleaning, and what is the main object of giving or sharing ?'

Yudhiṣṭhira uvāca:

svadharme sthiratā sthairyaṁ
dhairyamindriyanigrahaḥ
snānaṁ manomalatyāgo
dānaṁ vai bhūtarakṣanam (III. 313.96)

Simple Meaning—Yudhiṣṭhira replied, 'Real steadiness is a non-wavering commitment to one's duty, real patience is continued effort towards self-discipline, real cleanliness means getting rid of the impurities of the mind, and to protect all the creatures is the main object of giving or sharing.'

6.31. Yakṣa uvāca:

kaḥ paṇḍitaḥ pumānjñeyo
nāstikaḥ kaśca ucyate
ko mūrkhaḥ kaśca kāmaḥ syāt
ko matsara iti smṛtaḥ (III. 313.97)

Simple Meaning—Yakṣa asked, 'Who should be regarded as learned, who should be called an atheist, who should be called ignorant, what is the role of desire, and what is envy ?'

Yudhiṣṭhira uvāca:

dharmajñaḥ paṇḍito jñeyo
nāstiko mūrkha ucyate
kāmaḥ saṁsārahetuśca
hṛttāpo matsaraḥ smṛtaḥ (III. 313.98)

Simple Meaning—Yudhiṣṭhira replied, 'One who knows his duty should be regarded as learned, one who is ignorant should be called an atheist, also one who is an atheist should be called ignorant, desire is the root cause of saṁsāra (i.e. repeated cycle of births and deaths), and envy is the feeling of ill-will that burns your heart.'

6.32. Yakṣa uvāca:

ko'haṃkāra iti proktaḥ
kaśca daṃbhaḥ prakīrtitaḥ
kiṁ tad daivaṁ paraṁ proktaṁ
kiṁ tat paiśunyamucyate (III. 313.99)

Simple Meaning—Yakṣa asked, 'What is egotism, what is hypocrisy, what is called the grace of gods, and what is malicious talk ?'

Yudhiṣṭhira uvāca:

mahājñānamahaṁkāro
dambho dharmo dhvajocchrayaḥ
daivaṁ dānaphalaṁ proktaṁ
paiśunyaṁ paradūṣaṇam (III. 313.100)

Simple Meaning—Yudhiṣṭhira replied, 'Egotism is an expression of utter ignorance, hypocrisy consists in pretending as if you are the standard-bearer of dharma, what we call the grace of gods is in reality the fruit of what we have given to others, and malicious talk consists in speaking ill of others.'

6.33. Yakṣa uvāca:

dharmaścārthaśca kāmaśca
parasparavirodhinaḥ
eṣām nityaviruddhānāṁ
kathamekatra saṅgamaḥ (III. 313.101)

Simple Meaning—Yakṣa asked, 'The three Puruṣārtha's (goals of life), viz. dharma (duty), artha (wealth), and kāma (psychological value), are opposed to one another. How can these three exist together?'

Yudhiṣṭhira uvāca:

yadā dharmaśca bhāryā ca
parasparavaśānugau
tadā dharmārthakāmānāṁ
trayāṇāmapi sangamaḥ (III. 313.102)

Simple Meaning—Yudhiṣṭhira replied, 'When a man and his wife together become devoted to dharma (duty), then the three puruṣārtha's (goals of life) can exist together.'

6.34. Yakṣa uvāca:

akṣayo narakaḥ kena
prāpyate bharatarṣabha
etanme pṛcchataḥ praśnaṁ
tacchīghraṁ vaktumarhasi (III. 313.103)

Simple Meaning—Yakṣa asked, 'Who is he that is condemned to everlasting hell? Can you answer this question quickly?'

Yudhiṣṭhira uvāca:

brāhmaṇaṁ svayamāhūya
yācamānamakincanaṁ
paścānnāstīti yo brūyāt
so'kṣayaṁ narakaṁ vrajet (III. 313.104)

Simple Meaning—Yudhiṣṭhira replied, 'He who invites a poor brahmin, promising to make him a nice gift, and then tells him that he has nothing to give, goes to everlasting hell. (I want to mention two other types of persons who go to everlasting hell).'

vedeṣu dharmaśāstreṣu
mithyā yo vai dvijātiṣu
deveṣu pitṛdharmeṣu
so'kṣayaṁ narakaṁ vrajet (III. 313.105)

Simple Meaning—Yudhiṣṭhira continued, 'He who imputes falsehood to, and shows disrespect towards, Vedas, other scriptures, brahmins, gods, and ceremonies in honor of the ancestors, goes to everlasting hell.'

vidyamāne dhane lobhād
dānabhogavivarjitaḥ
paścānnāstīti yo brūyāt
so'kṣayaṁ narakaṁ vrajet (III. 313.106)

Simple Meaning—Yudhiṣṭhira concluded his reply about everlasting hell, 'He also goes to everlasting hell who, in spite of having money, but because of greed, does three things, viz., does not give in charity, does not spend money on pleasures that are consistent with dharma, and when approached by persons in need, tells them that he has nothing to give.'

6.35. Yakṣa uvāca:

rājan kulena vṛttena
svādhyāyena śrutena vā
brāhmaṇyaṁ kena bhavati
prabrūhyetat suniścitam (III. 313.107)

Simple Meaning—Yakṣa asked, 'Out of the four factors, viz. family, conduct, self-study, and listening to scriptures—which one contributes to brahminhood? Can you give me a definite answer?'

Yudhiṣṭhira uvāca:

śṛṇu yakṣa kulaṁ tāta
na svādhyāyo na ca śrutaṁ
kāraṇaṁ hi dvijatve ca
vṛttameva na saṁśayaḥ (III. 313.108)

Simple Meaning—Yudhiṣṭhira replied, 'I can say without any doubt that, out of the four factors that you mentioned, only one, viz. conduct, contributes to brahminhood—and the other three, viz. family, self-study, and listening to scriptures, are not so important. (And I want to explain this further.).'

vṛttaṁ yatnena saṁrakṣyaṁ
brāhmaṇena viśeṣataḥ
akṣīṇavṛtto na kṣīṇo
vṛttatastu hato hataḥ (III. 313.109)

Simple Meaning—Yudhiṣṭhira added, 'One's good conduct should always be maintained, and full effort should be devoted to this goal, particularly by a brahmin. One who maintains good conduct loses nothing, and one who loses his conduct loses everything.'

paṭhakāḥ pāṭhakāścaiva
ye cānye śāstracintakāḥ
sarve vyasanino mūrkhā
yaḥ kriyāvān sa paṇḍitaḥ (III. 313.110)

Simple Meaning—Yudhiṣṭhira continued, 'Even those who study the scriptures all the time, whether for self-study or for teaching, if their conduct is bad, they can be called ignorant and addicted. Only one whose conduct is good can be called learned.'

caturvedo'pi durvṛttaḥ
sa śūdrādatiricyate
yo'gnihotraparo dāntaḥ
sa brāhmaṇa iti smṛtaḥ (III. 313.111)

Simple Meaning—Yudhiṣṭhira concluded his reply about brahminhood, 'He whose conduct is bad, even if he knows all the four Vedas, is inferior to a śūdra (i.e. a person of the lowest caste). On the other hand, he whose conduct is good (i.e. who performs his duty and who keeps his senses under control) is surely a brahmin.'

6.36. Yakṣa uvāca:

priyavacanavādī kiṁ labhate
vimṛśitakāryakaraḥ kiṁ labhate
bahumitrakaraḥ kiṁ labhate
dharmarataḥ kiṁ labhate kathaya (III. 313.112)

Simple Meaning—Yakṣa asked, 'What does one gain who speaks sweet words, what does one gain who acts after considering the matter fully, what does one gain who makes many friends, and what does one gain who is devoted to righteousness ?'

Yudhiṣṭhira uvāca:
priyavacanavādī priyo bhavati
vimṛśitakāryakaro'dhikaṁ jayati
bahumitrakaraḥ sukhaṁ vasate
yaśca dharmarataḥ sa gatiṁ labhate (III. 313.113)

Simple Meaning—Yudhiṣṭhira replied , 'One who speaks sweet words endears oneself to all, one who acts after considering the matter fully has a very good chance of achieving success, one who makes many friends lives happily, and one who is devoted to righteousness attains a state of bliss.'

6.37. Yakṣa uvāca:
ko modate kimāścaryaṁ kaḥ panthāḥ kā ca vārtikā
mamaitāṁścaturaḥ praśnān kathayitvā jalaṁ piba
(III. 313.114)

Simple Meaning—Yakṣa said, 'Who lives joyfully, what is the greatest wonder, which is the right path to be followed, and what sort of conversation is full of meaning? After answering these four questions of mine, you may drink water.'

Yudhiṣṭhira uvāca:
pancame'hani ṣaṣṭhe vā śākaṁ pacati sve gṛhe
anṛṇī cāpravāsī ca sa vāricara modate (III. 313.115)

Simple Meaning—Yudhiṣṭhira replied, 'One who is not burdened with debt, and who is not away from home, lives joyfully, even if he eats only vegetables, cooked at home every fifth or sixth day.'

ahanyahani bhūtāni gacchantīha yamālayaṁ
śeṣāḥ sthāvaramicchanti kimāścaryamataḥ param
(III. 313.116)

Simple Meaning—Yudhiṣṭhira continued, 'People die every day, yet those who are alive want to live for ever—this is the greatest wonder.'

tarko'pratiṣṭhaḥ śrutayo vibhinnā
naiko ṛṣiryasya mataṁ pramāṇam
dharmasya tattvaṁ nihitaṁ guhāyām
mahājano yena gataḥ sa panthāḥ (III. 313.117)

Simple Meaning—Yudhiṣṭhira went on, 'About the right path to be followed, inferential logic alone can not help in making a clear and good choice. In the Śruti i.e. the Vedas and the Upaniṣads too, various answers to the same question can be found. As for the smṛties, it is difficult to identify a single Ṛṣi who can be considered more authoritative than others. So, in a way, it looks as if the essence of dharma is hidden in a cave. A practical solution to the problem is to follow the path shown by "mahājana" (which has two meanings, viz. "a great man" or "a majority of people").'[2]

asmin mahāmohamaye kaṭāhe
sūryāgninā rātridivendhanena
māsartudarvīparighattanena
bhūtāni kālaḥ pacatīti vārtā (III. 313.118)

Simple Meaning—Yudhiṣṭhira concluded his reply to the four questions, 'This world full of ignorance is like a pan. The sun is fire, the days and nights are fuel. The months and the seasons constitute the stirring spoon. Time is the cook. In this way all the beings in this world are being cooked. This sort of conversation is full of meaning.'

6.38. Yakṣa uvāca:

vyākhyātā me tvayā praśnā
yāthātathyaṁ parantapa
puruṣaṁ tvidānīṁ vyākhyāhi
yaśca sarvadhanī naraḥ (III. 313.119)

Simple Meaning—Yakṣa said, 'You have given right answers to all my questions. I now put two final questions—who is a puruṣa (i.e. a human being), and who can be said to possess limitless wealth?'

Yudhiṣṭhira uvāca:

divaṁ spṛśati bhūmiṁ ca
śabdaḥ puṇyena karmaṇā
yāvat sa śabdo bhavati
tāvat puruṣa ucyate (III. 313.120)

Simple Meaning—Yudhiṣṭhira replied to the first of the two questions, 'The title 'puruṣa' can be applied to a human being during that time when the popular appreciation of one's good actions spreads over the earth and reaches the heavens too.'

tulye priyāpriye yasya
sukhaduḥkhe tathaiva ca
atītānāgate cobhe
sa vai sarvadhanī naraḥ (III. 313.121)

Simple Meaning—Yudhiṣṭhira replied to the second question (i.e. the last question of Yakṣa), 'One can be said to possess limitless wealth if one is even-minded under all situations, i.e. if the pleasant and the unpleasant, joys and sorrows, and even the past and the future are the same to him or her.'

6.39. Yakṣa uvāca:
vyākhyātaḥ puruṣo rājan
yaśca sarvadhanī naraḥ
tasmāt tvamekaṁ bhrātṛṇāṁ
yamicchasi sa jīvatu (III. 313.122)

Simple Meaning—Yakṣa said, 'You have correctly answered both of my final questions. Therefore, I grant you a boon, viz. may one of your brothers, whom you choose, come back to life.'

Yudhiṣṭhira uvāca:
śyāmo ya eṣa raktākṣo
bṛhacchāla ivotthitaḥ
vyūḍhorasko mahābāhur
nakulo yakṣa jīvatu (III. 313.123)

Simple Meaning—Yudhiṣṭhira said, 'Let this one who is of dark color, whose eyes are red, who is tall like a tree, whose chest is broad and arms are long—let this Nakula come back to life.'

6.40. Yakṣa uvāca:
priyaste bhīmaseno'yaṁ
arjuno vaḥ parāyaṇaṁ
sa kasmānnakulaṁ rājan
sāpatnaṁ jīvamicchasi (III. 313.124)

Simple Meaning—Yakṣa asked, 'I am surprised at your choice. Why are you giving priority to Nakula (who is your step-brother) over Bhīma and Arjuna—this Bhīma who is dear to you, and this Arjuna on whom all of you depend?'

Yudhiṣṭhira uvāca:
kuntī caiva tu mādrī ca

dve bhārye tu piturmama
ubhe suputre syātāṁ vai
iti me dhīyate matiḥ (III. 313.131)

Simple Meaning—Yudhiṣṭhira replied, 'My father had two wives, Kuntī and Mādrī. I want that at least one son of each of them should be alive.'

yathā kuntī tathā mādrī
viśeṣo nāsti me tayoḥ
mātṛbhyām samamicchāmi
nakulo yakṣa jīvatu (III. 313.132)

Simple Meaning—Yudhiṣṭhira concluded his reply about his choice of Nakula, 'Although Kuntī is my mother, I do not make any distinction between her and Mādrī—both are the same to me. Because of this view of mine, I have given priority to Mādri's son Nakula, and I want him to come back to life.'

6.41. Yakṣa uvāca:

tasya te'rthācca kāmācca
ānṛśaṁsyaṁ paraṁ mataṁ
tasmāt te bhrātaraḥ sarve
jīvantu bharatarṣabha (III. 313.133)

Simple Meaning—Yakṣa said, 'You have demonstrated your highest devotion to 'ānṛśaṁsyam' (absence of cruelty)—even higher than to wealth and to psychological value. Therefore, I grant you a boon, viz. may all your brothers come back to life.'

6.42. We omit the rest of the dialogue between Yakṣa and Yudhiṣṭhira because it relates, not so much to issues of dharma, but more to how Yakṣa disclosed his real identity. Yakṣa said that he is Dharmarāja in disguise and that the drama of the deer running away with the brahmin's sticks was enacted by him—as a part of the test of Yudhiṣṭhira (whose success was certain because he was, after all, the son of Dharmarāja)

CHAPTER 7

Vidura-Nīti—Vidura's Advice to Dhṛtarāṣṭra

7.1. Vidura-Nīti is a well-known section of the Mahābhārata, located in Udyoga-Parva (i.e. Parva No.5). There are eight chapters in Vidura-Nīti, containing Vidura's advice to Dhṛtarāṣṭra, based on morality and justice. Besides dealing with specific problems faced by Dhṛtarāṣṭra, Vidura spoke on dharma in general also. Therefore keen interest in Vidura-Nīti exists in modern times too, particularly for members of the Swami Narayana religious group (for whom this by itself is an important scripture).

7.2. Before we look at the contents of Vidura-Nīti, we want to say a few words about Vidura. Ādi-Parva (i.e. Parva No.1) says that Vidura was a mortal incarnation of Dharma, śūdra by birth, but possessing deep knowledge of scriptures and always giving right advice to Dhṛtarāṣṭra. The birth of Dharma as a śūdra (i.e. low caste) is explained by means of the following story. Ṛṣi Māṇḍavya had his āśrama (hermitage) near a city. Some robbers, when pursued by king's men, hid themselves in that āśrama, without the knowledge of the Ṛṣi who was immersed in deep meditation. The king's men arrested the robbers and the Ṛṣi too, and the king punished all of them, without ascertaining whether the Ṛṣi had any connection with the robbery. Māṇḍavya asked Dharma, the divine dispenser of justice, why he (i.e. the Ṛṣi) had to suffer at the hands of the king. Dharma told Māṇḍavya that he (i.e. the latter) had tortured birds and bees in his childhood. The Ṛṣi then pronounced a curse on Dharma, 'You gave me punishment far in excess of what

I should have received for my childhood delinquency. Be born, therefore, as a śūdra in the world.' This is summarized in the following verse of Ādi-Parva :

dharmo vidurarūpeṇa
śāpāt tasya mahātmanaḥ
māṇḍavyasyārthatattvajñaḥ
kāmakrodhavivārjitaḥ (I. 105.29)

Simple Meaning—It was because of the curse of the Ṛṣi Māṇḍavya that Dharma was born as Vidura, who grew up to be an expert on governmental affairs, and at the same time, free from vices like selfishness and anger.[1]

7.3. Although the Vidura-Nīti covers a wide variety of topics, we shall here concentrate our attention on only four of them, viz.

(i) Need for unity, at the family level, and at higher levels too
(ii) Advice on behavior
(iii) What is right speech?
(iv) Importance of the goal of the good of all

7.4. Regarding unity, the specific problem facing Dhṛtarāṣṭra was the excessive greed and selfishness of his wicked son Duryodhana. Vidura advised Dhṛtarāṣṭra that, if Duryodhana remained adamant on depriving the Pāṇḍavas of their due share of the kingdom, then an individual (i.e. Duryodhana) should be given up in order not to hurt the interests of the family and larger groups :

tyajet kulārthe puruṣaṁ
grāmasyārthe kulaṁ tyajet
grāmaṁ janapadasyārthe
ātmārthe pṛthivīṁ tyajet (V. 37.17)

Simple Meaning—Vidura said to Dhṛtarāṣṭra, 'O king, it is better to give up one person (i.e. Duryodhana) for the sake of the family, similarly, give up the family for the village, and the village for the state. For the sake of Ātman (i.e. truth and high principles), even the whole world could be given up.'

7.5. Vidura-Nīti devotes much attention to convey the message : "Unity is strength". Just as a tree standing alone is uprooted by strong wind, said Vidura, similarly, a man depending solely on himself and feeling isolated, falls prey to enemies :

mahānapyekajo vṛkṣo
balavān supratiṣṭhitaḥ
prasahya eva vātena
saskandho marditum kṣaṇāt (V. 36.62)

Simple Meaning—Any tree that stands singly, though gigantic, strong and deep-rooted, has its trunk soon smashed and twisted by a mighty wind.

atha ye sahitā vṛkṣāḥ
sanghaśaḥ supratiṣṭhitāḥ
te hi śīghratamān vātān
sahante'nyonyasaṁśrayāt (V. 36.63)

Simple Meaning—Those trees that stand close to one another, are competent, owing to mutual dependence, to resist the strongest winds.

evaṁ manuṣyamapyekaṁ
guṇairapi samanvitaṁ
śakyaṁ dviṣanto manyante
vāyurdrumamivaikajam (V. 36.64)

Simple Meaning—Similarly, any man who is single, howsoever endowed with all the qualities, is viewed by enemies as weak and easy to vanquish, like an isolated tree that can be smashed by the wind.

7.6. Next, Vidura's advice on behavior is summarized in the following verse, which is one of the most well-known verses of the Mahābhārata :

na tat parasya sandadhyāt
pratikūlaṁ yadātmanaḥ
saṁgraheṇaiṣa dharmaḥ syāt
kāmādanyaḥ pravartate (V. 39.71)

Simple Meaning—That behavior, which is disagreeable to one's own self, should never be applied to others. This is the essence of dharma (righteousness). Whatever is contrary to this, is based on selfishness (and is therefore unrighteous).

Based on this principle, Vidura advised Dhṛtarāṣṭra to bring Duryodhana's greed under control so that a just settlement of the conflict with the Pāṇḍavas may be reached and mutual relationship guided by love and coöperation may be established.

pradāyaiṣāmucitaṁ tāta rājyaṁ
sukhī putraiḥ sahito modamānaḥ
na devānāṁ nāpi ca mānuṣāṇāṁ
bhaviṣyasi tvaṁ tarkaṇīyo narendra

(V. 33.123)

Simple Meaning—O my dear king, give back to the Pāṇḍavas their just share of the kingdom, and then you and your sons can live happily and joyfully. If you do this, then neither gods nor men will criticize you.

jñātibhirvigrahastāta
na kartavyaḥ śubhārthinā ....
sambhojanaṁ saṁkathanaṁ
samprītiśca parasparaṁ
jñātibhiḥ saha kāryāṇi
na virodhaḥ kadācana (V. 39.23-24)

Simple Meaning—He that desires his own good, should never quarrel with his relatives .... To eat with one another, to talk with one another, and to love one another—these are the things that relatives should do. And to repeat what they should not do—they should never quarrel.

7.7. The third important point covered by Vidura-Nīti is the question "What is right speech?", Vidura's answer to which is summarized in the following verse—and this again is a famous saying :

sulabhāḥ purūṣa rājan
satataṁ priyavādinaḥ
apriyasya tu pathyasya
vaktā śrotā ca durlabhaḥ (V. 37.15)

Simple Meaning—O king, there are plenty of people who will say to you what pleases you. However, it is difficult to find a person who will say what, though unpleasant, will do good to you—and similarly, a listener to such words is also difficult to find.

7.8. The concept of 'pathya' used in the above verse and carrying the meaning of 'doing good like medicine' is a speciality of Vidura-Nīti. In fact, Vidura identified four successive stages in regard to speech, viz. say what is true, say what is pleasant, say what is in accordance with dharma, and finally make sure that it will do good (to all). In the following verse, the starting point is 'not to speak at all' (which we have not counted as a speech-category :

avyāhṛtaṁ vyāhṛtācchreya āhuḥ
satyaṁ vaded vyāhṛtaṁ tad dvitīyaṁ
priyaṁ vaded vyāhṛtaṁ tat tṛtīyaṁ
dharmaṁ vaded vyāhṛtaṁ taccaturtham (V. 36.12)

Simple Meaning—There are occasions when 'not to speak at all' is better than speaking, if speak you must, then it is better to say what is true, going further, it is better to say what is pleasant; going still further, it is better to say what is in accordance with dharma (i.e. righteousness).

yo hi dharmaṁ samāśritya
hitvā bhartuḥ priyāpriye
apriyāṇyāha pathyāni
tena rājā sahāyavān (V. 37.16)

Simple Meaning—Since there are occasions when it may be difficult to determine what is in accordance with dharma, Vidura explained to Dhṛtarāṣṭra how such a determination can be made, 'O king, one who wants to be of real help to you, must say what is in accordance with dharma—and a practical way to determine this is to ignore whether it will please the king, and to say only what will do good to all.'

7.9. This is the role which Vidura played as adviser to Dhṛtarāṣṭra, and he repeated statements like the following :

mayā cāpi hitaṁ vācyaṁ
viddhi māṁ tvaddhitaiṣiṇam (V. 39.23)

Simple Meaning—O king, my function is to say what is good to all, therefore please look upon me as your well-wisher.

cakṣuṣā manasā vācā
karmaṇā ca caturvidhaṁ
prasādayati yo lokaṁ
taṁ loko'nuprasīdati (V. 34.25)

Simple Meaning—O king, only that person is liked by people who tries to win the hearts of the people by all means—for example, by his actions, by his speech, by the way he thinks about them, and by the way he looks at them.

7.10. An important guiding principle which Vidura suggested is 'apatrapā' i.e. to feel ashamed if you do or speak something wrong—because that will keep you away from wrong action and wrong speech :

ya ātmanāpatrapate bhṛśaṁ naraḥ
sa sarvalokasya gururbhavatyuta
anantatejāḥ sumanāḥ samāhitaḥ
sa tejasā sūrya ivāvabhāsate (V. 33.121)

Simple Meaning—That man who feels ashamed at his own faults, even though his faults are not pointed out to him by others, earns respect from all people. Possessed of a pure heart, boundless energy and balanced outlook, he shines like the sun.

7.11. The four-stage gradation suggested by Vidura in para 7.8 is applicable not only to speech but to all actions as well. That takes us to the final point which we want to pick up from Vidura-Nīti, viz. the importance that it attaches to the goal of the good of all. The relevant verses are the following :

hitaṁ yat sarvabhūtānāṁ
ātmanaśca sukhāvahaṁ
tat kuryādīśvare hyetan
mūlaṁ sarvārthasiddhaye (V. 37.40)

Simple Meaning—The guiding principle for achieving perfection in life can be summarized like this—do what contributes to the good of all, and do it happily, in the spirit of dedicating everything to God.

bhāvamicchati sarvasya
nābhāve kurute manaḥ
satyavādī mṛdurdānto
yaḥ sa uttamapūruṣaḥ (V. 36.16)

Simple Meaning—Best of all human beings is he who wishes the good of all, who never even thinks of harming anyone, who is truthful in speech, who is not harsh to anyone, and who has his senses under control.

7.12. Having specified the highest goal of the good of all, Vidura also advised about the technique of achieving that goal (and this can be called the technique of non-violence):

> *akrodhena jayet krodhamasādhuṁ sādhunā jayet*
> *jayet kadaryaṁ dānena jayet satyena nānṛtam* (V. 39.72)

Simple Meaning—Anger of others should be conquered by one's peacefulness; evil-doers should be conquered by saintliness; the miser should be conquered by gifts; and falsehood should be conquered by truth.

This verse has become famous because its Pali-language rendering forms part of Dhammapada (the Buddhistic scripture)

7.13. Before closing this brief account of Vidura-Nīti, we want to say that the advice about the highest goal and the non-violent technique has been given a practical shape by the supplementary advice called 'yathāśakti' which means 'take your capacity into consideration'. This point is stressed by Vidura in several verses, but we reproduce here only two of them :

> *yathāśakti cikīrṣanti yathāśakti ca kurvati*
> *na kincidavamanyante narāḥ paṇḍitabuddhayaḥ*
> (V. 33.21)

Simple Meaning—Wise people adjust their goals and actions according to their capacity—they do not ignore anything.

> *yathā yathā hi puruṣaḥ*
> *kalyāṇe kurute manaḥ*
> *tathā tathāsya sarvārthāḥ*
> *siddhyante nātra saṁśayaḥ* (V. 35.41)

Simple Meaning—If a man keeps on devoting his energies to the good of all, all the time adjusting his effort to his capacity, in the same proportion, he achieves success—and this is true without any doubt.

CHAPTER 8

Teachings of Ṛṣi Sanat-Sujāta

8.1. Udyoga-Parva (i.e. Parva No.5) says that immediately after listening to Vidura-Nīti (summarized by us in the preceding chapter), Dhṛtarāṣṭra expressed a desire for a continuation of similar conversation on dharma. Vidura suggested the name of Ṛṣi Sanat-Sujāta (immortal son of Brahmā who, even after attaining the status of a Ṛṣi, continued to look very young). Dhṛtarāṣṭra was happy to hear this but wondered how the Ṛṣi could be contacted. Vidura said, "That is not a problem because if we have a keen desire to hear the teachings of the Ṛṣi, he would appear before us here and now" :

cintayāmāsa viduras
tamṛṣiṁ śaṁsitavratam
sa ca taccintitaṁ jñātvā
darśayāmāsa bhārata (V.41.8)

Simple Meaning—Vidura concentrated his thoughts and silently expressed his keen desire to see that great Ṛṣi Sanat-Sujāta, who got this message and immediately appeared there (for the benefit of Dhṛtarāṣṭra).

8.2. Six chapters of Udyoga-Parva are devoted to the teachings that Ṛṣi Sanat-Sujāta gave to Dhṛtarāṣṭra. A part of the teachings is devoted to brahma-vidyā (i.e. knowledge of brahman) which is explained by the Ṛṣi from the Vedantic point of view. Our main interest in this book is in the application of brahma-vidyā for bringing about the good of the society. We shall therefore concentrate our attention on the following three points that are included in the teachings of the Ṛṣi :

(i) Knowledge that is confined to words or intellect is incomplete, i.e. it becomes complete only when it becomes a part of one's conduct.

(ii) Spiritual perfection is attained by dama (i.e. self-discipline) and by seeking the good of all.

(iii) It is particularly important to avoid cruel behavior (nṛśaṁsa)—which has as many as thirteen components—and mada (self-centered attitude)—which has as many as eighteen components.

8.3. About the first point relating to knowledge, the Ṛṣi takes great pains to clarify that merely knowing the words of the Vedas is not enough :

yo veda vedān na sa veda vedyaṁ
satye sthito yastu sa veda vedyam (V. 43.52)

Simple Meaning—One who knows merely the words of the Vedas, can not be said to know the knowable (i.e. brahman). However, if one is established in Truth (which is a synonym of brahman), then one can be said to know the knowable.

Although some of the Vedic scholars attached great significance to the correct pronunciation of the sacrificial mantras (hymns), in conformity with their metrical composition, Ṛṣi Sanat-Sujāta told Dhṛtarāṣṭra that even that was not enough :

chandovidaste ya uta nādhītavedā
na vedavedyasya vidurhi tattvam (V. 43.50)

Simple Meaning—Those who have knowledge of the metrical composition of the Vedic mantras can perform yajña's properly, but unless they realize brahman, the knowable, they can not be regarded as real knowers of the Vedas.

8.4. To obtain further clarification about the role of Vedic knowledge, Dhṛtarāṣṭra puts a question whether unrighteous conduct does the same type of harm to one who knows the words, metres, etc. of the Vedas as it does to common people :

Dhṛtarāṣṭra uvāca:
ṛco yajūṁṣi yo veda
sāmavedaṁ ca veda yaḥ

pāpāni kurvan pāpena
lipyate kiṁ na lipyate (V. 43.3)

Simple Meaning—Dhṛtarāṣṭra asked, 'O Ṛṣi, if someone is a Vedic scholar (say one who can recite Ṛgveda, Yajurveda as well as Sāmaveda), and if he does unrighteous acts, then does he have to suffer the consequences of his actions, or will his scholarship protect him?'

In his reply, the Ṛṣi states clearly that no one can take liberty in the matter of one's conduct, or in other words, the law of karma applies to everyone without exception :

Sanat-sujāta uvāca:
nainaṁ sāmānyṛco vāpi
na yajūṁṣyavicakṣaṇaṁ
trāyante karmaṇaḥ pāpān
na te mithyā bravīmyaham (V. 43.4)

Simple Meaning—Ṛṣi Sanat-Sujāta replied, 'O king, I do not want to give you any false hope in this matter. If one has no control on his senses and therefore commits sins, then he has to suffer the consequences of his actions, and even the Vedas can not protect him.'

nacchandāṁsi vṛjināt tārayanti
māyāvinaṁ māyayā vartamānaṁ
nīḍaṁ śakuntā iva jātapakṣāś
chandāṁsyenaṁ prajahatyantakāle (V. 43.5)

Simple Meaning—The Ṛṣi concluded his reply to the specific question raised by Dhṛtarāṣṭra, 'O king, Vedas never rescue from sin the deceitful person living by deceit. Just as newfledged birds forsake their nest, the Vedas forsake such a person at the end.'

8.5. On the second point (viz. on how to attain spiritual perfection), the Ṛṣi lays stress on the purification of heart by the cultivation of virtues. Lists of virtues are mentioned but, we want to focus attention on two of them. viz. 'hitam' i.e. desire to do good to all, and 'dama' i.e. self-discipline. Picking up the first one (i.e. hitam) fits in with the main theme of this book. Picking up the second one (i.e. dama) is prompted by the formulation adopted by the Ṛṣi, for example, he says, in a summarizd version, 'cultivate 'dama' and discard 'mada' (i.e. self-centered attitude). While verses referring to 'mada' will be presented under the third point, here we reproduce two verses that glorify, respectively, 'hitam' and 'dama' :

> Sanat-sujāta uvāca:
> *na darśane tiṣṭhati rūpamasya*
> *paśyanti cainaṁ suviśuddhasattvāḥ*
> *hito manīṣī manasā na tapyate*
> *ye pravrajeyuramṛtāste bhavanti*
> *yoginastaṁ prapaśyanti*
> *bhagavantaṁ sanātanam* (V. 46.20)

Simple Meaning—Ṛṣi Sanat-Sujāta said, 'That Eternal One endued with Divinity is beheld by Yogins by their mental eye—His form can not be seen by ordinary people with ordinary eyes. Those who want to see Him need to purify their heart, and this can be done by seeking the good of all. Such people have perfect control over their mind, and no worldly worry can cause pain to them, because they have no attachment to worldly objects. Such people are spiritually liberated even while they are physically living in the world.

> *damo hyaṣṭādaśaguṇaḥ ....*
> *damastyāgo'pramādaśca*
> *eteṣvamṛtamāhitaṁ*
> *tāni satyamukhānyāhur*
> *brāhmaṇā ye manīṣiṇaḥ* (V. 43.22-23)

Simple Meaning—'Dama' i.e. self-discipline has to be understood in a comprehensive sense, involving the cultivation of as many as eighteen virtues. (These are similar to what the Bhagavad-Gītā calls 'daivīsampat', a reference to which will be made in chapter twenty of this book) .... 'Dama' supplemented by 'tyāga' (non-attachment) and 'apramāda' (enthusiastic performance of one's duty), leads one to spiritual perfection. Wise people express this symbolically by saying that these virtues are sure to take you to 'satya' (truth) which is a synonym of brahman, the knowable.

8.6. Since the possibility of attaining spiritual liberation while one is physically living in this world is an important element of Ṛṣi Sanat-Sujāta's teachings, we feel it will be useful to draw attention to two more verses which convey the same message :

evaṁ yaḥ sarvabhūteṣu
ātmānamanupaśyati ....
yo vai taṁ puruṣaṁ veda
tasyehārtho na riṣyate (V. 46.18, 25)

Simple Meaning—One who understands that the same 'ātman' is in all beings, and further that 'ātman' and 'brahman' are identical, experiences spiritual bliss all the time, and in this very life. (The Ṛṣi uses the word 'iha' which means 'here, in this life'.

8.7. Inter-linking of the first two points (reference para 8.2) is also a part of Ṛṣi Sanat-Sujāta's teachings. He raises a question, 'What is the role of Vedic practices for one who is spiritually perfect?', and he himself gives the answer in the following verse :

yathodapāne mahati
sarvataḥ samplutodake
evaṁ sarveṣu vedeṣu
ātmānamanujānataḥ (V. 46.26)

Simple Meaning—Just as a well has only a minor role when we have access to a large lake filled with water, similarly Vedic practices have only a minor role when we have attained spiritual perfection through self-realization.

We must mention that this verse of Udyoga-Parva is a modified version of verse II.46 of Bhagavad-Gītā which is reproduced here for ready reference :

yāvānartha udapāne
sarvataḥ samplutodake
tāvān sarveṣu vedeṣu
brāhmaṇasya vijānataḥ (Gītā II.46)

(Simple meaning of this verse, being the same as that of the preceding verse of Udyoga-Parva, is not given here).

8.8. The third and the last point of this presentation relates to vices that need to be avoided by every spiritual aspirant. Out of the many vices listed by the Ṛṣi, we pay special attention to two (which are themselves interpreted by the Ṛṣi in a comprehensive sense)—viz. 'mada' (i.e. self-centered attitude) and 'nṛśaṁsa' (cruel behavior). As to the choice of 'mada', we have already given one reason in paragraph 8.5, the second reason being that anti-social activities (opposed to 'hitam' or good of all) are part of 'mada'. The second vice 'nṛśaṁsa' calls for our attention because Ṛṣi Sanat-Sujāta has probably written more about it than any other expert on dharma in the Mahābhārata.[1]

8.9. The Ṛṣi has warned against 'mada' by saying that it has as many as eighteen components (each of which is a vice by itself). In fact, there are two separate lists of these eighteen vices. The first of these two lists serves a double purpose, viz. that the vices are part of 'mada', but that the avoidance of these vices is part of 'dama' (explained in para 8.5). Here we pay special attention to the second list, because the Ṛṣi himself shows his preference to it, by saying :

mado'ṣṭādaśadośaḥ sa
syāt purā yo'prakīrtitaḥ (V. 45.9)

Simple Meaning—'mada' includes eighteen vices—and although I indicated them earlier (while talking of 'dama'), their wide-ranging damage to society was not specified.

After these introductory remarks, we now reproduce three verses in which Ṛṣi Sanat-Sujāta lists eighteen vices that form part of 'mada', and in which he also gives a strong warning against their evil effects :

lokadveṣyaṁ prātikūlyamabhyasūyā mṛṣā vacaḥ
kāmakrodhau pāratantryaṁ parivādo'tha paiśunam
arthahānirvivādaśca mātsaryaṁ prāṇipīḍanaṁ
īrṣyā modo'tivādaśca saṁjñānāśo'bhyasūyitā
tasmāt prājño na mādyeta sadā hyetad vigarhitam
(V. 45.9-11)

Simple Meaning—Eighteen vices forming part of 'mada' are—doing harm to people, doing things which people do not like, speaking ill of others, telling lies, selfishness, anger, taking away liberty of others, finding faults of others, misrepresenting others, misusing and wasting one's wealth, picking up quarrel with others, jealousy, hurting people, ill will, making fun of others, too much of argumentation, lack of discrimination, and disregarding the virtues of others. Therefore, one should clearly understand and avoid 'mada' which has been strongly condemned by good people.

8.10. Finally, about the second vice 'nṛśaṁsa' which means 'cruel behavior' and which has been characterized by Ṛṣi Sanat-Sujāta as having thirteen components :

nṛśāṁsāni daśatri rājan (V. 43.15)

Simple Meaning—O king, cruel behavior includes as many as thirteen vices.

The following two verses list thirteen types of vices included in 'nṛśaṁsa' :

vikatthanaḥ spṛhayālurmanasvī
bibhrat kopaṁ nirdayo'rakṣaṇaśca ....
sambhogasaṁvid viṣamo'timānī
dattānutāpī kṛpaṇo balīyān
vargapraśaṁsī vanitāsu dveṣṭā
ete hi daśatri nṛśaṁsavargāḥ (V. 43.18-19)

Simple Meaning—Thirteen types of 'nṛśaṁsa' (i.e. cruel) people are—those having superiority complex, lustful, those who humiliate others, wrathful, those who have no compassion, those who provide no protection to others, those who view enjoyment as the sole aim of life, those who don't believe in the spiritual equality of all human beings, those who are extremely arrogant, those who feel unhappy after having made a donation, those who are extremely miserly, those who violate dharma to pursue wealth and lust, and those who are biased against women.

CHAPTER 9

Lord Kṛṣṇa's Plea to Kauravas for Averting War

9.1. The primary aim of this book is to highlight the contribution of those who work for the good of all. Therefore, efforts made by Vidura and Lord Kṛṣṇa to avert the Mahābhārata war obviously deserve much attention. In chapter seven, we have summarized Vidura-Nīti, i.e. Vidura's advice to Dhṛtarāṣṭra oriented to the cause of peace. Subsequent to that, but still in Udyoga-Parva (i.e. Parva No.5), we have Lord Kṛṣṇa's strong plea to the Kaurava leaders for avoiding the war. Selected verses from this speech are presented below. But we also include in this chapter, a part of the description, in the words of Vaiśampāyana (the narrator), how Kṛṣṇa was welcomed by the residents of Hastinapur, when he was on his way to the Kaurava assembly :

puraṁ kurūṇāṁ saṁvṛttaṁ
draṣṭukāmaṁ janārdanaṁ
sabālavṛddhaṁ sastrīkaṁ
rathyāgatamarindama (V. 94.25)

Simple Meaning—All the citizens residing in the capital (i.e. Hastinapur), of all ages and both sexes, desirous of beholding Kṛṣṇa, came out into the streets.

9.2. *sa pūjyamānaḥ kurubhiḥ*
saṁśṛṇvan madhurāḥ kathāḥ
yathārhaṁ pratisatkurvan
prekṣamāṇaḥ śanairyayau (V. 94.27)

Simple Meaning—Honored by the Kauravas, and listening to their sweet words, Kṛṣṇa went along the main street, casting his eyes on all those present there, and also exchanging greetings :

pāṇau gṛhītvā viduraṁ
sātyakiṁ ca mahāyaśāḥ
jyotīṁṣyādityavad rājan
kurūn prācchādayacchriyā (V. 94.33)

Simple Meaning—Honorable Kṛṣṇa entered the Kaurava assembly, arm-in-arm with Vidura and Satyaki on either side, overshadowing with his own splendour, the lesser splendour of the Kauravas, like the sun over-shadowing the radiance of lesser lights in the firmament.

agrato vāsudevasya
karṇaduryodhanāvubhau
vṛṣṇayaḥ kṛtavarmā cā
pyāsan kṛṣṇasya pṛṣṭhataḥ (V. 94.34)

Simple Meaning—Karṇa and Duryodhana walked in front of Kṛṣṇa, while Kṛtavarman and other members of the Vṛṣṇi-family followed him.

9.3. *dhṛtarāṣṭraṁ puraskṛtya*
bhīṣmadroṇādayastataḥ
āsanebhyo'calan sarve
pūjayanto janārdanam (V. 94.35)

Simple Meaning—Bhīṣma, Droṇa and other prominent members of the Kaurava assembly—whose head was the blind king Dhṛtarāṣṭra—got ready to rise from their seats, to honor Kṛṣṇa.

abhyāgacchati dāśarhi
prajñācakṣurnareśvaraḥ
sahaiva droṇabhīṣmābhyāṁ
udatiṣṭhanmahāyaśāḥ (V. 94.36)

Simple Meaning—As soon as Kṛṣṇa entered the assembly hall, King Dhṛtarāṣṭra, along with Bhīṣma, Droṇa and other prominent members, rose from their seats.

9.4. *smayamānastu rājānaṁ*
bhīṣmadroṇau ca mādhavaḥ

abhyabhāṣata dharmātmā
rājñaścānyān yathāvahaḥ (V. 94.39)

Simple Meaning—After taking his seat, Kṛṣṇa smilingly exchanged greetings with Dhṛtarāṣṭra, Bhīṣma, Droṇa, and other prominent persons.

teṣvāsīneṣu sarveṣu
tūṣṇīmbhūteṣu rājasu
vākyamabhyādade kṛṣṇaḥ
sudaṁṣṭro dundubhisvanaḥ (V. 95.1)

Simple Meaning—After all the assembly members had been seated and perfect silence had ensued, Kṛṣṇa possessing fine teeth and having a voice deep as that of the drum, began to speak.

9.5. Śrī bhagavānuvāca:
kurūṇāṁ pāṇḍavānāṁ ca
śamaḥ syāditi bhārata
apraṇāśena vīrāṇāṁ
etad yācitumāgataḥ (V. 95.3)

Simple Meaning—Lord Kṛṣṇa said, 'Honorable descendant of Bharata, I have come here to seek your help so that peace may be established between the Kauravas and the Pāṇḍavas without any slaughter of the heroes.'

rājan nānyat pravaktavyaṁ
tava naiḥśreyasaṁ vacaḥ
viditaṁ hyeva te sarve
veditavyamarindama (V. 95.4)

Simple Meaning—'O king, my sole purpose is to affirm this goal of peace which will do good to all. In fact, you already know about all the issues that are involved in achieving this goal.'

9.6. *idaṁ hyadya kulaṁ śreṣṭhaṁ*
sarvarājasu pārthiva
śrutavṛttopasampannaṁ
sarvaiḥ samuditaṁ guṇaiḥ (V. 95.5)

Simple Meaning—'I want everyone to appreciate that this Kuru dynasty is currently the most distinguished of all royal dynasties, because it attaches great importance to scriptures and good conduct, and it has acquired admirable qualities.'

kṛpānukampā kāruṇyaṁ
ānṛśaṁsyaṁ ca bhārata
tathā'rjavaṁ kṣamā satyaṁ
kuruṣvetad viśiṣyate (V. 95.6)

Simple Meaning—'I want to make specific mention of virtues in the possession of which the Kuru dynasty has excelled, for example, to feel joy in the happiness of others, to feel sad at the sight of other people's misery, desire to alleviate distress, absence of cruelty, uprightness, forgiveness, and truth.'

9.7. *tasminnevaṁvidhe rājan*
kule mahati tiṣṭhati
tvannimittaṁ viśeṣeṇa
neha yuktamasāmpratam (V. 95.7)

Simple Meaning—'Such being the reputation of this dynasty, it would be a pity if anything improper were done by anyone belonging to it, and greater pity still if it were done by you, O king.'

tvaṁ hi dhārayitā śreṣṭhaḥ
kurūṇāṁ kurusattama
mithyā pracaratāṁ tāta
bāhyeṣvābhyantareṣu ca (V. 95.8)

Simple Meaning—'O chief of the Kurus, you as the great leader have to be the first to restrain any member of your dynasty, who may be guilty of misconduct, either openly or secretly.'

9.8. *te putrāstava kauravya*
duryodhanapurogamāḥ
dharmārthau pṛṣṭhataḥ kṛtvā
pracaranti nṛśaṁsavat (V. 95.9)

Simple Meaning—'O king, I want you to recognize that, your own sons headed by Duryodhana, have set aside dharma (righteousness) and artha (legitimate acquisition of wealth), and are behaving like cruel people.'

aśiṣṭā gatamaryādā
lobhena hṛtacetasaḥ

sveṣu bandhuṣu mukhyeṣu
tad vettha puruṣarṣabha (V. 95.10)

Simple Meaning—'Your sons' behavior towards their own cousins is highly improper. Their thinking is vitiated by excessive greed, and they have disregarded all norms of civilized conduct. I need not give specific examples because you know all this very well.'

9.9. *seyamāpanmahāghorā*
kuruṣveva samutthitā
upekṣyamāṇā kauravya
pṛthivīṁ ghātayiṣyati (V. 95.11)

Simple Meaning—'That terrible danger which threatens all, has its origin in the conduct of your sons. O king, if you ignore it, the result will be universal slaughter.'

śakyā ceyaṁ śamayituṁ
tvaṁ cedicchasi bhārata
na duṣkaro hyatra śamo
mato me bharatarṣabha (V. 95.12)

Simple Meaning—'O descendant of Bharata, if you have the necessary will-power, the approaching danger can still be averted. In my opinion, obstacles in the path of peace can be overcome.'

9.10. *tvayyadhīnaḥ śamo rājan*
mayi caiva viśāmpate
putrān sthāpaya kauravya
sthāpayiṣyāmyahaṁ parān (V. 95.13)

Simple Meaning—'O king, you and I (working in coordination) hold the key to peace. You bring the Kauravas to the path of peace, and I shall do the same with the Pāṇḍavas.'

ājñā tava hi rajendra
kāryā putraiḥ sahānvayaiḥ
hitaṁ balavadapyeṣāṁ
tiṣṭhatāṁ tava śāsane (V. 95.14)

Simple Meaning—I feel, O king, that your sons and their followers should obey your command, because they can achieve their highest good (hitam) only by acting in accordance with your directions.'

9.11. *tava caiva hitaṁ rājan*
pāṇḍavānāmatho hitaṁ
śame prayatamānasya
tava śāsanakāṁkṣiṇaḥ (V. 95.15)

Simple Meaning—'I must add, O king, that your own good (hitam)—as also the good (hitam) of the Pāṇḍavas—can be achieved if you exercise your authority properly and devote all your energies to the cause of peace.'

svayaṁ niṣphalamālakṣya
saṁvidhatsva viśāmpate
sahāyabhūta bharatās
tavaiva syurjaneśvara (V. 95.16)

Simple Meaning—'I suggest, O king, that you take the initiative, and realizing that no good result can come out of conflict, you try to lay the foundation for peace. If you do this, the Pāṇḍavas will cooperate with you.'

9.12. *dharmārthayostiṣṭha rājan*
pāṇḍavairabhirakṣitaḥ
na hi śakyāstathābhūtā
yatnādapi narādhipa (V. 95.17)

Simple Meaning—'O king, if you receive protective support of the Pāṇḍavas, you are sure to achieve high goals in the fields of dharma (righteousness) and artha (wealth). Please keep in mind that, howsoever hard you try, you cannot obtain allies who are as strong as the Pāṇḍavas .'

lokasyeśvaratāṁ bhūyaḥ
śatrubhiścāpyadhṛṣyatāṁ
prāpsyasi tvamamitraghna
sahitaḥ kurupāṇḍavaiḥ (V. 95.22)

Simple Meaning—'Once you have the support of both the Kauravas and the Pāṇḍavas, you will have the lordship of the entire world, which none of your enemies will be in a position to challenge.'

9.13. *saṁyuge vai mahārāja*
dṛṣyate sumahān kṣayaḥ

kṣaye cobhayato rājan
kaṁ dharmamanupaśyasi (V. 95.28)

Simple Meaning—'On the other hand, O king, if war breaks out between the Kauravas and the Pāṇḍavas, I foresee terrible destruction. What sort of dharma do you hope to accomplish if both the sides are destroyed?'

pāṇḍavairnihataiḥ saṁkhye
putrairvāpi mahābalaiḥ
yad vindethāḥ sukhaṁ rājaṁs
tad brūhi bharatarṣabha (V. 95.29)

Simple Meaning—'Even if you think that only one side will be destroyed in the war, i.e. either the Pāṇḍavas will be killed or your own mighty sons will perish—in either case, please tell me what kind of happiness will you be able to enjoy.'

9.14. *āhustvāṁ pāṇḍavā rājan*
abhivādya prasādya ca
bhavataḥ śāsanād duḥkhaṁ
anubhūtaṁ sahānugaiḥ (V. 95.40)

Simple Meaning—'O king, now I want to convey to you the message of the Pāṇḍavas—they have said, honored father, please accept our salutations, and listen to our petition, because although we have obeyed you, we and our followers have suffered great misery.'

dvādaśemāni varṣāṇi
vane nirvyuṣitāni naḥ
trayodaśaṁ tathājñātaiḥ
sajane parivatsaram (V. 95.41)

Simple Meaning—The Pāṇḍavas have said, 'For twelve years we lived in the woods, and for the thirteenth year we lived incognito (i.e. no one could recognize us).'

sthātā naḥ samaye tasmin piteti kṛtaniścayāḥ
nāhāsma samayaṁ tāta tacca no brāhmaṇāḥ viduḥ
(V. 95.42)

Simple Meaning—'O father, we did not break our pledge, firmly believing that you too will abide by yours. The fact that we kept our word is well-known to the brahmins who were with us.'

nityaṁ saṁkleśitā rājan
svarājyāṁśaṁ labhemahi (V. 95.43)

Simple Meaning—'O father, we have suffered great misery for such a long time—now we must receive our share of the kingdom.'

pitrā sthāpayitvā hi
vayamutpathamāsthitāḥ
saṁsthāpaya pathiṣvasmāṁs
tiṣtha dharme suvartmani (V. 95.46)

Simple Meaning—'O father, if we go astray from the path of dharma, it is your duty to bring us back to the right path. In that spirit, we appeal to you—please make sure that you too are following the path of dharma.'

9.15. *āhuścemāṁ pariṣadaṁ*
putrāste bharatarṣabha
dharmajñeṣu sabhāsatsu
neha yuktamasāmpratam (V. 95.47)

Simple Meaning—Lord Kṛṣṇa said to Dhṛtarāṣṭra, 'O king, the Pāṇḍavas have sent a message to this assembly also, which goes like this—Honorable members of the assembly, all of you are knowers of dharma, therefore please see that justice is done to us.'

9.16. *ye dharmamanupaśyantastūṣṇīṁ dhyāyanta āsate*
te satyamāhurdharmyaṁ ca nyāyyaṁ ca bharatarṣabha
(V. 95.51)

Simple Meaning—Lord Kṛṣṇa continued, 'O king, I have conveyed to you and to the assembly, the message of the Pāṇḍavas. Please appreciate that the Pāṇḍavas are sticking to the path of dharma. They are waiting patiently to receive their share of the kingdom—and their demand is in conformity with dharma, truth and justice.'

pitryaṁ tebhyaḥ pradāyāṁśaṁ
pāṇḍavebhyo yathochitaṁ
tataḥ saputraḥ siddhārtho
bhuṁkṣva bhogān parantapa (V. 95.54)

Simple Meaning—'O king, please give back to the Pāṇḍavas their due share of the ancestral kingdom, so that you and your children can peacefully rule over the rest of the kingdom and lead a happy life.'

ahaṁ tu tava teṣāṁ ca
śreya icchāmi bhārata
dharmādarthāt sukhāccaiva
mā rājan nīnaśaḥ prajāḥ (V. 95.60)

Simple Meaning—'O king, my suggestion will bring 'śreyas' (i.e. the highest good) to you as well as to the Pāṇḍavas—and that is what I want. Please do not take any action which may deprive all the people of dharma (righteousness), artha (wealth), and happiness.'

9.17. *anarthamarthaṁ manvāno'*
pyarthaṁ cānarthamātmanaḥ
lobhe'tiprasṛtān putrān
nigṛṇhīṣva viśāmpate (V. 95.61)

Simple Meaning—'O king, I have to tell you frankly that, at this moment, you are regarding evil as good and good as evil. Your sons have become extremely greedy. You have to control them so that they observe restraint.'

sthitāḥ śuśrūṣituṁ pārthāḥ
sthitā yoddhumarindamāḥ
yat te pathyatamaṁ rājaṁs
tasmiṁstiṣṭha parantapa (V. 95.62)

Simple Meaning—Lord Kṛṣṇa concluded his plea by saying, 'O king, please do not interpret my words to think that Pāṇḍavas are weak—they prefer peace but they have enough strength to fight also if their plea is rejected. Please choose the option which you think will do good (hitam) to you.'

9.18. We conclude this chapter by quoting only one line from Vaiśampāyana's remarks, made at the end of Lord Kṛṣṇa's address to the Kaurava assembly :

Vaiśampāyana uvāca:
tad vākyaṁ pārthivāḥ sarve
hṛdayaiḥ samapūjayan (V. 95.63)

Simple Meaning—Vaiśampāyana said to Janamejaya (who was great grandson of Arjuna), 'O king, all the members of the Kaurava assembly whole-heartedly applauded the statement of Lord Kṛṣṇa .'[1]

Chapter 10

Vidura's Portrayal of Life's Dilemma That has Appealed to Scholars in Many Countries

10.1. Vidura played an important role in the story of the Mahābhārata, mainly as an adviser to the blind king Dhṛtarāṣṭra. In Udyoga-Parva, i.e. prior to the great war between Pāṇḍavas and the Kauravas, the words of wisdom which Vidura spoke are known as 'Vidura-Nīti', extracts from which have been presented in Chapter Seven. Now our attention is focussed on what Vidura spoke to Dhṛtarāṣṭra in Strī-Parva, i.e. after the great war. Parva number eleven in the Mahābhārata is called Strī-Parva (i.e. Parva of the Women) because it describes the visit to what was the battle-field, by the grief-stricken widows of the soldiers who had lost their lives. Dhṛtarāṣṭra too was lamenting over the loss of his sons. To console him, Vidura related to him the story of the Man in the Well, which portrays the pitiable condition of everyone in this world, by means of a simile. B.A. van Nooten says that, over the centuries, Vidura's words contained in Strī-Parva have appealed to scholars in many countries.[1] Our own interest in Vidura's words is based partly on their appeal to so many scholars and partly on the message that they give in the end, viz.

dayā sarveṣu bhūteṣu (XI. 7.28)

i.e. show compassion to all the beings. The following presentation relates to the Mahābhārata story of the Man in the Well (together with its message), as also to van Nooten's account of the far-flung journey of this story.

10.2. Vidura uvāca:

atra te vartayiṣyāmi
namaskṛtvā svayambhuve
yathā saṁsāragahanaṁ
vadanti paramarṣayaḥ (XI. 5.2)

Simple Meaning—Vidura said to Dhṛtarāṣṭra, 'O King, after paying my respect to God (i.e. after being inspired by God), I want to portray (before your mental eye) the dilemma of human life, by means of a simile, as great Ṛṣi's in the past have done.'

kaścinmahati kāntāre
vartamāno dvijaḥ kila
mahad durgamanuprāpto
vanaṁ kravyādasaṁkulam (XI. 5.3)

Simple Meaning—A certain brahmin was journeying through a dense forest. He arrived in an impassable part of the forest, teeming with beasts of prey.

siṁhavyāghragajarkṣaughair
atighoraṁ mahāsvanaiḥ
piśitādairatibhayair
mahogrākṛtibhistathā
samantāt samparikṣiptaṁ
yat sma dṛṣṭvā trased yamaḥ (XI.5.4)

Simple Meaning—There were hordes of lions, tigers, elephants and bears, all of which were engaged in roaring aloud. Because of the dangerous beasts, the forest looked so terrifying that even Yama himself would take fright at it.

10.3. *tadasya dṛṣṭvā hṛdayaṁ*
udvegamagamat paraṁ
abhyucchayaśca romṇāṁ vai
vikriyāśca parantapa (XI. 5.5)

Simple Meaning—Beholding such a forest, the heart of the brahmin became exceedingly aGītāted. His hair stood on end, and other signs of fear also manifested themselves.

sa tad vanaṁ vyanusaran
sampradhāvannitastataḥ

vīkṣamāṇo diśaḥ sarvāḥ
śaraṇaṁ kva bhavediti (XI. 5.6)

Simple Meaning—Wondering how to escape from the forest, he began to run hither and thither, casting his eyes on every point of the compass, for finding out some source of protection whose shelter he might seek.

sa teṣāṁ chidramanvicchan
pradruto bhayapīḍitaḥ
na ca niryāti vai dūraṁ
na vā tairvipramocyate (XI. 5.7)

Simple Meaning—Wishing to find some point of escape from those terrible creatures, he ran in fright, but he could neither escape nor take himself away from their threatening presence.

10.4. *athāpaśyad vanaṁ ghoraṁ*
samantād vāgurāvṛtaṁ
bāhubhyāṁ samparikṣiptaṁ
striyā paramaghorayā (XI. 5.8)

Simple Meaning—He then saw that the terrible forest was surrounded with a net, and that a frightful woman stood there, stretching her arms as if to hold him in her grip.

pañcaśīrṣadharairnāgaiḥ
śailairiva samunnataiḥ
nabhaḥspṛśairmahāvṛksaiḥ
parikṣiptaṁ mahāvanam (XI. 5.9)

Simple Meaning—That large forest was also encompassed by many five-headed snakes of dreadful forms, tall as cliffs, and there were huge trees too, which touched the skies.

vanamadhye ca tatrābhūd
udapānaḥ samāvṛtaḥ
vallībhistṛṇachannābhir
dṛḍhābhirabhisaṁvṛtaḥ (XI. 5.10)

Simple Meaning—In the middle of that forest, there was a concealed well, entirely covered with invisible creepers, hidden as they were by grass.

papāta sa dvijastatra
nigūḍhe salilāśaye

vilagnaścābhavat tasmin
latāsantānasaṁkule (XI. 5.11)

Simple Meaning—The brahmin fell into that hidden well, but he did not go down because he was hung up in that interlacing tangle of creepers.

panasasya yathā jātaṁ
vṛntabaddhaṁ mahāphalaṁ
sa tathā lambate tatra
hyūrdhvapādo hyadhaḥśirāḥ (XI. 5.12)

Simple Meaning—The brahmin, hanging into the well, with his feet up and his head down, looked like a large fruit of a jack tree (i.e. breadfruit tree) hanging by its stalk.

10.5. *atha tatrāpi cānyo'sya*
bhūyo jāta updravaḥ
kūpamadhye mahānāgaṁ
apaśyata mahābalam (XI. 5.13)

Simple Meaning—Then another calamity overtook the brahmin—he saw a large and mighty snake within the well.

kūpavīnāhavelāyāṁ
apaśyata mahāgajaṁ
ṣaḍvaktraṁ kṛṣṇaśuklaṁ ca
dviṣaṭkapadacāriṇam (XI. 5.14)

Simple Meaning—On the circular masonry of the well, the brahmin saw a huge elephant, dark in complexion with white spots, having six faces and twelve feet.

krameṇa parisarpantaṁ
vallīvṛkṣasamāvṛtaṁ (XI. 5.15)

Simple Meaning—The elephant moved slowly, approaching the well that was covered with creepers and trees.

10.6. *tasya cāpi praśākhāsu*
vṛkṣaśākhāvalambinaḥ
nānārūpā madhukarā
ghorarūpā bhayāvahāḥ
āsate madhusaṁvṛtya
pūrvameva niketajāḥ (XI. 5.16)

Simple Meaning—Around the twigs of the tree (from a branch of which the brahmin was hanging), roved many bees of frightful forms, employed from before in collecting the honey gathered in their comb about which they swarmed in large numbers.

bhūyo bhūyaḥ samīhante
madhūni bharatarṣabha
svādanīyāni bhūtānāṁ
yairbālo viprakṛṣyate (XI. 5.17)

Simple Meaning—The bees repeatedly endeavoured to collect honey, which is the sweetest thing in which even a fool among creatures takes pleasure.

teṣāṁ madhūnāṁ bahudhā
dhārā prasravate tadā
ālambamānaḥ sa pumān
dhārāṁ pibati sarvadā (XI. 5.18)

Simple Meaning—The honey collected in the comb fell downwards in many streams, and the brahmin hanging upside down in the well drank that honey.

10.7. *na cāsya tṛṣṇā viratā*
pibamānasya saṁkaṭe
abhīpsyati tadā nityaṁ
atṛptaḥ sa punaḥ punaḥ (XI. 5.19)

Simple Meaning—Although the brahmin faced danger to his life, his thirst for honey was not allayed. He desired it all the time, unsatiated time and again.

na cāsya jīvite rājan
nirvedaḥ samajāyata
tatraiva ca manuṣyasya
jīvitāśā pratiṣṭhitā (XI. 5.20)

Simple Meaning—Even under such circumstances, he did not become disgusted with life. He continued his hope to live on because he wanted to drink more honey.

kṛṣṇāḥ śvetāśca taṁ vṛkṣaṁ
kuṭṭayanti ca mūṣikāḥ (XI. 5.21)

Simple Meaning—A number of black and white rats were eating away the roots of that tree (from a branch of which the brahmin was hanging).

10.8. *vyālaiśca vanadurgānte*
striyā ca paramograyā
kūpādhastācca nāgena
vīnāhe kunjareṇa ca
vṛkṣaprapātācca bhayaṁ
mūṣikebhyaśca pancamaṁ
madhulobhān madhukaraiḥ
ṣaṣṭhamāhur mahad bhayam (XI. 5.22-23)

Simple Meaning—After having indicated six different sources of danger to the brahmin's life, Vidura listed them in a summarized form—The first danger was from snakes that were in the forest, the second danger was from the frightful woman who stood there, the third danger was from the snake within the well, the fourth danger was from the huge elephant that stood on the circular masonry of the well, the fifth danger was from the approaching fall of the tree (because rats were eating away its roots and the brahmin was hanging from one of its branches), and the sixth danger was from the bees (although they supplied the honey which was a source of pleasure to the brahmin).

10.9. *evaṁ sa vasate tatra*
kṣiptaḥ saṁsārasāgare
na caiva jīvitāśāyāṁ
nirvedamupagacchati (XI. 5.24)

Simple Meaning—Vidura said to Dhṛtarāṣṭra, 'O king, the plight of that brahmin is symbolic of the plight of every human being in this world because, in spite of so many dangers to life, one hopes to live on and remains attached to life.'

upamānamidaṁ rājan
mokṣavidbhirudāhṛtaṁ
sukṛtaṁ vindate yena
paralokeṣu mānavaḥ (XI. 6.4)

Simple Meaning—'O king, Ṛṣis possessing knowledge of mokṣa (liberation) cite this as a simile, a proper understanding of which could inspire a person to orient one's life in the right direction.'

10.10. *ucyate yat tu kāntāraṁ*
mahāsaṁsāra eva saḥ
vanaṁ durgaṁ hi yaccaitat
saṁsāragahanaṁ hi tat (XI. 6.5)

Simple Meaning—The dangerous environment pictured for the brahmin is symbolic of this great world. The dense forest represents this 'saṃsāra' (i.e. the cycle of births and deaths).

ye ca te kathitā vyālā
vyādhayaste prakīrtitāḥ
yā sā nārī bṛhatkāyā
adhyatiṣṭhata tatra vai
tāmāhustu jarāṁ prājñā
rūpavarṇavināśinīm (XI. 6.6)

Simple Meaning—Different types of beasts of prey are the diseases which afflict human life. The frightful woman standing and stretching her arms is the old age which destroys complexion and beauty.

yastatra kūpo nṛpate
sa tu dehaḥ śarīriṇāṁ
yastatra vasate'dhastān
mahāhiḥ kāla eva saḥ
antakaḥ sarvabhūtānāṁ
dehināṁ sarvahāryasau (XI. 6.7-8)

Simple Meaning—The well is the human body. The huge snake dwelling in the bottom of the well is time which destroys all embodied creatures and every other thing too.

10.11. *kūpamadhye ca yā jātā*
vallī yatra sa mānavaḥ
pratāne lambate lagno
jīvitāśā śarīriṇām (XI. 6.9)

Simple Meaning—The cluster of creepers growing in the well and attached to whose spreading stems the man hangs down is the hope for life which is cherished by every creature.

sa yastu kūpavīnāhe
taṁ vṛkṣaṁ parisarpati
ṣaḍvaktraḥ kunjaro rājan
sa tu saṁvatsaraḥ smṛtaḥ (XI. 6.10)

Simple Meaning—The six-faced elephant which proceeds towards the tree standing at the mouth of the well is the year.

mukhāni ṛtavo māsāḥ
pādā dvādaśa kīrtitāḥ
ye tu vṛkṣaṁ nikṛntanti
mūṣikāḥ satatotthitāḥ
rātryahāni tu tānyāhur
bhūtānāṁ paricintakāh (XI. 6.11)

Simple Meaning—The six faces of the elephant are the six seasons of the year, and its twelve feet are the twelve months. The rats that are cutting away the roots of the tree (without taking any time off) are the days and nights (which denote the constant revolving of the wheel of time).

ye te madhukarāstatra
kāmāste parikīrtitāḥ
yāstu tā bahuśo dhārāḥ
sravanti madhunisravaṁ
tāṁstu kāmarasān vidyād
yatra majjanti mānavāḥ (XI. 6.12-13)

Simple Meaning—Bees represent desires. Streams of honey are the pleasures derived from the gratification of desires in which human beings drown themselves.

10.12. *evaṁ saṁsāracakrasya*
parivṛttiṁ vidurbudhāḥ
yena saṁsāracakrasya
pāśāṁśchindanti vai budhāḥ (XI. 6.14)

Simple Meaning—Wise people who understand clearly why saṁsāra binds the ignorant, succeed in finding a way to tear off its bonds.

na vikramo na cāpyartho
na mitraṁ na suhṛjjanaḥ
tathonmocayate duḥkhād
yathā'tmā sthirasaṁyamaḥ (XI. 7.22)

Simple Meaning—The spiritual path that can take one beyond the sorrows of the world does not depend on physical strength nor wealth nor worldly supporters—what is needed is moral strength that comes from self-discipline.

> *abhayaṁ sarvabhūtebhyo yo dadāti mahīpate*
> *sa gacchati paraṁ sthānaṁ viṣṇoḥ padamanāmayaṁ ....*
> *tasmāt sarveṣu bhūteṣu dayā kāryā vipaścitā*
>
> (XI. 7.25,28)

Simple Meaning—Vidura summarized the message based on the story of Man in the Well—One who gives to all beings an assurance of fearlessness, achieves spiritual perfection. Therefore, compassion to all beings is the characteristic of the wise.

10.13. Before closing this chapter, we give an extract from B.A. van Nooten's account of the far-flung journey of the story of Man in the Well :

"The literatue of the Middle Ages in Europe contains one story that originated in the Mahābhārata. John of Damascus (eighth century) composed a set of fables which included the story of the Man in the Well, which he had based on a set of legends describing the life of the Buddha. The work, under the name of Barlaam and Josaphat was translated into Latin A.D. 1048-49. By the early thirteenth century it had found its way into the Gesta Romanorum where the story of the Man in the Well appears as Chapter 168, 'On Eternal Damnation...."

The moral of the story is expounded as follows :

"The unicorn (who was an elephant in the Indian story) is Death, the pit is this life, the white and black mouse are day and night, the four vipers are the four humors of the body which is the tree; the dragon is the devil, the well in the bottom is hell; the sweetness of the honey is the delight in sinning, tempting the human being; the friend is Christ, the ladder penitence which if refused leads to a precipitous fall into the Devil's mouth."

"The purpose of the story has certainly undergone some changes, more than the details in fact. From Vidura's attempt to console old Dhṛtarāṣṭra and set him at peace with the world, it has been transformed into an eloquent admonition from the Church Militant to abide by its doctrines of salvation. The story has been rendered into a bas-relief by the thirteenth-century

Italian sculptor Benedetto Antelami, or one of his pupils, on the Porta della Vita (1260-62) of the Battistero in Parma ...."

"Through the agency of Christian missionaries, the story reached Japan in the sixteenth century. It seems to be the only and very remote connection of that country with the Mahābhārata."

"As late as the nineteenth century, this episode in a Russian translation from the Georgian version, exerted a powerful influence on the thinking of the youthful Leo Tolstoy and contributed to his resolve to lead an unconventional life."[2]

CHAPTER 11

Various Gītās included in Śānti-Parva

11.1. According to B.G. Tilak, "The word 'Gītā' is applied not only to the Bhagavad-Gītā but also to many other works dealing with spiritual knowledge."[1] In fact, Tilak has given a list of nine Gītās that are included in Śānti-Parva (i.e. Parva no. 12)—these nine Gītās being Pingalā-Gītā, Śampāka-Gītā, Manki-Gītā, Bodhya-Gītā, Vicakhnu-Gītā, Hārīta-Gītā, Vṛtra-Gītā, Parāśara-Gītā, and Haṁsa-Gītā[2]. Prior to these Gītās in the Mahābhārata, there is Vyādha-Gītā in Vana-Parva (i.e. Parva no. 3) and Bhagavad-Gītā (which is the main Gītā) in Bhīṣma-Parva (i.e. Parva no. 6). Subsequent to Śānti-Parva, there are two Gītās in Aśvamedha-Parva (i.e. Parva no. 14), viz. Kāma-Gītā (which is a short one) and Anu-Gītā (which, in importance, is next only to Bhagavad-Gītā, and a part of which is, by itself, also called Brāhmaṇa-Gītā). We have already summarized Vyādha-Gītā in chapter four. We shall give the main points of Anu-Gītā and Kāma-Gītā in chapter eighteen. In the rest of this chapter, we shall present summaries of the nine Gītās included in Śānti-Parva.

11.2. Pingalā- Gītā is the name given to a group of seven verses that occur in the beginning of mokṣa-dharma sẹction of Śānti-Parva. The message of this Gītā is based on the enlightenment that dawned on a prostitute (named Pingalā)—she realized that by giving up the desire for worldly pleasures, she could attain peace.

Pingalovāca:
pratibuddhāsmi jāgṛmi ....
nāhamadyājitendriyā ....
sukhaṁ nirāśaḥ svapiti
nairāśyaṁ paramaṁ sukhaṁ
āśāmanāśāṁ kṛtvā hi
sukhaṁ svapiti pingalā (XII. 174.60-62)

Simple Meaning—Pingalā declared (after enlightenment had dawned on her), 'I have been aroused from the sleep of ignorance. I am now awake .... I am no longer a slave of my senses .... One freed from desire and hope sleeps in felicity. Freedom from hope and desire makes one happy. Let everyone listen to my declaration, 'Having driven off desire and hope, Pingalā sleeps in felicity'.'

11.3. Śampāka-Gītā consists of twenty-one verses through which a learned brahmin (whose name was Śampāka) gave the message that renunciation was the right way to attain happiness :

nātyaktvā sukhamāpnoti
nātyaktvā vindate paraṁ
nātyaktvā cābhayaḥ śete
tyaktvā sarvaṁ sukhī bhava (XII. 176.22)

Simple Meaning—Śampāka gave the message through Bhīṣma—Without renunciation one can never attain happiness. Without renunciation one can never obtain what is for one's highest good. Without renunciation one can never sleep fearlessly. Therefore, renouncing every thing, make happiness thy own.

11.4. Manki-Gītā consists of fifty verses which begin with the story of two bullocks belonging to a Muni (spiritual aspirant) named Manki. The Muni tied the two bullocks to a yoke with the intention of training them so that he could earn more money by utilizing them for agricultural work. Unfortunately, the bullocks hit a camel that was lying on the field. When the camel rose up, he found the two bullocks dangling on either side of his (i.e. camel's) neck. The camel started running and the Muni realized that his bullocks would be injured and might even die. This sudden loss brought the Muni to a state of enlightenment :

damyanāśakṛte mankir
amṛtatvaṁ kilāgamat (XII. 177.54)

Simple Meaning—After the sudden loss of his two bulls, Manki attained wisdom and immortality.

The message of Manki-Gītā is—give up desire and greed, and have compassion on all beings :

prahāya kāmaṁ lobhaṁ ca sukhaṁ prāpto'smi sāmpratam ....
sarvabhūtadayāṁ caiva viddhi māṁ samupāgatam
(XII. 177.45, 47)

Simple Meaning—Manki said, 'By giving up desire and greed, I have attained happiness .... Compassion towards all beings is now a part of my spontaneous activity.'

11.5. Bodhya-Gītā was stated in a condensed form by Ṛṣi Bodhya to King Yayāti. When the king asked the Ṛṣi, 'How and from where did you learn the way to attain peace?', the Ṛṣi said, 'I have six gurus' :

Bodhya uvāca:
pingalā kuraraḥ sarpaḥ
sāraṇgānveṣaṇaṁ vane
iṣukāraḥ kumārī ca
ṣaḍete guravo mama (XII. 178.7)

Simple Meaning—Ṛṣi Bodhya said to King Yayāti, 'I have six gurus, viz. Pingalā, osprey (i.e. a fish-eating bird), snake, a flock of birds staying together, craftsman-artist, and kumārī (i.e. a girl who performed household work noiselessly).'

Bhīṣma then explained to Yudhiṣṭhira the six messages that Ṛṣi Bodhya's six gurus give. The first guru is Pingalā (already referred to by us in para 11.2). She gives the message of giving up the desire for worldly pleasures. The second guru is a fish-eating bird (osprey)—when pursued by other birds, the osprey realizes that by dropping the fish, it becomes free. So the osprey gives the message of not possessing an object of pleasure which others try to snatch. The third guru is a snake, who does not build its own house but lives happily in a hole dug by others. So the snake gives the message of 'aniketa' i.e. non-attachment to one's house. The fourth guru is a flock of birds who stay together under all circumstances—they give the message of 'adroha' i.e. absence of ill-will. The fifth guru is a craftsman-artist who was concentrating all his attention on his work so much so that he did not even notice the king's procession passing by. So the message of the craftsman-artist is 'single-mindedness'. The sixth guru is Kumārī, i.e. a girl who performed household work noiselessly by reducing the number of armlets to one. K.M. Ganguli explains this further :

> "The story of Kumārī, evidently a very ancient one, is given in full in the Bhāgavat-Mahāpurāṇa. Once upon a time, a maiden, residing in her father's house, wished to feed a number of brahmins. While removing the grain from the barn, her armlets, made of shells, began to jingle. To avoid making that noise, she broke all her armlets except one for each hand, thus giving the message of non-interference."[3]

11.6. Vicakhnu-Gītā makes a strong plea for ahiṁsā (non-violence). Although there are only eleven verses in this Gītā, the brief description that it gives of King Vicakhnu's visit to a yajña (performed with animal sacrifice) is very moving. This is how the king's visit to the yajña and his plea for ahiṁsā are narrated by Bhīṣma to Yudhiṣṭhira :

Bhīṣma uvāca:
atrāpyudāharantīmaṁ
itihāsaṁ purātanaṁ
prajānāmanukampārthaṁ
gītaṁ rājñā vicakhnunā (XII. 265.1)

Simple Meaning—Bhīṣma said, 'Words spoken by King Vicakhnu, long ago, because of his compassion for all beings, are of an exemplary nature'.

chinnasthūṇaṁ vṛṣaṁ dṛṣṭvā
vilāpaṁ ca gavāṁ bhṛśaṁ
gograhe yajñavāṭasya
prekṣamāṇaḥ sa pārthivaḥ (XII. 265.2)

Simple Meaning—'The occasion for King Vicakhnu to express his feelings was the following—He saw that a yajña was being performed with animal sacrifice, and he even heard painful groans of cows.'

svasti gobhyo'stu lokeṣu
tato nirvacanaṁ kṛtaṁ
hiṁsāyām hi pravṛttāyāṁ
āśīreṣā tu kalpitā (XII. 265.3)

Simple Meaning—The king said, 'May all the cows in the world live happily'. This was a spontaneous expression of the king's good wishes for cows and other animals, because he did not approve of animal sacrifice.

avyavasthitamaryādairvimūḍhairnāstikairnaraiḥ
saṁśayātmabhiravyaktairhiṁsā samanuvarṇitā
(XII. 265.4)

Simple Meaning—The king said, 'Only those who violate norms of righteous conduct, and who are ignorant or atheists or sceptics, want to acquire fame through rituals and take recourse to animal sacrifice.'

sarvakarmasvahiṁsā hi
dharmātmā manurabravīt
kāmakārād vihiṁsanti
bahirvedyāṁ paśūn narāḥ (XII. 265.5)

Simple Meaning—The king continued, 'The righteous-souled Manu has applauded the observance of ahiṁsā (non-violence) in all acts. Indeed, only those people who are motivated by selfish desires (i.e. who violate the principle of niṣkāma-karma of Bhagavad-Gītā) perform yajña by sacrificing animals'.

tasmāt pramāṇataḥ kāryo
dharmaḥ sūkṣmo vijānatā
ahiṁsā sarvabhūtebhyo
dharmebhyo jyāyasī matā (XII. 265.6)

Simple Meaning—Although King Vicakhnu spoke a little longer on the same subject, we present this verse as his concluding words, viz. 'Dharma should not be practiced blindly and thoughtlessly as is done by people who sacrifice animals. Subtle issues of dharma should be settled in the light of proper authority. I firmly believe that to practice ahiṁsā towards all beings is dharma at its best'.

11.7. Hārīta-Gītā too glorifies ahiṁsā (non-violence), but this Gītā associates it with Saṁnyāsa āśrama, i.e. the fourth stage of life (normally covering the years seventy-five and beyond). This Gītā contains twenty verses attributed to Hārīta Muni, but we reproduce only three of them :

svagṛhādabhinissṛtya
lābhelābhe samo muniḥ
samupoḍheṣu kāmeṣu
nirapekṣaḥ parivrajet (XII. 278.3)

Simple Meaning—Retiring from one's home, regarding gain and loss in the same light, restraining the senses, and disregarding all objects of desire even when they are readily available for enjoyment, the spiritual aspirant in the fourth stage of life should follow the path of renunciation.

na cakṣuṣā na manasā
na vācā dūṣayedapi
na pratyakṣaṁ parokṣaṁ vā
dūṣaṇaṁ vyāharet kvacit (XII. 278.4)

Simple Meaning—Neither with eyes, nor with word, nor in thought, should one disparage another. Nor should one speak evil of any person, either in or out of his hearing.

na hiṁsyāt sarvabhūtāni
maitrāyaṇagataścaret
nedaṁ jīvitamāsādya
vairaṁ kurvīta kenacit (XII. 278.5)

Simple Meaning—One should abstain from injuring any creature, maintaining a friendly behavior towards all. After all, one lives in this world for a limited time only, so avoiding enmity should be the goal of life.

11.8. Vṛtra-Gītā (consisting of two chapters) is based on the dialogue that took place between Vṛtrāsura (a fierce demon), on the one hand, and Śukrācārya (the guru of the demons) on the other. Śānti-Parva says that, after being defeated by the gods, Vṛtrāsura gave up the vices normally associated with the demons. Śukrācārya asked Vṛtrāsura how the latter reconciled himself with the defeat :

bhraṣṭaiśvaryaṁ purā vṛtraṁ
uśanā vākyamabravīt
kācit parājitasyādya
na vyathā te'sti dānava (XII. 279.15)

Simple Meaning—When Vṛtrāsura was bereft of glory, his guru Śukrācārya asked, 'How is it that, although you have been defeated, you do not seem to harbour any grievance?'

"Vṛtrāsura replied that, as a result of his defeat, enlightenment dawned on him and he realized that his downfall was due to his own misdeeds. Also, virtuous thoughts were strengthened in him when he saw Śrī Nārāyaṇa Hari (who was helping the gods in the battle against the demons) :

aiśvaryaṁ tapasā prāptaṁ bhraṣṭaṁ tacca svakarmabhiḥ
dhṛtimāsthāya bhagavan na śocāmi tatastvaham
(XII. 279.27)

Simple Meaning—Vṛtrāsura said, 'O honorable guru, I realized that the glory that I had achieved by tapas (austerity) was taken away from me because I did not act properly. I learnt patience and how not to grieve.'

yuyutsunā mahendreṇa
puṁsā sārdhaṁ mahātmanā
tato me bhagavān dṛṣṭo
harirnārāyaṇaḥ prabhuḥ (XII. 279.28)

Simple Meaning—Although Vṛtrāsura spoke in some detail, we present this verse as his concluding words. He said, 'When I was fighting against Indra, I noticed that Śrī Nārāyaṇa Hari was helping the gods. This opportunity of seeing Hari came as a boon to me.'

11.9. Parāśara-Gītā, consisting of nine chapters, is the longest of all the Gītās of Śānti-Parva. This Gītā is based on a dialogue between the famous King Janaka and the great Ṛṣi Parāśara (who was the father of Vyāsa). King Janaka asked :

Janaka uvāca:
kiṁ śreyaḥ sarvabhūtānāṁ
asmin loke paratra ca
yad bhavet pratipattavyaṁ
tad bhavān prabravītu me (XII. 290.4)

Simple Meaning—Janaka asked, 'What is it that contributes to the Śreyas (i.e. good) of all the beings, both in this world and the next? Please explain the main points that I should know in this connection.'

In reply, Ṛṣi Parāśara explained varṇa-dharma (i.e. dharma of the four varṇas—brahmin, kṣatriya, vaiśya, śūdra), as well as sāmānyadharma (i.e. dharma common to all). Here we present selected verses pertaining to sāmānyadharma only.

11.10. While listing virtues that all members of the society need to practice for achieving the good of all, Parāśara starts with 'ānṛśaṁsyam' (i.e. absence of cruelty) :

> *ānṛśaṁsyamahiṁsā cāpramādaḥ saṁvibhāgitā*
> *śrāddhakarmātitheyaṁ ca satyamakrodha eva ca*
> *sveṣu dāreṣu santoṣaḥ śaucaṁ nityānasūyatā*
> *ātmajñānaṁ titikṣā ca dharmāḥ sādhāraṇā nṛpa*
> (XII. 296.23-24)

Simple Meaning—O king, I list thirteen virtues that all members of the society should practice—absence of cruelty, non-violence, diligence, allowing others what is due to them, respect for ancestors, serving guests, truthfulness, never giving way to anger, observing marriage vows, purity, never being envious, spiritual knowledge, and tolerance.

Earning money only by just means (nyāya) is stressed, and in this context again, says Parāśara, 'Avoid cruelty (nṛśaṁsa)' :

> *nyāyāgataṁ dhanaṁ caiva nyāyenaiva vivardhitaṁ*
> *saṁrakṣyaṁ yatnamāsthāya dharmārthamiti niścayaḥ*
> *na dharmārthī nṛśaṁsena karmaṇā dhanamarjayet*
> *śaktitaḥ sarvakāryāṇi kuryānnarddhimanusmaret*
> (XII. 292.4-5)

Simple Meaning—Wealth should be acquired only by just means, increase of wealth should also be achieved only by just means, and all wealth should be carefully protected and used for righteous causes. This should be understood as the teaching of scriptures. Another aspect of this teaching is that the process of earning money should not involve cruelty to anyone. Furthermore, all acts should be performed within one's capacity, and there is no need to worry about increasing one's wealth because one may be tempted to do so by unjust means.

11.11. As in Bhagavad-Gītā, Parāśara-Gītā also takes the view that whatever wealth and qualities we have, we owe them to God, family support and to the society as a whole, or in other words, we are indebted to all of them. So we must try to discharge this debt, by contributing whatever we can, to the good of family members, guests, and of those in need :

devatātithibhṛtebhyaḥ
pitṛbhyaścātmanastathā
ṛṇavān jāyate martyas
tasmādanṛṇatām vrajet (XII. 292.9)

Simple Meaning—Everyone should realize that during the course of one's life, one takes help from five main sources and therefore one is indebted to them—these sources being gods (i.e. god-like beings like teachers), guests, general helpers and supporters, ancestors, and one's own 'ātman' (which is the same as brahman or God). One must try to do those things in one's life which can be considered as discharging (or repaying) one's debt.

11.12. Parāśara-Gītā's plea to people to adopt the path of righteousness and to stay away from unrighteousness, is linked with the general advice : 'Do not do that action which, when done by others, is condemned by you':

pareṣāṁ yadasūyeta
na tat kuryāt svayaṁ naraḥ (XII. 290.24)

Simple Meaning—One should not oneself do that act which, if done by someone else, would be criticized by one.

We draw attention to Vidura-Nīti (para 7.6) which gives a similar message.

Coming back to Parāśara-Gītā's advice about how to behave with others, we want to briefly mention the following two points :

karma hiṁsātmakaṁ tyajet (XII. 294.24)
sāntvena hi mahīyate (XII. 297.36)

Simple Meaning—Give up those acts which involve violence to others .... One who sympathizes with others is worthy of great respect.

11.13. Haṁsa-Gītā (consisting of forty-one verses) is the ninth and the last Gītā which occurs in Śānti-Parva, and it is so called because Brahmā assumed the form of a 'haṁsa' (i.e. swan) to give the teaching about right discrimination. Indian literature views a swan as having the unique power to be able to separate milk from a mixture of milk and water, thereby giving the following message—That the world is a mixture of good and bad, virtues and vices, but be like a swan i.e. make a clear distinction between good and bad, and adopt only virtues, discarding the vices. A practical form of such discrimination, according to Haṁsa-Gītā, is—Return good for evil :

ākruśyamāno na vadāmi kiṁcid
kṣamāmyahaṁ tāḍyamānaśca nityam (XII. 299.12)

Simple Meaning—The swan says, 'Even if someone speaks ill of me, I do not speak ill of that person. When someone assails me, I forgive the assailant'.

We draw attention to Vidura-Nīti (para 7.12) which gives a similar message.

CHAPTER 12

Dialogue between Tulādhāra and Jājali

12.1. The dialogue between Tulādhāra (a person engaged in trade) and Jājali (a brahmin) is a very important part of the Mahābhārata. Bhīṣma tells Yudhiṣṭhira about this dialogue in Śānti-Parva. Although it is not called a Gītā, the teachings given by Tulādhāra are quoted by scholars with practically the same reverence as, shown to any of the Gītā's. In fact, this dialogue reminds one of Vyādha-Gītā (occurring in Vana-Parva and summarized by us in chapter four), because both have a similar setting. Jājali was engaged in severe austerities (standing still for a long time and giving shelter to birds in his hair). Then feelings of arrogance arose in him (as was the case with the brahmin in Vyādha-Gītā). Jājali heard a heavenly voice, 'Don't think too much of yourself. Go and see Tulādhāra in Vārāṇasī who is a more genuine follower of dharma' (In Vyādha-Gītā, the brahmin went to the butcher in Mithilā). Here Jājali went to Vārāṇasī and listened to Tulādhāra's teachings, which helped him attain salvation by going along a new spiritual path.

12.2. With this background, we present selected verses from Śānti-Parva which begin with Jājali's tapas (austerities) :

atīva tapasā yukto ghoreṇa sa babhūva ha
tathopasparśanarataḥ sāyaṁ prātar mahātapāḥ

(XII. 261.13)

Simple Meaning—Jājali was engaged in tapas (austerities) which kept him busy in the mornings as well as evenings, but his tapas was 'ghora' (i.e. extremely austere).

About 'ghora tapas' we want to mention that it does not find favour with Bhagavad-Gītā (XVII. 5-6).

sa kadācinnirāhāro
vāyubhakṣo mahātapāḥ
tasthau kāṣṭhavadavyagro
na cacāla ca karhi-cit (XII. 261.19)

Simple Meaning—On one occasion, that great ascetic, abstaining entirely from food, and living upon air only, stood in the forest like a log of wood. Unmoved at heart, Jājali stood there, without once stirring an inch.

tasya sma sthāṇubhūtasya
nirviceṣṭasya bhārata
kuliṅgaśakunau rājan
nīḍaṁ śirasi cakratuḥ (XII. 261.20)

Simple Meaning—Since Jājali stood there like a log of wood, not moving at all, a pair of birds built their nest on his head.

ahanyahani cāgatya
tatastau tasya mūrdhani
āśvāsitau nivasataḥ
samprahṛṣṭau tadā vibho (XII. 261.26)

Simple Meaning—That pair of birds lived happily on Jājali's head, flying away to collect foodgrains but returning to their nest (which they had built on that head).

aṇḍebhyastvatha puṣṭebhyaḥ prājāyanta śakuntakāḥ
vyavardhanta ca tatraiva na cākampata jājaliḥ
(XII. 261.27)

Simple Meaning—With the passage of time, the eggs laid by the birds became mature and young ones came out, but they too began to grow up in that nest because Jājali did not move at all.

kadācinmāsamātreṇa
samutpatya vihaṅgamāḥ
naivāgacchaṁstato rājan
prātiṣṭhata sa jājaliḥ (XII. 261.37)

Simple Meaning—With further passage of time, the young ones became independent, and they (as well as the parent birds) flew away. Jājali waited for their return for one month (but in vain), and then he too left that spot.

12.3. *tatasteṣu pralīneṣu*
jājalirjātavismayaḥ
siddho'smīti matiṁ cakre
tatastaṁ māna āviśat (XII. 261.38)

Simple Meaning—The birds disappeared. Jājali wondered how successfully he stood motionless for such a long time. 'I have achieved perfection', he thought. Then egotism entered his heart.

sambhāvya caṭakān mūrdhni
jājalirjapatāṁ varaḥ
āsphoṭayat tathā'kāśe
dharmaḥ prāpto mayeti vai (XII. 261.41)

Simple Meaning—Jājali began to declare, 'I have attained the highest level of dharma through my tapas. I gave shelter to birds and their young ones for such a long time.'

12.4. *athāntarikṣe vāgāsīt tāṁ ca śuśrāva jājaliḥ*
dharmeṇa na samastvaṁ vai tulādhārasya jājale
(XII. 261.42)

Simple Meaning—Then an invisible voice arose in the sky and Jājali heard the following words, 'O Jājali, You have not attained the highest level of dharma. In fact, you are not even equal to Tulādhāra in this respect'.

vārāṇasyāṁ mahāprājñas
tulādhāraḥ pratiṣṭhitaḥ
so'pyevaṁ nārhate vaktuṁ
yathā tvaṁ bhāṣase dvija (XII. 261.43)

Simple Meaning—Jājali further heard the invisible voice say to him, 'O brahmin, Tulādhāra is engaged in trade in Vārāṇasī. He has great wisdom, but even he is not fit to say such words of self-admiration as you have spoken.'

12.5. *so'marṣavaśamāpannas*
tulādhāradidṛkṣayā

pṛthivīmacarad rājan
yatra sāyaṁgṛho muniḥ (XII. 261.44)

Simple Meaning—Upon hearing those words, Jājali became filled with anger. However, motivated by the desire to meet Tulādhāra, Jājali walked towards Vārāṇasī, passing the nights at those places where evening overtook him.

kālena mahatāgacchat
sa tu vārāṇasīṁ purīṁ
vikrīṇantaṁ ca paṇyāni
tulādhāraṁ dadarśa saḥ (XII. 261.45)

Simple Meaning—After having walked for many days, Jājali reached the city of Vārāṇasī (i.e. Banaras). There he saw Tulādhāra engaged in selling miscellaneous articles.

12.6. *so'pi dṛṣṭvaiva taṁ vipraṁ*
āyāntaṁ bhāṇḍajīvanaḥ
samutthāya susaṁhṛṣṭaḥ
svāgatenābhyapūjayat (XII. 261.46)

Simple Meaning—As soon as Tulādhāra, the shop-keeper saw that Jājali has arrived there, he cheerfully stood up and welcomed Jājali with proper salutations.

Tulādhāra uvāca:
āyānevāsi vidito
mama brahman na saṁśayaḥ ....
amarṣavaśamāpannas
tataḥ prāpto bhavāniha
karavāṇi priyaṁ kiṁ te
tad brūhi dvijasattama (XII. 261.47,51)

Simple Meaning—Tulādhāra said, 'Honorable brahmin, I already know why you have come here—the invisible voice spoke words which made you angry. I shall do whatever you want, so please let me know'.

12.7. Jājaliruvāca:
adhyagā naiṣṭhikīṁ buddhiṁ
kutastvāmidamāgataṁ
etadācakṣva me sarvaṁ
nikhilena mahāmate (XII. 262.3)

Simple Meaning—Jājali asked, 'O wise man, I want to know how (in spite of remaining busy with trade) you have succeeded in attaining such stable wisdom as well as such deep knowledge.'

12.8. Tulādhāra uvāca:

vedāhaṁ jājale dharmaṁ sarahasyaṁ sanātanaṁ
sarvabhūtahitaṁ maitraṁ purāṇaṁ yaṁ janā viduḥ
(XII. 262.5)

Simple Meaning—Tulādhāra replied, 'O Jājali, the dharma that I have learnt is based on deep knowledge of values like the good of all and universal friendliness. This dharma is old i.e. it has stood the test of time.'

Tulādhāra wanted to convey the message to Jājali that 'ghora tapas' was not a part of such dharma.

adroheṇaiva bhūtānāṁ
alpadroheṇa vā punaḥ
yā vṛttiḥ sa paro dharmas
tena jīvāmi jājale (XII. 262.6)

Simple Meaning—Tulādhāra continued, 'I not only have knowledge of dharma, but I also try to live according to it. For example, my goal is to have no ill-will towards any being, but if I am unable to achieve that goal, then minimization of ill-will becomes my objective. I believe that such an approach leads me to the highest level of practicable dharma.'

rasāṁśca tāṁstān viprarṣe
madyavarjyān bahūnahaṁ
krītvā vai prativikrīṇe
parahastādamāyayā (XII. 262.8)

Simple Meaning—Tulādhāra talked of principles underlying his trading policy, 'O learned brahmin, I do not sell wines in my store. Of course, there are several non-alcoholic drinks which I buy from other stores and which I sell here. But complete honesty is the guiding principle of my entire trading activity.'

sarveṣāṁ yaḥ suhṛnnityaṁ sarveṣāṁ ca hite rataḥ
karmaṇā manasā vācā sa dharmaṁ veda jājale
(XII. 262.9)

Simple Meaning—Tulādhāra highlighted the importance of doing good to all, 'O Jājali, in the field of dharma, theoretical knowledge is not enough. A real knower of dharma is one who is friendly to all and who is always engaged in doing good to all, in thought, word and deed.'

samo'haṁ sarvabhūteṣu
paśya me jājale vrataṁ
tulā me sarvabhūteṣu
samā tiṣṭhati sarvadā (XII. 262.10)

Simple Meaning—Tulādhāra spoke about the value of even-mindedness and equality of treatment towards all, 'O Jājali, in my behavior towards fellow beings, I practice equal vision. The same is true about my trading practice—all my customers are guaranteed equal treatment.'

12.9. *yadā na kurute bhāvaṁ*
sarvabhūteṣu pāpakaṁ
karmaṇā manasā vācā
brahma sampadyate tadā (XII. 262.16)

Simple Meaning—Tulādhāra condemned sinful conduct, 'O Jājali, only that person can attain brahman (i.e. spiritual perfection) who does not conduct himself sinfully towards any being in thought, word or deed.

na bhūtānāmahiṁsāyā
jyāyān dharmo'sti kaścana (XII. 262.30)

Simple Meaning—Although Tulādhāra went on, we conclude his initial statement by quoting his admiration for ahiṁsā, 'O Jājali, there is no greater dharma than the practice of non-violence towards all creatures.'

12.10. Jājali expressed his disagreement with Tulādhāra's view on non-violence. Just as 'ghora tapas' was a part of Jājali's dharma, the performance of yajña with animal sacrifice was also necessary according to him. Here are Jājali's words :

Jājaliruvāca:
paśubhiścauṣadhībhiśca
martyā jīvanti vāṇija ....
tato yajñaḥ prabhavati
nāstikyamapi jalpasi (XII. 263.2-3)

Simple Meaning—Jājali said, 'O expert in trade, it seems that you are an atheist because you are against the killing of animals even for yajña. But animals and herbs not only support human life, they also enable us to perform yajña.'

12.11. Tulādhāra uvāca:

vakṣyāmi jājale vṛttiṁ
nāsmi brāhmaṇa nāstikaḥ
na yajñaṁ ca vinindāmi
yajña vit tu sudurlabhaḥ (XII. 263.4)

Simple Meaning—Tulādhāra replied, 'O Jājali, please do not think that I am an atheist. I am not against yajña itself. I am only against animal sacrifice. My view may not be supported by many people, but those who know the real meaning of yajña (and such persons are rare) are in agreement with me.'

On the topic under discussion, Nicholas Sutton has made the following remarks :

"Tulādhāra refutes this (i.e. Jājali's) accusation and says that he does not deny the Vedas because in ancient times sacrifice did not involve animal killing and was performed with plants and herbs as the offerings".[1]

12.12. Although Tulādhāra opposed animal sacrifice by saying that this was not a part of yajña in the past, he put forth another idea to prove the same point. He said that a practice does not become doable simply because ancient people did it. In other words, there is no need to follow our ancestors blindly. So, even if animal sacrifice was performed for yajña by some people in the past, that would not make it acceptable now. Here are Tulādhāra's words :

īdṛśānaśivān ghorān
ācārāniha jājale
kevalācaritatvāt tu
nipuṇo nāvabuddhyase
kāraṇād dharmamanvicchen
na lokacaritaṁ caret (XII. 262.52-53)

Simple Meaning—Tulādhāra said, 'O Jājali, I am pained to see that some of the unrighteous and violent practices keep going in the world, only because people like you, in spite of being scholars, ignore their anti-social drawbacks. My advice in such cases is this—do not follow old practices blindly, and examine whether they can stand to reason.'

12.13. At this point Jājali gave up his opposition to Tulādhāra's ideas, and practically like a disciple, asked whether visiting centers of pilgrimage would make him happy :

Jājaliruvāca:
sukhaṁ tu kena karmaṇā ....
śaṁsa me tanmahāprajña
bhṛśaṁ vai śraddhāmi te (XII. 263.38-39)

Simple Meaning—Jājali said, 'O honorable man of great wisdom, please show me the way to be happy, e.g. should I visit centers of pilgrimage? I have full confidence in you.'

12.14. In reply, Tulādhāra explained further his ideas on non-violence (which we need not repeat), and then spoke about pilgrimage centers :

Tulādhāra uvāca:
sarvā nadyaḥ sarasvatyaḥ
sarve puṇyāḥ śiloccayāḥ
jājale tīrthamātmaiva
mā sma deśātithir bhava (XII. 263.42-43)

Simple Meaning—Tulādhāra replied, 'O Jājali, happiness comes from purity of heart, and not from ritualistic acts like visiting centers of pilgrimage. All rivers are as sacred as Sarasvatī, and all mountains are as sacred as Himalayas. One's 'ātman' itself is a tīrtha (i.e. a center of pilgrimage), so you need not wander about on earth for visiting sacred places.'

12.15. Tulādhāra concluded his statement on an emotional and startling suggestion, by referring to birds who had grown up on Jājali's head :

sambhāvayanti pitaraṁ
tvayā sambhāvitāḥ khagāḥ
asaṁśayaṁ pitā vai tvaṁ
putrānāhūya jājale (XII. 264.4)

Simple Meaning—'O Jājali, you are like father to the birds who grew up on your head. They have great regard for you. I suggest that you summon them like your children.'

12.16. Bhīṣma told Yudhiṣṭhira that the birds came and spoke to Jājali in human voice :

> Bhīṣma uvāca:
> *tato jājalinā tena*
> *samāhūtāḥ patattriṇaḥ*
> *vācamuccārayanti sma*
> *dharmasya vacanāt kila* (XII. 264.5)

Simple Meaning—Bhīṣma said, 'Jājali summoned the birds with fatherly love, and because of his righteousness, the birds came and spoke clearly in human voice.'

> *ahiṁsādikṛtaṁ karma*
> *ihaiva caiva paratra ca*
> *śraddhāṁ nihanti vai brahman*
> *sā hatā hanti taṁ naram* (XII. 264.6)

Simple Meaning—Birds said, 'All acts that are done non-violently bring good to the doer, both here and hereafter. On the other hand, acts done violently destroy faith, and that leads to total destruction.'

> *jyāyasī yā pavitrāṇāṁ*
> *nivṛttiḥ śraddhayā saha ....*
> *śraddhāmayo'yaṁ puruṣo*
> *yo yacchraddhaḥ sa eva saḥ* (XII. 264.16-17)

Simple Meaning—Birds went on, 'Faith is important, and if one is able to get rid of mental impurities also, then a combination of faith and purity is the best .... Man is of the nature of his faith; what his faith is, that, verily, he is.'

We want to mention that the above-quoted part of verse XII. 264.17 is the same as the second half of verse XVII.3 of Bhagavad-Gītā.

> *śraddhāṁ kuru mahāprajña*
> *tataḥ prāpsyasi yat paraṁ*
> *śraddhāvānśraddadhānaśca*
> *dharmaścaiva hi jājale* (XII. 264.19)

Simple Meaning—Birds concluded their statement by saying,

'Honorable Jājali, we have faith in you, and we think you have faith in Tulādhāra. This will lead you to spiritual perfection. A person with sāttvika (i.e. pure) faith is an embodiment of dharma.'

12.17. Bhīṣma uvāca:

tato'cireṇa kālena
tulādhāraḥ sa eva ca
divaṁ gatvā mahāprājñau
viharetāṁ yathāsukham (XII. 264.20)

Simple Meaning—As the concluding verse of this chapter, we have Bhīṣma's words addressed to Yudhiṣṭhira, 'After a short while, Tulādhāra and Jājali, both of whom had acquired great wisdom, attained the state of perfection and supreme bliss.'[2]

CHAPTER 13

Nārāyaṇīya Dharma

13.1. This book pays special attention to those sections of the Mahābhārata which support Bhagavad-Gītā's approach to dharma. The Nārāyaṇīya dharma portion of Śānti-Parva is one such section. A striking point of structural similarity between this section and Bhagavad-Gītā is that there are eighteen chapters in either of them. There are similarities in regard to the spiritual content of their dharma, and also about the names of famous entities through whom the dharmic tradition spread in the world. However, before we go into specific details of similarities, we present the stories of Ṛṣi Nārada and King Uparicara, by means of which Nārāyaṇīya dharma is explained in Śānti-Parva.

13.2. Bhīṣma, narrating the stories to Yudhiṣṭhira, begins with Ṛṣi Nārada's visit to Badarikāśrama in the northern mountains :

nāradaḥ sumahadbhūtaṁ
sarvalokānacīcarat
taṁ deśamagamad rājan
badaryāśramamāśugaḥ (XII. 334.14)

Simple Meaning—Ṛṣi Nārada, who is known for his travels to different places all over the world, arrived at the sacred place known as Badarikāśrama.

aho hyanugṛhīto'dya dharma ebhiḥ surairiha
naranārāyaṇābhyāṁ ca kṛṣṇena hariṇā tathā
(XII. 334.17)

Simple Meaning—Nārada said to himself, 'How wonderful it is that the strong foundations of dharma have been laid by four deities, viz. Nara, Nārāyaṇa, Hari and Kṛṣṇa.'

atra kṛṣṇo hariścaiva
kasmiṁścit kāraṇāntare
sthitau dharmottarau hyetau
tathā tapasi dhiṣṭhitau (XII. 334.18)

Simple Meaning—Nārada went on, 'At this point of time, Hari and Kṛṣṇa are not here. However, Nara and Nārāyaṇa are here, deeply engaged in tapas (austerity) for promoting the cause of dharma.'

Nārada uvāca:
pitā mātā ca sarvasya
jagataḥ śāśvato guruḥ
kiṁ tvadya yajase devaṁ
pitaraṁ kaṁ na vidmahe (XII. 334.27)

Simple Meaning—Nārada said to Nara and Nārāyaṇa, 'O Great Lords, you are the father and mother of all and the supreme guru. I wonder who that deva or power could be whom you are worshipping today.'

Śrībhagavān uvāca:
sa hyantarātmā bhūtānām
kṣetrajñaśceti kathyate ....
āvābhyāṁ pūjyate'sau hi
daive pitrye ca kalpate (XII. 334.30,32)

Simple Meaning—Śrī Bhagavān in the form of Nara and Nārāyaṇa replied, 'O Ṛṣi, we are worshipping the original entity of whom we are forms. He is the ātman of all beings and is called 'Kṣetrajña' (i.e. the knower of all forms).'

13.3. Nārada, eager to see 'kṣetrajña', went to śvetadvīpa and devoted himself to prayers :

prāpya śvetaṁ mahādvīpaṁ
nārado bhagavānṛṣiḥ ....
stotraṁ jagau sa viśvāya
nirguṇāya guṇātmane (XII. 338.1,3)

Simple Meaning—After arriving at the spacious realm called 'śvetadvīpa' (i.e. White Island), Ṛṣi Nārada prayed to Nārāyaṇa, the Lord of the universe, who is formless, but who also assumes form for the good of the world.

13.4. Śrībhagavān uvāca:

ekataśca dvitaścaiva
tritaścaiva maharṣayaḥ
imaṁ deśamanuprāptā
mama darśanalālasāḥ (XII. 339.12)

Simple Meaning—The Lord of the universe said to Nārada, 'You are devoted to me, so you can see me. Those who follow the path of 'tapas ' (i.e. austerity), ignoring devotion, can not see me even when they come here (for example, Ṛṣi's named Ekata, Dvita and Trita).'

na ca māṁ te dadṛśire
na ca drakṣyati kaścana
ṛte hyaikāntikaśreṣṭhāt
tvaṁ caivaikāntikottamaḥ (XII. 339.13)

Simple Meaning—'O devoted Ṛṣi, 'Ekata, Dvita, and Trita could not see me. In fact, only 'ekāntin' (i.e. those exclusively devoted to Him) can get my vision. You being the best of 'ekāntin' have seen me.'

13.5. Bhīṣma uvāca:

nārado'pi mahātejāḥ
prāpyānugrahamīpsitaṁ
naranārāyaṇau draṣṭuṁ
badaryāśramamādravat (XII. 339.110)

Simple Meaning—Bhīṣma said to Yudhiṣṭhira, 'After having successfully completed his mission, Ṛṣi Nārada returned to Badarikāśrama to see Nara and Nārāyaṇa.'

13.6. Next, the story of King Uparicara (as narrated by Bhīṣma to Yudhiṣṭhira) :

rajoparicaro nāma
babhūvādhipatirbhuvaḥ ....
ātmarājyaṁ dhanaṁ caiva
kalatraṁ vāhanaṁ tathā
yattadbhāgavataṁ sarvaṁ
iti tat prokṣitaṁ sadā (XII. 335.17,23)

Simple Meaning—There was, in times past, a famous king named Uparicara .... He was devoted to Nārāyaṇa. All that he had, e.g. kingdom, wealth, family and glory, he viewed them as God-given, and so he dedicated all his actions to Nārāyaṇa (i.e. to selfless service of mankind).

tasya yajño mahānāsīd
aśvamedho mahātmanaḥ ....
na tatra paśughāto'bhūt
sa rājaivaṁ sthito'bhavat (XII. 336.5,10)

Simple Meaning—King Uparicara performed a grand yajña. Although this yajña was called 'aśvamedha' (literally meaning horse sacrifice), no animal was killed, because the king believed in ahiṁsā (non-violence).

prītastato'sya bhagavān
devadevaḥ purātanaḥ
sākṣāt taṁ darśayāmāsa
so'dṛśyo'nyena kenacit (XII. 336.12)

Simple Meaning—Nārāyaṇa, the Lord of the universe, accepted the prayers of Uparicara, and revealed Himself to him (i.e. to King Uparicara), but no one else could see Him (because they lacked devotion—reference para 13.4)

13.7. This is a summary of the first part of the story of Uparicara. The second part of his story is rather complicated, and it describes how he committed a mistake and was cursed, but also how his devotion to Nārāyaṇa ultimately brought bliss to him. Uparicara (also called Vasu) was requested to mediate in a religious controversy between Ṛṣis and devas (probably priests arguing in the name of devas i.e. gods) :

bho rājan kena yaṣṭavyaṁ
ajenahosvidauṣadhaiḥ
etannaḥ saṁśayaṁ chindhi
pramāṇaṁ no bhavān mataḥ (XII. 337.10)

Simple Meaning—Since there was a difference of opinion (Ṛṣis opposing animal sacrifice and devas or priests supporting it), they said to Uparicara, 'O king, how should a yajña be performed—with a goat or with foodgrains? Kindly settle this dispute. We believe you will be the right judge.'

13.8. Although Uparicara had performed his own yajña without killing any animal (reference para 13.6), it is obviously a matter of great surprise that, in the present case, he gave his opinion in favor of devas :

devānāṁ tu mataṁ jñātvā
vasunā pakṣasaṁśrayāt ....
kupitāste tataḥ sarve
munayaḥ sūryavarcasaḥ (XII. 337.13-14)

Simple Meaning—Uparicara gave his judgment in favor of gods. Hearing this, the Ṛṣis, whose radiance was comparable to that of the sun, became extremely angry with the king.

13.9. *brahmaśāpād divo bhraṣṭaḥ ....*
rajoparicarastadā
adho vai sambabhūvāśu
bhūmervivarago nṛpa (XII. 336.62, 337.17)

Simple Meaning—Cursed by the Ṛṣis, Uparicara fell down, into a hole in the earth.

smṛtistvenam na hi jahau
tadā nārāyaṇājñayā ...
ayajaddhariṁ surapatiṁ
bhūmervivarago'pi san (XII. 337.18,30)

Simple Meaning—Since Uparicara's misjudgment was due to some momentarily unrighteous influence, he did not lose the grace of Nārāyaṇa. So even after having fallen into a hole, he retained his memory and continued worshipping Hari.

varado bhagavān viṣṇuḥ
samīpasthaṁ dvijottamaṁ
garutmantaṁ mahāvegaṁ
ābabhāṣepsitaṁ tadā (XII. 337.32)

Simple Meaning—Bhagavān Viṣṇu, the giver of boons, moved with the desire of doing good to Uparicara, gave instructions to Garuḍa, the foremost of birds who was capable of travelling at great speed.

tata enaṁ samutkṣipya
sahasā vinatāsutaḥ
utpapāta nabhastūrṇe
tatra cainamamuncata (XII. 337.37)

Simple Meaning—Garuḍa took no time in lifting Uparicara from the hole and restoring him to the high status that he earlier had.

13.10. We now take up the question of similarities between Nārāyaṇīya dharma and the ideas of Bhagavad-Gītā. The first point of similarity is that they both advocate an activist approach to life. In the Gītā it is called Karmayoga. Nārāyaṇīya dharma uses the expression 'Pravṛtti' to convey the same idea :

pravṛttilakṣaṇaścaiva
dharmo nārāyaṇātmakaḥ (XII. 347.83)

Simple Meaning—Pravṛtti (i.e. activism) is the characteristic mark of the Nārāyaṇīya dharma.

We should mention that the opposite of 'Pravṛtti' in this context is 'Nivṛtti' (i.e. renunciation). It is a special feature of the Gītā that it re-interpreted 'nivṛtti' to denote 'a renunciatory mental attitude' rather than 'outward renunciation'—thus enabling harmonization of 'pravṛtti' and 'nivṛtti'.

13.11. The second point of similarity between Nārāyaṇīya dharma and the Gītā is the importance given to 'bhakti' (devotion to God) in both of them. In the Gītā, a combination of selfless action (karma) and devotion (bhakti) is called by Lord Kṛṣṇa as 'mat-karma' (i.e. My work or God's work), one form of which is to dedicate all one's actions to God. The text of the Nārāyaṇīya dharma states (reference para 13.6) that this is what King Uparicara did. In fact, because of the importance attached to bhakti, the Nārāyaṇīya dharma is also called Bhāgavata dharma.

13.12 The third point of similarity between Nārāyaṇīya dharma and the Gītā is their opposition to animal sacrifice. Chapters III and IV of the Gītā indicate various ways of performing 'yajña', but there is no place for animal sacrifice in any of them. Nārāyaṇīya dharma's opposition to animal sacrifice is brought out through the story of King Uparicara (reference paras 13.6-9)

13.13 The fourth point of similarity between Nārāyaṇīya dharma and the Gītā is their advocacy of actions for the good of all. Chapters V and XII of the Gītā glorify 'sarvabhūtahitam' (i.e. the good of all beings). In Nārāyaṇīya dharma, King Uparicara is described (in an early part of the text) as :

satyaparaḥ sarvabhūteṣvahiṁsakaḥ (XII. 335.20)

i.e. devoted to truth and practising non-violence towards all beings. And it is made clear towards the end of the text that 'sarvabhūtahitam' was a part of non-violence :

ahiṁsakairātmavidbhiḥ sarvabhūtahite rataiḥ
bhavet kṛtayugaprāptirāśīḥ karmavivarjitā (XII. 348.63)

Simple Meaning—If more and more people would be like Uparicara, i.e. devoted to non-violence, possessing knowledge of ātman, and engaged in doing good to all, without desiring any return for themselves, then it would be like living in Satyayuga.

13.14. The fifth point of similarity between Nārāyaṇīya dharma and the Gītā is their lack of support to rituals and 'ghora tapas' (violent austerities). For ready reference, we give below verse XI.53 of the Gītā :

nāhaṁ vedairna tapasā
na dānena na cejyayā
śakya evaṁvidho draṣṭuṁ
dṛṣṭavānasi māṁ yathā (Gītā XI.53)

Simple Meaning—Lord Kṛṣṇa told Arjuna (after showing him His form), 'O Arjuna, in the form in which you have seen Me, I can not be seen by the Vedas, or tapas (austerities) or gifts or sacrifices.'

In the context of Nārāyaṇīya dharma, we have quoted (in para 13.4) the Lord's words spoken to Ṛṣi Nārada, indicating that tapas-oriented Ṛṣis like Ekata, Dvita, and Trita failed to see Him because they did not have the necessary devotion. Later portions of the same chapter of Nārāyaṇīya dharma mention that Bṛhaspati himself, who adopted the sacrificial mode of worship, could not see Him. When Bṛhaspati felt angry, Uparicara and Ṛṣi's consoled him by pointing out that devotion and grace of God was needed to see Him—

na roṣaṁ kartumarhasi ....
yasya prasādaṁ kurute
sa eva draṣṭumarhati (XII. 336.18,20)

Simple Meaning—Uparicara and Ṛṣis said to Bṛhaspati, 'Honorable guru, please don't be angry. Only those who have the grace of the Lord, are able to see Him.'

13.15. Having looked at points of similarity in regard to the spiritual content of the Gītā and Nārāyaṇīya dharma, we need to draw attention to a point of dissimilarity also—and that relates to 'vyūha' i.e. steps of evolution. Nārāyaṇīya dharma speaks of 'caturvyūha' i.e. four steps of evolution :

ekavyūhavibhāgo vā
kvacid dvirvyūhasaṁjñitaḥ
trirvyūhaścāpi saṁkhyātaś
caturvyūhaśca dṛśyate (XII. 348.57)

Simple Meaning—The number of vyūha's or steps of evolution could range from one to four, in the order of Vāsudeva, Saṁkarṣaṇa, Pradyumna, and Aniruddha—their metaphysical equivalents being brahman, jīva, mind, and individuation.

On the other hand, the Gītā takes the Vedantic approach which says that brahman is the only reality.

We need not go into further details on this point of dissimilarity between the Gītā and Nārāyaṇīya dharma,[1] because our focus in this book is only on practical applications of spiritual ideas for the good of all.

13.16. The final point that we want to include in this chapter is again a point of similarity between the Gītā and Nārāyaṇīya dharma, but this similarity relates, not to the spiritual contents of their dharma, but to the names of famous entities through whom their dharmic tradition spread in the world. For this purpose, we first look at verse IV.1 of the Gītā :

imaṁ vivasvate yogaṁ
proktavānahamavyayaṁ
vivasvān manave prāha
manurikṣvākave'bravīt (Gītā IV.1)

Simple Meaning—Lord Kṛṣṇa said to Arjuna, 'I proclaimed this imperishable yoga to Vivasvān (sun), Vivasvān told it to Manu, and Manu spoke it to Ikṣvāku'.

It is significant that the same names occur in the following verse of Nārāyaṇīya dharma :

tretāyugādau ca tato
vivasvān manave dadau
manuśca lokabhūtyarthaṁ
sutāyekṣvākave dadau (XII. 348.51)

Simple Meaning—In the beginning of Tretāyuga, Vivasvān (Sun) taught this dharma to Manu, who in turn passed it on to his son Ikṣvāku, for the good of all mankind.

CHAPTER 14

Two Dialogues of Janaka—One with the Saintly Woman Sulabhā, and Another with His Wife

14.1. King Janaka plays an important role in the dharma-related dialogues in the Mahābhārata. One of these dialogues was with Sulabhā, a saintly woman, to which scholars have paid a good deal of attention. Another dialogue of Janaka was with his wife—but this dialogue has practically been ignored. We feel that both these dialogues are important, but in their own respective ways. In brief, Sulabhā was critical of Janaka as a karmayogin (although, to be a karmayogin was his speciality), while his wife was critical of his assumption of external features of saṁnyāsa (i.e. renunciation, which was a temporary assumption only). In this chapter, we present selected verses from the two dialogues, one after the other. Both of them occur in Śānti-Parva—the dialogue of Janaka with Sulabhā being in the mokṣa-dharma section, and that with his wife in the rāja-dharma section—the two narrators being Bhīṣma and Vaiśampāyana, respectively.

14.2. The first dialogue is between Janaka and Sulabhā. The Mahābhārata presents it in four parts, viz. introduction by Bhīṣma, Janaka's statement, Sulabhā's statement, and closing remarks by Bhīṣma. Here we follow the same sequence :

Bhīṣma uvāca:
maithilo janako nāma dharmadhvaja iti śrutaḥ
(XII. 320.4)

Simple Meaning—Bhīṣma said to Yudhiṣṭhira, 'In the dialogue that I am going to narrate, one of the participants was Janaka, King of Mithilā, whose fame as a spiritually perfect person had spread far and wide.'

mahīmanucacāraikā
sulabhā nāma bhikṣukī (XII. 320.7)

Simple Meaning—'The other participant in this dialogue was Sulabhā, who had renounced the world, and who wandered alone, from one place to another.'

sātisūkṣmāṁ kathāṁ śrutvā
tathyaṁ neti sasaṁśayā
darśane jātasaṁkalpā
janakasya babhūva ha (XII. 320.9)

Simple Meaning—When Sulabhā heard about the spiritual attainments of Janaka, she wondered whether all this was true or not. To ascertain this personally, Sulabhā became desirous of seeing Janaka.

14.3. *sā prāpya mithilāṁ ramyāṁ*
prabhūtajanasaṁkulāṁ
bhaikṣyacaryāpadeśena
dadarśa mithileśvaram (XII. 320.12)

Simple Meaning—Sulabhā arrived at the beautiful city of Mithilā where a large number of people lived. She went to the King's palace and saw Janaka. At that time, Sulabhā had the appearance of a mendicant.

tato'syāḥ svāgataṁ kṛtvā
vyādiśya ca varāsanaṁ
pūjitāṁ pādaśaucena
varānnenāpyatarpayat (XII. 320.14)

Simple Meaning—Janaka welcomed Sulabhā, offered her an excellent seat, gave water to wash her feet, and served nice refreshments which she liked.

14.4. *sulabhā tvasya dharmeṣu*
mukto neti sasaṁśayā
sattvaṁ sattvena yogajñā
praviveśa mahīpateḥ (XII. 320.16)

Simple Meaning—Sulabhā had a doubt whether Janaka had really become jīvan-mukta (i.e. liberated while still living) by following the karma-yoga path of dharma. Since Sulabhā possessed special yogic power, she adopted a special technique of seeking clarification of her doubt, viz. that she made her own intellect enter into Janaka's intellect.

netrābhyāṁ netrayorasya
raśmīn saṁyamya raśmibhiḥ
sā sma taṁ codayiṣyantī
yogabandhairbabandha ha (XII. 320.17)

Simple Meaning—Because of her yogic power, Sulabhā was able to restrain the rays issuing from the eyes of the king, by means of the rays emanating from her own eyes. In this way, she bound up the king's mind with yoga bonds, in the hope that this will enable her to know the truth about Janaka's spiritual attainments.

14.5. *janako'pyutsmayan rājā*
bhāvamasyā viśeṣayan
pratijagrāha bhāvena
bhāvamasyā nṛpottama (XII. 320.18)

Simple Meaning—But Janaka too had great mental strength. He understood Sulabhā's intention, and without losing control of his mind, he allowed her intellect to interact with his own.

tadekasminnadhiṣṭhāne
saṁvādaḥ śrūyatāmayaṁ
chatrādiṣu vimuktasya
muktāyāśca tridaṇḍake (XII. 320.19)

Simple Meaning—In this closing verse of Bhīṣma's introduction, a mental picture is drawn as to how the dialogue between Janaka and Sulabhā began. Bhīṣma said to Yudhiṣṭhira, 'As a result of the simultaneous application of the special powers that these two great personalities had, their subtle bodies stayed together, and although Janaka and Sulabhā spoke to each other, it appeared as if the former was without the symbols of royalty and the latter was without the symbols of saṁnyāsa (i.e. renunciation).'

14.6. Janaka uvāca:
chatrādiṣu viśeṣeṣu

muktaṁ māṁ viddhi tattvataḥ
sa tvāṁ sammantumicchāmi
mānārhā hi matāsi me (XII.320.22)

Simple Meaning—Janaka's statement forms part two of the dialogue between the King and Sulabhā. Janaka began like this, 'I want you to know that I have no attachment to symbols of royalty. I have great regard for you, although, before closing my statement, I shall indicate some points about which I would like to have more information.'

parāśarasagotrasya
vṛddhasya sumahātmanaḥ
bhikṣoḥ pañcaśikhasyāhaṁ
śiṣyaḥ paramasammataḥ (XII. 320.24)

Simple Meaning—Janaka continued, 'I am the beloved disciple of the high-souled and venerable Pañcaśikha, who belongs to the mendicant order named after the great Ṛṣi Parāśara.'

14.7. *seyaṁ paramikā buddheḥ*
prāptā nirdvandvatā mayā
ihaiva gatamohena
caratā muktasanginā (XII. 320.31)

Simple Meaning—'Since I have become free from attachment, I do not see this householder-status as an obstacle to even-mindedness. I am free from delusion, and dualities (i.e. pairs of opposites like heat and cold) do not disturb my intellect.'

yaśca me dakṣiṇaṁ bāhuṁ
candanena samukṣayet
savyaṁ vāsyāpi yastaśnet
samāvetāvubhau mama (XII. 320.36)

Simple Meaning—'I have equal vision towards all the people, for example, a person who puts the pleasing sandal-paste on my right hand and another person who cuts or hurts my left hand—I have equal regard for both of them.'

14.8. *sukhī so'hamavāptārthaḥ*
samaloṣṭāśmakāncanaḥ
muktasaṅgaḥ sthito rājye
viśiṣṭo'nyaistridaṇḍibhiḥ (XII. 320.37)

Simple Meaning—Janaka went on, 'Having fulfilled the purpose of human life, I feel inner happiness. To me there is no difference between a clod of earth, a piece of stone, and a lump of gold. Although I am engaged in ruling a kingdom, I am free from all attachments. I believe that such practice of karma-yoga with inner renunciation is better (for the society) than external renunciation (which assumes no responsibility for socially useful work).'

We should mention that the compound word

'samaloṣṭāśmakāncanaḥ'

which occurs in this verse, also occurs in Gītā, verse XIV.24.

kāṣāyadhāraṇaṁ mauṇḍyaṁ
triviṣṭabdhaṁ kamaṇḍaluṁ
liṅgānyutpathabhūtāni
na mokṣāyeti me matiḥ (XII. 320.47)

Simple Meaning—'In my opinion, external things are not important for spirituality, for example, wearing of brown clothes, shaving of the head, bearing of the triple stick and the begging bowl—these are outward signs of renunciation, but they do not help in attaining spiritual perfection.'

14.9. *kṛteyaṁ hi vijijñāsā*
mukto neti tvayā mama
etat sarvaṁ praticchannaṁ
mayi nārhasi gūhituṁ (XII. 320.70)

Simple Meaning—Having stated his own opinion, Janaka started mentioning the points on which he wanted Sulabhā to respond, 'I believe the main question in your mind was whether I was jīvan-mukta (i.e. liberated while still living), and I have expressed my own point of view on that. Now I want you not to hide whatever your other purposes might have been.'

praveśaste kṛtaḥ kena
mama rāṣṭre pure'pi vā
kasya vā sannikarṣāt tvaṁ
praviṣṭā hṛdayaṁ mama (XII. 320.58)

Simple Meaning—Janaka continued listing his questions for Sulabhā, 'What was your intention (other than the desire to find out about my spiritual status) when you entered my kingdom and my city? How can you justify entering into my heart (with your yoga power) because no initiative was taken by me in this regard?'

sā tvaṁ jātiṁ śrutaṁ vṛttaṁ
bhāvaṁ prakṛtimātmanaḥ
kṛtyamāgamane caiva
vaktumarhasi tattvataḥ (XII. 320.75)

Simple Meaning—Concluding his statement, Janaka said to Sulabhā, 'Since I have told you clearly about my guru, philosophy, status, etc., I feel, I am justified in seeking similar information about you, for example, your family, education, philosophy, approach to life, and your real motive underlying the visit to this place.'

14.10. Sulabhovāca:
pradhāno nāma rājarśir
vyaktaṁ te śrotramāgataḥ
kule tasya samutpannāṁ
sulabhāṁ nāma viddhi mām (XII. 320.184)

Simple Meaning—Sulabhā's statement forms part three of the dialogue between her and Janaka. In the summarized version that we present here, we have brought forward the verses in which she answers the questions raised by Janaka. For example, Sulabhā tells about her family, 'You must have heard about a kṣatriya Ṛṣi whose name was 'Pradhāna'. I was born in his family, and my name is Sulabhā.'

sāhaṁ tasmin kule jātā
bhartaryasati madvidhe
vinītā mokṣadharmeṣu
carāmyekā munivratam (XII. 320.186)

Simple Meaning—Sulabhā continued, 'As I told you, I was born in a well-known kṣatriya family. Since no suitable match could be found for me, I took to saṁnyāsa-order and received instruction in mokṣa-dharma (also called 'nivṛtti' i.e. renunciatory path to spiritual perfection). I wander alone, from one place to another.'

14.11. *nāsmi satrapraticchannā*
na parasvāpahāriṇī

na dharmasankarakarī
svadharme'smi dhṛtavratā (XII. 320.187)

Simple Meaning—Sulabhā went on, 'I practice no hypocrisy in the matter of leading a life of renunciation. I am not a thief that appropriates what belongs to others. I do not create confusion about practices that belong to different orders. I am firm in the practices belonging to that mode of life to which I properly belong.'

nāsthirā svapratijñāyāṁ nāsamīkṣya pravādinī
nāsamīkṣyāgatā ceha tvatsakāśaṁ janādhipa
(XII. 320.188)

Simple Meaning—'I am firm and steady in my vows. I never utter any word without reflecting on its propriety. I did not come to thee, without having deliberated properly'.

14.12. *mokṣe te bhāvitāṁ buddhiṁ*
śrutvāhaṁ kuśalaiṣiṇī
tava mokṣasya cāpyasya
jijñāsārthamihāgatā (XII. 320.189)

Simple Meaning—Sulabhā, answering Janaka's question as to why she came there, said, 'I had heard that you are firmly devoted to 'mokṣa-dharma' (i.e. practices that lead to spiritual perfection). I wanted to know about the essence of your philosophy. So it is clear that I came here with very good intentions.'

14.13. *ātmanyevātmanā'tmānaṁ*
yathā tvamanupaśyasi
evamevātmanā'tmānaṁ
anyasmin kiṁ na paśyasi (XII. 320.127)

Simple Meaning—Sulabhā showed appreciation of Janaka's Vedantic knowledge, but she also expressed a doubt about its completeness, 'Although you see nothing but 'ātman' in your own body, mind and intellect, it seems that you are unable to do the same when it comes to some one else's body, mind and intellect.'

yadyātmani parasmiṁśca
samatāmadhyavasyasi

atha māṁ kāsi kasyeti
kimarthamanupṛcchasi (XII. 320.128)

Simple Meaning—Sulabhā justified her criticism by referring to the questions that Janaka had asked her, 'If you were really even-minded, as between yourself and others, you would not have asked me questions like who I am and to what family I belong.'

14.14. *paratantraḥ sadā rājā*
svalpeṣvapi prasajjate ....
ko rājyamabhipadyeta
prāpya copaśamaṁ labhet (XII. 320.140, 155)

Simple Meaning—As a follower of the path of nivṛtti (i.e. renunciation), Sulabhā expressed the view that kingship and freedom cannot go together, 'In my opinion, a king can never be free. The act of ruling goes hand-in-hand with attachment to so many things, small as well as big .... How can a man, desiring freedom, agree to be a ruler, and if he agrees, how can he attain peace?'

14.15. We omit philosophical details contained in Sulabhā's statement,[1] and move on to Bhīṣma's closing remarks (which constitute part four of the dialogue between Janaka and Sulabhā) :

Bhīṣma uvāca:
ityetāni sa vākyāni
hetumantyarthavanti ca
śrutvā nādhijagau rājā
kincidanyadataḥ param (XII. 320.193)

Simple Meaning—Bhīṣma said to Yudhiṣṭhira, 'Having heard Sulabhā's statement, which was logical as well as meaningful, King Janaka did not pursue the matter any further.'

Bhīṣma's closing remarks do not imply that Janaka accepted Sulabhā's point of view—they only mean that the king did not want to drag on the debate between pravṛtti (activism) and nivṛtti (renunciation).

14.16. The second dialogue is between Janaka and his wife, and this was narrated by Vaiśampāyana to Janamejaya. The Mahābhārata presents it in three parts, viz. introduction by Vaiśampāyana, statement by Janaka's wife, and closing remarks by Vaiśampāyana. Here we follow the same sequence :

> Vaiśampāyana uvāca:
> *dhanānyapatyaṁ dārāśca*
> *ratnāni vividhāni ca*
> *panthānaṁ pāvakaṁ hitvā*
> *janako mauḍhyamāsthitaḥ* (XII. 18.4)

Simple Meaning—Vaiśampāyana said to Janamejaya, 'One day, a sudden mood of renunciation gripped King Janaka, who cast off wealth, children, wife, symbols of royalty, and even the philosophy of pravṛtti (i.e. activism)'.

> *taṁ dadarśa priyā bhāryā*
> *bhaikṣyavṛttimakincanaṁ ....*
> *kruddhā manasvinī bhāryā*
> *vivikte hetumad vacaḥ* (XII. 18.5-6)

Simple Meaning—'When the queen saw that her husband had shaved off his head and assumed the garb of a mendicant, she realized what her duty was. She chose the right moment when no third person was around. Then, showing anger on her face, she spoke to her husband (i.e. King Janaka), presenting logical arguments against the assumption of external features of saṁnyāsa'.

14.17. Bhāryovāca:

> *kathamutsṛjya rājyaṁ svaṁ*
> *dhanadhānyasamanvitaṁ*
> *kāpālīṁ vṛttimāsthāya*
> *dhānāmuṣṭirna te varaḥ* (XII. 18.7)

Simple Meaning—The statement by Janaka's wife forms part two of the dialogue between her and her husband. She began by criticizing the step suddenly taken by the king, 'Why have you adopted a life of mendicancy, abandoning such a wealthy and prosperous kingdom? To take to begging for a handful of fallen off barley can not be proper for you.'

> *pratijñā te'nyathā rājan*
> *viceṣṭā cānyathā tava*
> *yad rājyaṁ mahadutsṛjya*
> *svalpe tuṣyasi pārthiva* (XII. 18.8)

Simple Meaning—Janaka's wife went on, 'The vow that you had taken was of one kind, while the renunciatory step that you are now taking is of another kind. You had resolved to be a great ruler, but now you want to be satisfied with small things.'

naitenātithayo rājan
devarṣipitarastathā
adya śakyāstvayā bhartuṁ
moghaste'yaṁ pariśramaḥ (XII. 18.9)

Simple Meaning—'By begging, you will be able to get only a handful of grain, but that will not enable you to fulfil your obligations towards guests, gods, Ṛṣis and ancestors. So the labour that you will put into the act of begging will not serve your purpose.'

14.18. *naiva te'sti paro loko*
nāparaḥ pāpakarmaṇaḥ
dharmyān dārān parityajya
yastvamicchasi jīvitum (XII. 18.15)

Simple Meaning—Janaka's wife objected to her being ignored, 'I want you to understand that, to leave your wedded wife and to think of living alone, will be a sinful act for you, which will cause unhappiness, in this life as well as in the next.'

14.19. *nipānaṁ sarvabhūtānāṁ*
bhūtvā tvaṁ pāvanaṁ mahat
āḍhyo vanaspatirbhūtvā
so'nyāṁstvaṁ paryupāsase (XII. 18.17)

Simple Meaning—The queen reminded the king of the help that he used to give to so many people, 'I also want you to understand the adverse effect that your action will have on a large number of persons, because you were like a large and sacred lake giving water to all, or like a mighty tree giving food and shelter to many. Now, instead of helping others, you will depend on others.'

14.20. *annād gṛhasthā loke'smin bhikṣavastata eva ca*
annāt prāṇaḥ prabhavati annadaḥ prāṇado bhavet
(XII. 18.28)

Simple Meaning—The queen put forth the view that to give up the householder-status would be a mistake, 'If you are under the impression that, as a mendicant, you could serve the society better, then I want to point out why such an impression is wrong. Since all life subsists on food, we must accord the highest status to householders who maintain stocks of food not only for themselves but for mendicants too.'

gṛhasthebhyo'pi nirmuktā
gṛhasthāneva saṁśritāḥ
prabhavaṁ ca pratiṣṭhāṁ ca
dāntā vindanta āsate (XII. 18.29)

Simple Meaning—'Householders supply not only food, but other things too. In fact, mendicants themselves come from households, and even after they leave households, they depend on them for their maintenance. It is through the householders again that mendicants acquire fame.'

14.21. *tyāgānna bhikṣukaṁ vidyān*
na mauḍhyānna ca yācanāt
ṛjustu yo'rthaṁ tyajati
nasukhaṁ viddhi bhikṣukam (XII. 18.30)

Simple Meaning—The queen drew the king's attention to the very concept of renunciation, 'Finally, I want to say that real renunciation is a state of mind. To leave the home and to take a begging bowl do not mean renunciation—they only denote ignorance. On the other hand, by giving up attachment, crookedness and selfishness (while staying at home), one is entitled to be regarded as a true mendicant.'

samaḥ śatrau ca mitre ca sa vai mukto mahīpate
(XII. 18.31)

Simple Meaning—The queen added, 'O my husband, you are a great king, and even staying as a king, you will attain salvation if you become even-minded towards all and have an equal vision towards friends and foes.'

aniṣkaṣāye kāṣāyaṁ
īhārthamiti viddhi taṁ
dharmadhvajānāṁ muṇḍānāṁ
vṛttyarthamiti me mitih (XII. 18.34)

Simple Meaning—The queen concluded her plea to the king,

'I do not attach any importance to the putting on of brown robe—the main thing is to purify one's mind. If the mind is impure, then brown robe is just a means to become a beggar and to survive on charity. Such persons of clean-shaven heads that pretend to set up a banner of virtue have no higher goal in life than begging and surviving on charity.'

14.22. Vaiśampāyana uvāca:
tattvajño janako rājā
loke'sminniti gīyate
so'pyāsīnmohasampanno
mā mohavaśamanvagāḥ (XII. 18.37)

Simple Meaning—Vaiśampāyana's closing remarks constitute part three of the dialogue between Janaka and his wife, 'O Janamejaya, after listening to his wife's plea, King Janaka changed his mind and continued to rule as before. But this narration has a message for you and for everyone, viz. that even Janaka, who was famous for his wisdom, temporarily became a victim of ignorance and confusion about dharma, therefore beware and protect yourself from attacks of ignorance which can occur at any time.'

CHAPTER 15

Two More Stories from Śānti-Parva Condemning Animal Sacrifice

15.1. Śānti-Parva has several stories that condemn animal sacrifice. We have already referred to three of them in chapters 11-13, in the context of Vicakhnu-Gītā, Tulādhāra-Jājali dialogue, and Nārāyaṇīya dharma, respectively. In this chapter, we present summaries of two more of such stories which can be considered special because they stand on their own (in condemning animal sacrifice), rather than form a part of any wide-ranging text (which was the case for the earlier three stories). The narrator for both the stories of this chapter is Bhīṣma.

15.2. Bhīṣma uvāca:

rāṣṭre dharmottare śreṣthe
vidarbheṣvabhavad dvijaḥ
uñchavṛttirṛṣiḥ kaścid
yajñaṁ yaṣṭuṁ samādadhe (XII. 272.3)

Simple Meaning—Bhīṣma said to Yudhiṣṭhira, 'Once upon a time, there lived in Vidarbha, a brahmin who followed the 'uncha' mode (i.e. he subsisted on grains of corn picked up from the fields after the reapers had abandoned them). Influenced by the dharmic practices of the region (i.e. Vidarbha), this brahmin believed in the importance of performing a yajña.'

upagamya vane siddhiṁ
sarvabhūtāvihiṁsayā
api mūlaphalairiṣṭo
yajñaḥ svargyaḥ parantapa (XII. 272.5)

Simple Meaning—'Abstaining from injuring any creature, and leading the life of a forest recluse, he attained to ascetic success. With roots and fruits, he used to perform sacrifices that were believed to confer heaven upon him.'

15.3. *tasya bhāryā vratakṛśā*
śuciḥ puṣkaradhāriṇī
yajñapatnī samānītā
satyenānuvidhīyate (XII. 272.6)

Simple Meaning—'The brahmin's name was Satya and his wife's name was Puṣkaradhāriṇī. She was pure-minded and had emaciated herself by the observance of many austere vows. She co-operated with her husband and took her seat by his side as his spouse for the performance of sacrifices (although she was not sure whether her husband's faith in non-violence was as firm as hers).'

15.4. *śukrasya punarājātiḥ*
parṇādo nāma dharmavit
tasmin vane samīpastho
mṛgo'bhūt sahavāsikaḥ (XII. 272.8)

Simple Meaning—'In that forest, not far from the brahmin's asylum, lived the virtuous Parṇāda who could trace his lineage back to Śukrācarya. (It is mentioned later in this story that Lord Dharma himself had assumed the form of Parṇāda). In order to give the message of non-violence to Satya, Parṇāda assumed the form of a deer.'

vacobhirabravīt satyaṁ
tvayedaṁ duṣkṛtaṁ kṛtaṁ ....
māṁ bhoḥ prakṣipa hotre
tvaṁ gaccha svargamaninditaḥ (XII. 272.9-10)

Simple Meaning—'The deer spoke to Satya in human voice, 'Your yajña is incomplete without animal sacrifice .... I, therefore, ask you to slay me so that your yajña may become complete and you may go to heaven.'

15.5. *tatastu yajñe sāvitrī*
sākṣāt taṁ sannyamantrayat
nimantrayantī pratyuktā
na hanyāṁ sahavāsinam (XII. 272.11)

Simple Meaning—'Goddess Sāvitrī appeared there and advised Satya to do what the deer had asked him to do. (This was obviously to test Satya). The brahmin (Satya) firmly replied, "I shall not slay this deer who lives with me in this same neighborhood." '

sa tu baddhāñjaliṁ satyaṁ
ayācaddhariṇaḥ punaḥ
satyena sa pariṣvajya
sandiṣṭo gamyatāmiti (XII. 272.13)

Simple Meaning—'The deer, then, with folded hands, once more begged of Satya (to be cut into pieces and poured into the sacrificial fire). However, Satyā embraced him in friendship and asked him to go away, in a tone full of love.'

15.6. *tataḥ sa hariṇo gatvā*
padānyaṣṭau nyavartata
sādhu hiṁsaya māṁ satya
hato yāsyāmi sadgatim (XII. 272.14)

Simple Meaning—'At this, the deer seemed to leave that place. But after he had gone only eight steps, he returned and said to Satya, 'Verily, do thou slay me. Truly do I say, slain by thee I am sure to attain to a righteous end.'

paśya hyapsaraso divyā
mayā dattena cakṣuṣā
vimānāni vicitrāṇi
gandharvāṇāṁ mahātmanām (XII. 272.15)

Simple Meaning—'The deer added, "Look, Satya, I give you heavenly vision—behold the celestial apsarās (i.e. nymphs) and the beautiful planes of the high-souled gandharvas (i.e. benevolent, heavenly musicians)." '

15.7. *tataḥ sa suciraṁ dṛṣṭvā*
spṛhālagnena cakṣuṣā
mṛgamālokya hiṁsāyāṁ
svargavāsaṁ samarthayat (XII. 272.16)

Simple Meaning—'Beholding that heavenly sight for a long time, with longing eyes, and succumbing to the temptation given by the deer, and thinking that residence in heaven is attainable only by animal sacrifice, Satya mentally gave up the opposition that he had so far expressed (regarding animal sacrifice).'

15.8. *sa tu dharmo mṛgo bhūtvā*
bahuvarṣoṣito vane
tasya niṣkṛtimādhatta
na tvasau yajñasaṁvidhiḥ (XII. 272.17)

Simple Meaning—'It was the Lord Dharma himself who (had assumed the form of Parṇāda and who in turn) became a deer that lived in those woods for many years. Seeing that Satya (the brahmin) was tempted by the heavenly prospect, Dharma provided for his salvation and counselled him, saying, 'This (i.e. even the thought of animal sacrifice) is a violation of the right method of performing yajña.'

15.9. *tasya tenānubhāvena*
mṛgahiṁsātmanastadā
tapo mahatsamucchinnaṁ
tasmāddhiṁsā na yajñiyā (XII. 272.18)

Simple Meaning—'Since Satya (the brahmin) had mentally given up the opposition to animal sacrifice, he lost a large part of dharma that he had accumulated, because of that improper thought itself. However, in the end, he did get the message that animal sacrifice in any form and under any circumstances forms no part of yajña.'

tatastaṁ bhagavān dharmo
yajñaṁ yājayata svayaṁ
samādhānaṁ ca bhāryāyā
lebhe sa tapasā paraṁ (XII. 272.19)

Simple Meaning—'After giving the message of non-violence, Lord Dharma (assumed his real form) and helped Satya (the brahmin) in performing yajña with roots and fruits. Satya's wife (Puṣkaradhāriṇī) was happy that her husband's faith in non-violence was now as firm as hers.'

15.10. The second story (narrated by Bhīṣma, like the first one, but much longer) is based on a dialogue between Ṛṣi Kapila (who opposed animal sacrifice)and Syūmaraśmi (who sought advice because he had doubts). The occasion was the arrival of a guest (named Tvaṣṭā) at the residence of King Nahuṣa. Initially, the king had planned to perform yajña with animal sacrifice, but Ṛṣi Kapila intervened and gave the message of non-violence which was finally accepted by all those present there.

15.11. Bhīṣma uvāca:
āmnāyamanupaśyan hi
purāṇaṁ śāśvataṁ dhruvaṁ
nahuṣaḥ pūrvamālebhe
tvaṣṭurgāmiti naḥ śrutam (XII. 268.6)

Simple Meaning—Bhīṣma said to Yudhiṣṭhira, 'Once upon a time, when Tvaṣṭā arrived as a guest, King Nahuṣa, for discharging the duties of hospitality, was on the point of sacrificing a cow, thinking that this would be in conformity with the true, ancient and eternal teachings of the Vedas.'

15.12. *tāṁ niyuktāmadīnātmā*
sattvasthaḥ saṁyame rataḥ
jñānavān niyatāhāro
dadarśa kapilastathā (XII. 268.7)

Simple Meaning—'Ṛṣi Kapila of liberal soul, firmly holding sāttvika (i.e. good) values, self-disciplined, possessing true knowledge, and whose food was excellent (i.e. vegetarian), saw that cow tied for slaughter.'

sa buddhimuttamāṁ prāpto
naiṣṭhikīmakutobhayāṁ
satīmaśithilāṁ satyāṁ
vedā ityabravīt sakṛt (XII. 268.8)

Simple Meaning—'Ṛṣi Kapila, whose understanding was excellent, who was perfectly fearless, and whose devotion to truth was unshakable, spoke these words from his heart—"Alas ye Vedas (in whose name this cow is going to be slaughtered)." '

15.13. *tāṁ gāmṛṣiḥ syūmaraśmiḥ*
praviśya yatimabravīt
na hi vedā yadi matā
dharmāḥ kenāpare matāḥ (XII. 268.9)

Simple Meaning—'At that time, another Ṛṣi, of the name of Syūmaraśmi, entering by yoga-power the form of that cow, spoke to Ṛṣi Kapila, "If you have doubts about the validity of animal sacrifice, then what criterion (other than Vedas) can you use to justify other practices of dharma?" '

15.14. Kapila uvāca:
nāhaṁ vedān vinindāmi

na vivakṣyāmi karhicit
pṛthagāśramiṇāṁ karmāṇy
ekārthānīti naḥ śrutam (XII. 268.12)

Simple Meaning—Ṛṣi Kapila replied to Syūmaraśmi, 'My criticism of animal sacrifice is on the grounds that this is done (wrongfully) in the name of Vedas—so this is not a criticism of the Vedas, but only of those who have interpreted them incorrectly. Although dharmas assigned to different stages of life may look different, the goal achieved by them is the same, i.e. spiritual perfection (although it may be called by different names).'

anālambhe hyadoṣaḥ syād
ālambhe doṣa uttamaḥ ....
yadyatra kincit pratyakṣaṁ
ahiṁsāyāḥ paraṁ mataṁ
ṛte tvāgamaśāstrebhyo
brūhi tad yadi paśyasi (XII. 268.16-17)

Simple Meaning—Ṛṣi Kapila added, 'You asked me about the basic criterion, and my answer is 'non-violence'. I believe that animal sacrifice is unrighteous, and to abstain from it is righteous .... If you know of any principle as being superior to non-violence, which is supported by direct experience rather than by a wrong interpretation of scriptures, then you please tell me about it.'

15.15. Syūmaraśmiruvāca:
syūmaraśmirahaṁ brahman
jijñāsārthamihāgataḥ
śreyaskāmaḥ pratyavocaṁ
ārjavānna vivakṣayā (XII. 269.41)

Simple Meaning—Syūmaraśmi said, 'O learned Ṛṣi, my name is Syūmaraśmi and I have come here for acquiring knowledge. Desirous of doing good to myself, I have started this conversation in good faith and not for the sake of disputation.'

nāstikyamanyathā ca syād
vedānāṁ pṛṣṭhataḥ kriyā
etasyānantyamicchāmi
bhagavañśrotumañjasā (XII. 269.67)

Simple Meaning—Syūmaraśmi went on, 'According to my limited understanding, if Vedic rituals are not performed, one runs the risk of being called an atheist. I want to hear from you about 'mokṣa' (i.e. liberation), which comes in the Vedas after the declarations in favor of rituals.'

15.16. Kapila uvāca:
anāgamamanaitihyaṁ
pratyakṣaṁ lokasākṣikaṁ
dharma ityeva ye yajñān
vitanvanti nirāśiṣaḥ (XII. 270.4)

Simple Meaning—Ṛṣi Kapila replied to Syūmaraśmi, 'I begin by indicating the right approach to yajña. Those who perform yajña as a duty, without any desire for fruits, (and also without violence), attain purity of heart, as all the people who come in direct contact with them can testify—and you do not need to verify this with the help of Vedas or other books.'

15.17. *utpannatyāgino'lubdhāḥ*
kṛpāsūyāvivarjitāḥ
dhanānāmeṣa vai panthās
tīrtheṣu pratipādanaṃ (XII. 270.5)

Simple Meaning—Kapila went on, 'Next, I indicate the right approach to 'dānam' (i.e. sharing). Only those persons can give 'dānam' to deserving people who are not greedy, who have no attachment to wealth, who are free from miserliness and jealousy, and who regard sharing (rather than storing) as the best use of money.'

15.18. *anāśritāḥ pāpakarma*
kadācit karmayoginaḥ
manaḥsaṃkalpasaṁsiddhā
viśuddhajñānaniścayāḥ (XII. 270.6)

Simple Meaning—Kapila continued, 'Next, I mention the spiritual benefits of karma-yoga (which means performing one's duty without attachment to results). Since a karmayogin concentrates on karma and not on results, he stays away from sinful acts. Furthermore, since karma-yoga is skill in action, he is sure to achieve success in fulfilling the main objective (i.e. purity of heart). Finally, such yoga culminates in true knowledge of the ultimate reality (i.e. brahman).'

15.19. *akrudhyanto'nasūyanto*
nirahaṃkāramatsarāḥ
jñānaniṣṭhāstriśuklāśca
sarvabhūtahite ratāḥ (XII. 270.7)

Simple Meaning—Kapila linked non-violence to the good of all, 'Those who follow the non-violent approach, never give way to wrath, never look to other people's faults and never become victims of arrogance and malice. Through such self-discipline, their spiritual practices are well-maintained, leading to three-fold purity (i.e. of birth, conduct, and learning). To be devoted to the good of all, becomes their spontaneous activity.'

15.20. *āsan gṛhasthā bhūyiṣṭhā*
avyutkrāntāḥ svakarmasu
rājānaśca tathā yuktā
brāhmaṇāśca yathāvidhi (XII. 270.8)

Simple Meaning—Kapila said that these ideas have stood the test of time, 'There have been, in the ages gone by, many men, leading lives as householders and thoroughly devoted to their own duties. These included many kings (like Janaka, Aśvapati, etc.) who combined their royal duties with knowledge leading to spiritual perfection. Learned brahmins too (like Yājñavalkya) set examples for others.'

15.21. *ānṛśaṁsyaṁ kṣamā śāntir*
ahiṁsā satyamārjavam
adroho'nabhimānaśca
hrīstitikṣā śamastathā
panthāno brahmaṇastvete
etaiḥ prāpnoti yatparam (XII. 270.39-40)

Simple Meaning—Kapila concluded his reply to Syūmaraśmi by recapitulating the linkage between avoidance of animal sacrifice and attainment of brahman, 'Virtues leading to mokṣa start with absence of cruelty (i.e. avoidance of animal sacrifice), which is closely linked with forgiveness, tranquility, and non-violence. Other related virtues are truth, uprightness, absence of ill-will, freedom from arrogance, modesty, endurance, and serenity. These constitue the path leading to brahman, which is the highest state of mokṣa, and about which you wanted to hear from me.'

15.22. The substance of the second story is summarized by Sutton in the following words :

> "Three chapters of Śānti-Parva describe a conversation between Kapila and Syūmaraśmi, who has taken the form of a cow awaiting slaughter. Kapila, famous as the original propounder of Sāṃkhya, condemns the killing of animals, and a debate follows, ... at the end of which Kapila emerges victorious and Syūmaraśmi accepts his teachings."[1]

CHAPTER 16

How a Monster was Won over by Ahiṁsā

16.1. In Anuśāsana-Parva (i.e. Parva no.13), Bhīṣma told Yudhiṣṭhira a story in which a brahmin was captured by a violent Rākṣasa (monster), but instead of yielding or fighting, the former (i.e. the brahmin) won over the latter (i.e. the rākṣasa) by ahiṁsā (non-violence). Such stories occurring in Buddhist literature are well-known[1], but this Mahābhārata story does not seem to have attracted much attention, partly because the brahmin's name is not specified here. We attach great importance to this story, and so we reproduce it in full as told by Bhīṣma.

16.2. Bhīṣma uvāca:

kaścid vāgbuddhisampanno
brāhmaṇo vijane vane
gṛhītaḥ kṛcchramāpanno
rakṣasā bhakṣayiṣyatā (XIII. 124.5)

Simple Meaning—Bhīṣma said to Yudhiṣṭhira, 'A certain brahmin, endued with eloquence as well as intelligence, fell into distress, because he was seized in a lone forest by a rākṣasa (monster) who wished to feed on him.'

sa buddhiśrutisampannas
taṁ dṛṣṭvātīva bhīṣaṇaṁ
sāmaivāsmin prayuyuje
na mumoha na vivyathe (XIII. 124.6)

Simple Meaning—'Since the brahmin was learned and wise, he kept his calm. Without allowing himself to be stupefied at the sight of that terrible cannibal, he resolved to apply the method of non-violence.'

16.3. *rakṣastu vācaṁ sampūjya*
praśnaṁ papraccha taṁ dvijaṁ
mokṣyase brūhi me praśnaṁ
kenāsmi hariṇaḥ kṛśaḥ (XIII. 124.7)

Simple Meaning—The rākṣasa was impressed by the brahmin's sweet words and calm face. He did not carry out his initial intention of killing the brahmin. Rather he offered to give him a chance by saying, 'I shall release you if give me a satisfactory reply to my question : why am I pale of hue and so lean?'

muhūrtamatha saṁcintya
brāhmaṇastasya rakṣasaḥ
ābhirgāthābhiravyagraḥ
praśnaṁ pratijagāda ha (XIII. 124.8)

Simple Meaning—After reflecting for a while, the brahmin calmly accepted the conditional offer of the rākṣasa and proceeded to give his reply in the following well-spoken words.

16.4. Brāhmaṇa uvāca:
videśastho vilokastho
vinā nūnaṁ suhṛjjanaiḥ
viṣayānatulān bhuṅkṣe
tenāsi hariṇaḥ kṛśaḥ (XIII. 124.9)

Simple Meaning—The brahmin replied to the rākṣasa, 'Dwelling in a place that is distant from your normal abode, moving in a different environment, and deprived of the companionship of your friends and kinsmen, you find yourself in possession of unusual sense objects. Such a situation makes you pale and lean.'

nūnaṁ mitrāṇi te rakṣaḥ
sādhūpacaritānyapi
svadoṣādaparajyante
tenāsi hariṇaḥ kṛśaḥ (XIII. 124.10)

Simple Meaning—'Your friends, though well-treated by you, are still not well-disposed towards you—and this is not due to your fault, but because of their own vicious nature. This makes you pale and lean.'

16.5. *dhanaiśvaryādhikāḥ stabdhās*
tvadguṇaiḥ paramāvarāḥ
avajānanti nūnaṁ tvāṁ
tenāsi hariṇaḥ kṛśaḥ (XIII. 124.11)

Simple Meaning—The brahmin went on, 'Persons less qualified than you, happen to get greater wealth and prosperity than you. When they look down upon you, then you become pale and lean.'

guṇavān viguṇānanyān
nūnaṁ paśyasi satkṛtān
prājño'prājñān vinītātmā
tenāsi hariṇaḥ kṛśaḥ (XIII. 124.12)

Simple Meaning—'In spite of deserving honor due to your qualities, wisdom and modesty, you do not get it, while you see that honor bestowed on those who have no qualities and no wisdom—this makes you pale and lean.'

16.6. *avṛttyā kliśyamāno'pi*
vṛttyupāyān vigarhayan
māhātmyād vyathase nūnaṁ
tenāsi hariṇaḥ kṛśaḥ (XIII. 124.13)

Simple Meaning—The brahmin went on, 'Though distressed through want of means of support, you are led by the greatness of your soul to disregard unworthy means (like living on charity). This dilemma makes you pale and lean.'

16.7. *sampīḍyātmānamāryatvāt*
tvayā kaścidupaskṛtaḥ
jitaṁ tvāṁ manyate sādho
tenāsi hariṇaḥ kṛśaḥ (XIII. 124.14)

Simple Meaning—The brahmin went on, 'Even when you do good to someone (and this might involve sacrifice on your part but you still do it because of your good nature), that person (in stead of appreciating your help) thinks that your action is only a sign of your defeat. Such an unpleasant experience makes you pale and lean.'

16.8. *kliśyamānān vimārgeṣu*
kāmakrodhāvṛtātmanaḥ
manye tvaṁ dhyāyasi janāṁs
tenāsi hariṇaḥ kṛśaḥ (XIII. 124.15)

Simple Meaning—The brahmin went on, 'Perhaps you feel sorry for those persons who follow a wrong path under the influence of lust and anger, and who therefore suffer misery in this world. Such sympathy for incurable sinners makes you pale and lean.'

16.9. *prajñāsambhāvito nūnaṁ*
aprajñairupasaṁhitaḥ
hīyamāno'si durvṛttais
tenāsi hariṇaḥ kṛśaḥ (XIII. 124.16)

Simple Meaning—The brahmin went on, 'Even though you deserve honor due to your wisdom, you find that unwise persons laugh at you and wicked persons insult you. To be a victim of such baseless ill-treatment makes you pale and lean.'

nūnaṁ mitramukhaḥ śatruḥ
kaścidāryavadācaran
vañcayitvā gatastvāṁ vai
tenāsi hariṇaḥ kṛśaḥ (XIII. 124.17)

Simple Meaning—'Perhaps some enemy of yours pretended to be friendly with you, spoke sweet words and behaved nicely, but subsequently cheated you and went away. To be a victim of such hypocrisy and cheating makes you pale and lean.'

16.10. *prakāśārthagatirnūnaṁ*
rahasyakuśalaḥ kṛtī
tajjñairna pūjyase nūnaṁ
tenāsi hariṇaḥ kṛśaḥ (XIII. 124.18)

Simple Meaning—The brahmin went on, 'Even those people do not respect you who know about your learning, your skill in understanding different issues and your method of work. Such non-recognition of your talent makes you pale and lean.'

asatsvapi niviṣṭeṣu
bruvato muktasaṁśayaṁ
guṇāste na virājante
tenāsi hariṇaḥ kṛśaḥ (XIII. 124.19)

Simple Meaning—'Even though you speak clearly and remove the confusion from which wicked and untruthful persons suffer, you do not get due credit for the fine contribution that you make. Such non-recognition of your qualities makes you pale and lean.'

16.11. *dhanabuddhiśrutairhīnaḥ*
kevalaṁ tejasānvitaḥ
mahat prārthayase nūnaṁ
tenāsi hariṇaḥ kṛśaḥ (XIII. 124.20)

Simple Meaning—The brahmin went on, 'Perhaps you wanted a high position, merely on the basis of your physical strength, and you were unsuccessful because you did not have the necessary wealth, intelligence and scriptural knowledge. Such failure makes you pale and lean.'

16.12. *tapaḥpraṇihitātmānaṁ*
manye tvāraṇyakāṅkṣiṇaṁ
bāndhavā nābhinandanti
tenāsi hariṇaḥ kṛśaḥ (XIII. 124.21)

Simple Meaning—The brahmin went on, 'It seems that, although you are keen to retire into the forest to carry out your plan to practice severe austerities, yet your kinsmen are not favorably inclined towards this plan of yours. Such non-cooperation from your kinsmen makes you pale and lean.'

16.13. *iṣṭabhāryasya te nūnaṁ*
prātiveśyo mahādhanaḥ
yuvā sulalitaḥ kāmī
tenāsi hariṇaḥ kṛśaḥ (XIII. 124.22)

Simple Meaning—The brahmin went on, 'While living in the city, you may notice that, some neighbor of yours, who is rich, young and handsome, is trying to attract the attention of your dear wife. Such threat from your neighbor makes you pale and lean.'

nūnamarthavatāṁ madhye
tava vākyamanuttamaṁ
na bhāti kāle'bhihitaṁ
tenāsi, hariṇaḥ kṛśaḥ (XIII. 124.23)

Simple Meaning—'While in the company of rich persons, you may find that, howsoever wisely you speak, they criticize your words as being unwise and inappropriate to the occasion. Such criticism makes you pale and lean.'

dṛḍhapūrvaṁ śrutaṁ mūrkhaṁ
kupitaṁ hṛdayapriyaṁ

anunetuṁ na śaknoṣi
tanāsi hariṇaḥ kṛśaḥ (XIII. 124.24)

Simple Meaning—'While in the company of your dear kinsmen, you may find that one of them, though exposed to scriptures for a long time, acts foolishly and becomes angry with you, and you are unable to pacify him. Such inability makes you pale and lean.'

16.14. *nūnamāsaṁjayitvā tvāṁ*
kṛtye kasmiṁścidīpsite
kaścidarthayate nityaṁ
tenāsi hariṇaḥ kṛśaḥ (XIII. 124.25)

Simple Meaning—The brahmin went on, 'While dealing with a business partner, you may find that, although outwardly he gives the impression that the work allotted to you is to fulfill your desires and your purposes, in reality he only wants to promote his own selfish interest. Such disillusionment makes you pale and lean.'

nūnaṁ tvāṁ suguṇairyuktaṁ
pūjayānaṁ suhṛddhruvaṁ
mamārtha iti jānīte
tenāsi hariṇaḥ kṛśaḥ (XIII. 124.26)

Simple Meaning—'While dealing with a friend, you may find that, although people known to both of you honor you for your qualities, still your friend thinks that such honor is given to you because of him. Such betrayal by a friend makes you pale and lean.'

16.15. *antargatamabhiprāyaṁ*
nūnaṁ necchasi lajjayā
vivektuṁ prāptiśaithilyāt
tenāsi hariṇaḥ kṛśaḥ (XIII. 124.27)

Simple Meaning—'While dealing with a potential donor, you may find that two reasons prevent you from stating clearly what you want—the first reason being that you have doubts about getting what you want, and the second reason being that you feel ashamed in exposing your weakness. Such an awareness about your own problems makes you pale and lean.'

16.16. *nānābuddhiruco loke*
manuṣyān nūnamicchasi
grahītuṁ svaguṇaiḥ sarvāṁs
tenāsi hariṇaḥ kṛśaḥ (XIII. 124-28)

Simple Meaning—The brahmin went on, 'You might have set before you an impossible goal, viz. to bring under your control, all the people who have diverse kinds of understandings and inclinations. Such an over-estimation of your own capability makes you pale and lean.'

avidvān bhīruralpārthe
vidyāvikramadānajaṁ
yaśaḥ prārthayase nūnaṁ
tenāsi hariṇaḥ kṛśaḥ (XIII. 124.29)

Simple Meaning—'Another impossible goal that you might have set before yourself is this, viz. that you seek such fame as is won by knowledge, prowess and gifts, but you do not have learning, courage and wealth. Such an unbalanced approach on your part makes you pale and lean.'

16.17. *cirābhilaṣitaṁ kincit*
phalamaprāptameva te
kṛtamanyairapahṛtaṁ
tenāsi hariṇaḥ kṛśaḥ (XIII. 124.30)

Simple Meaning—The brahmin went on, 'You might have been trying hard to acquire some long-desired object, only to find that some other persons have taken it away, leaving you disappointed. Such a failure after a long struggle makes you pale and lean.'

nūnamātmakṛtaṁ doṣaṁ
apaśyan kincidātmanaḥ
akāraṇe'bhiśapto'si
tenāsi hariṇaḥ kṛśaḥ (XIII. 124.31)

Simple Meaning—'The unhelpful attitude of other persons might hurt you in another way, viz. that, although you are completely innocent and are not able to detect any error on your part, but still other persons curse you, apparently for no good reason. Such a false criticism by other persons makes you pale and lean.'

16.18. *sādhūn gṛhasthān dṛṣtvā ca*
tathāsādhūn vanecarān
muktāṁścāvasathe saktāṁs
tenāsi hariṇaḥ kṛśaḥ (XIII. 124.32)

Simple Meaning—The brahmin went on, 'As a well-wisher of others, you may feel disappointed when you see strange behavior on their part, for example, saṃnyāsins reverting to householders' way of life, worldly persons living in forests, and liberated souls getting attached to property. Such disappointment makes you pale and lean.'

suhṛdāṁ duḥkhamārtānāṁ
na pramokṣyasi cārtijaṁ
alamarthaguṇairhīnaṁ
tenāsi hariṇaḥ kṛśaḥ (XIII. 124.33)

Simple Meaning—'As a well-wisher of others, you may also feel unhappy that you do not have the necessary wealth and qualities, to dispel the grief of your friends and the sufferings of sorrowing men. Such unhappiness makes you pale and lean.'

dharmyamarthyaṁ ca kāmyaṁ ca
kāle cābhihitaṁ vacaḥ
na pratītayanti te nūnaṁ
tenāsi hariṇaḥ kṛśaḥ (XIII. 124.34)

Simple Meaning—'As a well-wisher of others, you may also feel rejected when they do not trust you, although you speak well-timed words, consistent with dharma, to promote wealth and psychological values. Such rejection makes you pale and lean.'

16.19. *dattānakuśalairarthān*
manīṣī sañjijīviṣuḥ
prāpya vartayase nūnaṁ
tanāsi hariṇaḥ kṛśaḥ (XIII. 124.35)

Simple Meaning—The brahmin went on, 'As a believer in the law of karma, you might be afraid of evil consequences when you accept a gift from a person of evil conduct, to help you maintain yourself, particularly because you are wise enough to understand what dharma means. Such fear makes you pale and lean.'

pāpān pravardhato dṛṣṭvā
kalyāṇānāvasīdataḥ
dhruvaṁ garhayase nityaṁ
tenāsi hariṇaḥ kṛśaḥ (XIII. 124.36)

Simple Meaning—'As a believer in the law of karma, you might be confused when you see unrighteous people advancing and righteous people suffering, although you try to restore dharma by condemning the system which violates the law of karma. Such confusion makes you pale and lean.'

16.20. *parasparaviruddhānāṁ priyaṁ nūnaṁ cikīrṣasi*
suhṛdāmuparodhena tenāsi hariṇaḥ kṛśaḥ (XIII. 124.37)

Simple Meaning—The brahmin, approaching the end of his reply to the rākṣasa, devoted the last two verses to an appreciation of the reformist attitude of the rākṣasa, 'Desirous of reforming your friends, who fight among themselves, you try to bring them together, for their good, but probably you are worried about the degree of success. Such worry makes you pale and lean.'

śrotriyāṁśca vikarmasthān
prājñāṁścāpyajitendriyān
manye'nudhyāyasi janāṁs
tenāsi hariṇaḥ kṛśaḥ (XIII. 124.38)

Simple Meaning—'Desirous of reforming important persons, you try to help, for example, you try that Vedic scholars should get away from improper acts, and other learned persons should similarly get out of the slavery of their senses, but probably you are worried about the degree of success. Such worry makes you pale and lean.'

16.21. *evaṁ sampūjitaṁ rakṣo*
vipraṁ taṁ pratyapūjayat
sakhāyamakaroccainaṁ
saṁyojyārthairmumoca ha (XIII. 124.39)

Simple Meaning—In conclusion, Bhīṣma said to Yudhiṣṭhira, 'After getting such a fine and respectful reply to his question, the rākṣasa too adopted a worshipful attitude, viz. that he made the brahmin his friend, and (instead of eating him up), gave him a nice gift of money, and let him off to freedom.'

CHAPTER 17

Anuśāsana-Parva's Plea for Extending Ahiṁsā to Include Vegetarian Food

17.1. This chapter is a continuation of the preceding one in the sense that it is based on the same Parva (i.e. Anuśāsana) and the main topic of discussion is also the same i.e. ahiṁsā (non-violence). In the previous chapter, the efficacy of ahiṁsā in winning over a monster was demonstrated by Bhīṣma through a story. In the present chapter, Bhīṣma does not tell Yudhiṣṭhira any story, but expresses his opinion (supported by Ṛṣis) in favor of extending ahiṁsā to include vegetarian food.

17.2. Bhīṣma uvāca:

caturvidheyaṁ nirdiṣṭā
hyahiṁsā brahmavādibhiḥ
ekaikato'pi vibhraṣṭā
na bhavatyarisūdana (XIII. 114.4)

Simple Meaning—Bhīṣma said to Yudhiṣṭhira, 'Ṛṣis possessing knowledge of brahman (the only reality) have said that the practice of ahiṁsā (non-violence) is complete only if it is done in a comprehensive way, covering four dimensions (viz. thought, word, deed, and food). As soon as any one of these four dimensions is neglected, then the completeness of ahiṁsā is lost—and such an incomplete practice does not deserve the title 'ahiṁsā.'

yathā sarvaścatuṣpād vai
tribhiḥ pādairna tiṣṭhati

tathaiveyaṁ mahīpāla
kāraṇaiḥ procyate tribhiḥ (XIII. 114.5)

Simple Meaning—'Just as no four-footed animal can stand on three legs, similarly if the practice of ahiṁsā is done in only three dimensions, then the word 'ahiṁsā' can not be used for it.'

17.3. *yathā nāgapade'nyāni*
padāni padagāminām
sarvāṇyevāpidhīyante
padajātāni kauñjare
evaṁ lokeṣvahiṁsā tu
nirdiṣṭā dharmataḥ purā (XIII. 114.6)

Simple Meaning—'Just as the foot of the elephant, being the largest, can contain the foot of any animal, similarly the religion based on ahiṁsā is capable of containing any important element of dharma—and this was declared by the Ṛṣis long ago.'

17.4. *karmaṇā lipyate jantur*
vācā ca manasāpi ca
purvaṁ tu manasā tyaktvā
tathā vācātha karmaṇā
na bhakṣayati yo māṁsaṁ
trividhaṁ sa vimucyate (XIII. 114.7-8)

Simple Meaning—'The sins of hiṁsā (violence) can be committed in three ways viz. by sinful act, or by violent speech, or by mentally thinking of harming someone. If one abstains from eating meat, one can get rid of these three types of sins, because all three processes are involved in this single act, for example, one gives up mentally the desire to eat meat, one avoids violent speech, and one stays away from the violent act of killing the animal.'

17.5. *trikāraṇaṁ tu nirdiṣṭaṁ*
śrūyate brahmavādibhiḥ
mano vāci tathā'svāde
doṣā hyeṣu pratiṣṭhitāḥ (XIII. 114.9)

Simple Meaning—'Ṛṣis possessing knowledge of brahman have identified three main causes which lead people to the sin involved in eating meat—and these causes are mental (i.e. desire to eat meat), vocal (i.e. advice regarding meat-eating), and those related to taste (i.e. the process of developing a liking for the taste of meat).'

na bhakṣayantyato māṁsaṁ
tapoyuktā manīṣiṇaḥ
doṣāṁstu bhakṣaṇe rājan
māṁsasyeha nibodha me (XIII. 114.10)

Simple Meaning—'Therefore, (i.e. in order to stay away from the three-fold sin), wise and self-disciplined persons do not eat meat. Since this is an important subject, I want to go into some detail for clarifying to you the harm that is caused by meat-eating, and I hope you will listen to it with due attention'.

17.6. *rasaṁ ca pratijivhāyā*
jñānaṁ prajñāyate yathā
tathā śāstreṣu niyataṁ
rāgo hyāsvāditāt bhavet (XIII. 114.13)

Simple Meaning—'The first harm caused by meat-eating is that it is likely to turn into addiction. The tongue provides the sensation of taste, and that leads to attachment (i.e. the desire to eat it again and again). Harmful effects of attachment are pointed out by the scriptures.'

duṣkaraṁ ca rasajñāne
māṁsasya parivarjanaṁ (XIII. 115.17)

Simple Meaning—'Once the taste of meat is acquired, it becomes very difficult to give up meat-eating'.

17.7. *yasmād grasati caivāyur*
hiṁsakānāṁ mahādyute
tasmād vivarjayenmāṁsaṁ
ya icched bhūtimātmanaḥ (XIII. 115.31)

Simple Meaning—'The second harm caused by meat-eating is the adverse effect on health and longevity. The period of life is shortened, of persons who slaughter living creatures or cause them to be slaughtered. Therefore, any person who wishes his own good, should give up meat entirely.'

17.8. *bherīmṛdaṅgaśabdāṁśca*
tantrīśabdāṁśca puṣkalān

niṣeviṣyanti vai mandā
māṁsabhakṣāḥ kathaṁ narāḥ (XIII. 114.15)

Simple Meaning—'The third harm caused by meat-eating is the adverse effect on spiritual progress. How will those foolish men that subsist upon meat succeed in listening to the sweet music of heavenly drums, cymbals, lyres and harps?'

17.9. *ye bhakṣayanti māṁsāni*
bhūtānāṁ jīvitaiṣiṇāṁ
bhakṣyante te'pi bhūtaistair
iti me nāsti saṁśayaḥ (XIII. 116.24)

Simple Meaning—'The fourth harm caused by meat-eating can be understood by applying the law of karma. Those who eat the flesh of animals (who are themselves desirous of life), will, in turn, be eaten up by the animals they eat—and I have no doubts in this matter.'

māṁ sa bhakṣayate yasmād
bhakṣayiṣye tamapyahaṁ
etanmāṁsasya māṁsatvaṁ
anubuddhyasva bhārata (XIII. 116.25)

Simple Meaning—'If you break the word 'māṁsa' into two parts, you get the meaning 'Me ... He', as if the animal is saying 'Me he eateth, therefore I shall eat him.' Since the word 'māṁsa'means 'meat', this etymology of the word conveys very effectively the message, from the animal to the meat-eater, based on the law of karma. In other words, the 'māṁsa-hood' of 'māṁsa' lies in the warning that underlies this message.'

17.10. *māṁsasyābhakṣaṇāt rājan*
yo dharmaḥ kurunandana
tanme śṛṇu yathātattvaṁ
yathāsya vidhiruttamaḥ (XIII. 115.5)

Simple Meaning—'Next, listen to me what benefits one gets by abstaining from meat. My opinion is based on views expressed by other authorities on dharma.'

rūpamavyaṅgatāmāyur
buddhiṁ sattvaṁ balaṁ smṛtiṁ
prāptukāmairnarairhiṁsā
varjitā vai mahātmabhiḥ (XIII. 115.6)

Simple Meaning—'Those high-souled persons who desire beauty, faultlessness of limbs, long life, proper understanding, mental and physical strength, and right functioning of memory, need to stay away from all acts of violence.'

17.11. *ṛṣīṇāmatra saṁvādo*
bahuśaḥ kurunandana
babhūva tesāṁ tu mataṁ
yat tacchṛṇu yudhiṣṭhira (XIII. 115.7)

Simple Meaning—'On this topic, innumerable discussions took place amongst the Ṛṣis. Listen, O Yudhiṣṭhira, what their common opinion was.'

saptarṣayo vālakhilyās
tathaiva ca marīcipāḥ
amāṁsabhakṣaṇaṁ rājan
praśaṁsanti manīṣiṇaḥ (XIII. 115.9)

Simple Meaning—'All the Ṛṣis—including the seven celestial Ṛṣis, the Vālakhilyās, and those Ṛṣis who drink the rays of the sun—whose wisdom has guided mankind, applaud abstention from meat.'

adhṛṣyaḥ sarvabhūtānāṁ
viśvāsyaḥ sarvajantuṣu
sādhūnāṁ sammato nityaṁ
bhavenmāṁsaṁ vivarjayan (XIII. 115.10)

Simple Meaning—'All the Ṛṣis say that one who stays away from meat, enjoys the approbation and commendation of the righteous people. No living creature thinks of oppressing him. In fact, all living beings have confidence in him.'

17.12. *na bhakṣayati yo māṁsaṁ*
na ca hanyānna ghātayet
tanmitraṁ sarvabhūtānāṁ
manuḥ svāyambhuvo'bravīt (XIII. 115-11)

Simple Meaning—'After giving the general opinion of the Ṛṣis, I want to mention three individual opinions. First, the self-born Manu said that the man, who does not eat meat, or who does not slay living creatures, or who does not cause them to be slain, is a friend of all creatures.'

svamāṁsaṁ paramāṁsena
yo vardhayitumicchati
nāradaḥ prāha dharmātmā
niyataṁ so'vasīdati (XIII. 115.12)

Simple Meaning—'Second, the righteous-souled Nārada said that the man who wishes to increase his own flesh by eating the flesh of other creatures, is bound to meet with calamity.'

dadāti yajate cāpi
tapasvī ca bhavatyapi
madhumāṁsanivṛttyeti
prāha caivaṁ bṛhaspatiḥ (XIII. 115.13)

Simple Meaning—'Third, Bṛhaspati, the guru of the gods, said that the man who stays away from wine and meat, acquires the merit of gifts, sacrifices and austerities.'

17.13. *sadā yajati satreṇa*
sadā dānaṁ prayacchati
sadā tapasvī bhavati
madhumāmsavivarjanāt (XIII. 115.15)

Simple Meaning—'I have a special fascination for what Bṛhaspati said, and so I want to repeat it, viz. that the man who stays away from wine and meat, acquires as much merit as one who gives lots of gifts, who performs lots of yajña's, and who observes lots of austerities.'

sarve vedā na tat kuryuḥ
sarve yajñāśca bhārata
yo bhakṣayitvā māṁsāni
paścādapi nivartate (XIII. 115.16)

Simple Meaning—'I have a message of encouragement for those, who, being meat-eaters, want to change. Ṛṣis have declared that a man, who having eaten meat gives it up afterwards, acquires merit by such an act that is so great that a study of all the Vedas, or a performance of all the sacrifices, can not bestow its like.'

17.14. *sarvabhūteṣu yo vidvān*
dadātyabhayadakṣiṇāṁ
dātā bhavati loke sa
prāṇānāṁ nātra saṁśayaḥ (XIII. 115.18)

Simple Meaning—'Abstention from meat is one of the steps leading to the high ideal of abhaya-dāna' i.e. giving an assurance of fearlessness. That learned person who gives such an assurance to all living creaturs, comes to be regarded, without doubt, as the giver of life-breaths in this world.'

evaṁ vai paramaṁ dharmaṁ
praśaṁsanti manīṣiṇaḥ
prāṇā yathā'tmano'bhīṣṭā
bhūtānāmapi vai tathā (XIII. 115.19)

Simple Meaning—'This is the supreme dharma of ahiṁsā (non-violence) which wise people applaud. A follower of this dharma believes that life-breaths of other creatures are as dear to them as those of one's to one's own self.'

17.15. *mṛtyuto bhayamastīti*
viduṣāṁ bhūtimicchatāṁ
kiṁ punarhanyamānānāṁ
tarasā jīvitārthināṁ
arogāṇāmapāpānāṁ
pāpairmāṁsopajīvibhiḥ (XIII. 115.20-21)

Simple Meaning—'It is seen that even those men who are possessed of learning and who seek to achieve the highest good in the form of emancipation, are not free from the fear of death. No wonder that such fear has a more disturbing hold on those innocent and healthy creatures endued with love of life, who are sought to be slain by sinful wretches subsisting by slaughter.'

tasmād viddhi mahārāja
māṁsasya parivarjanaṁ
dharmasyāyatanaṁ śreṣṭhaṁ
svargasya ca sukhasya ca (XIII. 115.22)

Simple Meaning—'In view of this, O Yudhiṣṭhira, know that the discarding of meat is the highest refuge of religion, of heaven, and of happiness.'

dhanyaṁ yaśasyamāyuṣyaṁ
svargyaṁ svastyayanaṁ mahat
māṁsasyābhakṣaṇaṁ prāhur
niyatāḥ paramarṣayaḥ (XIII. 115.35)

Simple Meaning—'Great Ṛṣis devoted to the observance of vows and self-restraint have said that abstention from meat is productive of long life, fame and heaven, is worthy of every praise, and a great propitiation by itself.'

17.16. *na hi prāṇāt priyataraṁ*
loke kincana vidyate
tasmād dayāṁ naraḥ kuryād
yathā'tmani tathā pare (XIII. 116.8)

Simple Meaning—'Next, I want to draw your attention to a great virtue connected with abstention from meat. Since one's life is the dearest thing to every creature, the virtue of compassion deserves the highest place, and the same degree of compassion needs to be shown to the lives of others as one does to one's own life.'

nātmano'sti priyataraḥ
pṛthivīmanusṛtya ha
tasmāt prāṇiṣu sarveṣu
dayāvānātmavān bhavet (XIII. 116.22)

Simple Meaning—'The same message is given by wise men through a different formulation based on 'ātman' (self), rather than on 'prāṇa' (life). Since 'ātman' is the dearest essence to every creature, and since the identity of one's 'ātman' with the 'ātman' of others is the highest knowledge, the virtue of compassion deserves the highest place.'

abhayaṁ sarvabhūtebhyo
yo dadāti dayāparaḥ
abhayaṁ tasya bhūtāni
dadatītyanuśuśruma (XIII. 116.13)

Simple Meaning—'That man who is devoted to compassion, gives an assurance of fearlessness to all creatures, who in turn give similar assurance of fearlessness to that man—this we have heard from Ṛṣis.'

17.17. *ahiṁsā paramo dharmas*
tathāhiṁsā paro damaḥ
ahiṁsā paramaṁ dānaṁ
ahiṁsā paramaṁ tapaḥ (XIII. 116.28)

Simple Meaning—'The essence of what I have told you is this—ahiṁsā is the supreme religion, ahiṁsā is the supreme self-discipline, ahiṁsā is the supreme gift, and ahiṁsā is the supreme austerity.'[1]

CHAPTER 18

Anu-Gītā and Kāma-Gītā—Follow-up of Bhagavad-Gītā

18.1. Gītā-narrations of the Mahābhārata (i.e. texts known by titles that include the word 'Gītā') have been given the pride of place in this book. For example, chapter four was devoted to Vyādha-Gītā (narrated in Vana-Parva), and in chapter eleven we summarized nine Gītā's included in Śānti-Parva. All these are important Gītā's but, unlike Bhagavad-Gītā, none of them came directly from the mouth of Lord Kṛṣṇa. The main topic of the present chapter, viz. Anu-Gītā, occupies a special position from this point of view because this Gītā too, like Bhagavad-Gītā, contains words spoken by Lord Kṛṣṇa to Arjuna. The narrator in both the cases is Vaiśampāyana. However, there are two points of difference that need to be taken into consideration. The first one is the nature of the occasion when the dialogue between Lord Kṛṣṇa and Arjuna took place. More specifically, the occasion for the utterance of Bhagavad-Gītā was the time of crisis when the Mahābhārata war was about to start. Thus the narration of Bhagavad-Gītā occurs in Bhīṣma-Parva (i.e. Parva no.6). On the other hand, the occasion for the dialogue of Anu-Gītā came much later when the war was over and Bhīṣma too had departed from the world after having given all the instructions to Yudhiṣṭhira. Thus Anu-Gītā belongs to a post-war state of relaxation described in Aśvamedha-Parva (i.e. Parva no.14). The second point of difference between Bhagavad-Gītā and Anu-Gītā was pointed out by Lord Kṛṣṇa himself in the beginning of Anu-Gītā, viz. that he was, as if, completely immersed in yoga when he gave the teachings of Bhagavad-Gītā, and that it was not such a simple matter (even for him) to be in that state again. Consequently, we present Anu-Gītā in this chapter, mainly as a follow-up of Bhagavad-Gītā, which supplements and clarifies some of the points that needed to be explained further.

18.2. Before we write more about Anu-Gītā, we want to point out that a small part of Aśvamedha-Parva (occurring before Anu-Gītā) is called 'Kāma-Gītā' which was spoken by Lord Kṛṣṇa to Yudhiṣṭhira. Although there are eleven verses in Kāma-Gītā, the main message is contained in the following verse (which is a triplet) :

atra gāthāḥ kāmagītāḥ
kīrtayanti purāvidaḥ
śṛṇu saṁkīrtyamānāstā
akhilena yudhiṣṭhira
nāhaṁ śakyo'nupāyena
hantuṁ bhūtena kenacit (XIV. 13.12)

Simple Meaning—Lord Kṛṣṇa said to Yudhiṣṭhira, 'Sages versed in ancient lore recite 'gāthās' (stories) which are known as 'Kāma-Gītā'. Please listen carefully because I want to give you the essence of 'Kāma-Gītā', viz. 'Kāma (i.e. desire) says that no one can destroy me without resorting to proper methods.'

The question as to what methods are proper is answered briefly by saying that suppression of desire by resorting to violent austerities (tapas) is unlikely to succeed. Referring to the specific situation of Yudhiṣṭhira at that time, Lord Kṛṣṇa advised :

dharme kuru mahārāja (XIV. 13.19)

Simple Meaning—'O king, channelize your desire in the direction of dharma i.e. virtuous acts.'

18.3. Now we take up the task of summarizing Anu-Gītā which consists of thirty-six chapters. Arjuna took the initiative and expressed his desire to Lord Kṛṣṇa, to listen to the Gītā again, because he (i.e. Arjuna) had forgotten what he had heard earlier :

Arjuna uvāca:
viditaṁ me mahābāho
saṅgrāme samupasthite
māhātmyaṁ devakīmātas
tacca te rūpamaiśvaram (XIV. 16.5)

Simple Meaning—Arjuna said, 'O Kṛṣṇa, when the war was about to begin, your greatness became known to me—and I also saw your divine form as the Lord of the universe.

yat tad bhagavatā proktam
purā keśava sauhṛdāt
tat sarvaṁ puruṣavyāghra
naṣṭaṁ me bhraṣṭacetasaḥ (XIV. 16.6)

Simple Meaning—'O Keśava, what you as the Lord said unto me at that time, because of your affection for me, has all been forgotten by me—and for this I only blame myself, in the sense that I lost my mental concentration.'

mama kautūhalaṁ tvasti
teṣvartheṣu punaḥ punaḥ
bhavāṁstu dvārakāṁ gantā
nacirādiva mādhava (XIV. 16.7)

Simple Meaning—'O Mādhava, again and again, my desire becomes prominent, to listen to what you had told me earlier—and I am expressing that desire to you now, because you will soon be leaving for Dvārakā.'

18.4. Śrībhagavān uvāca
śrāvitastvaṁ mayā guhyaṁ
jñāpitaśca sanātanaṁ
dharmaṁ svarūpiṇaṁ pārtha
sarvalokāṁśca śāśvatān (XIV. 16.9)

Simple Meaning—Lord Kṛṣṇa said, 'O Arjuna, what you heard from me at that time was the supreme mystery, that is, knowledge based on eternal truths, and an elucidation of the broadest concept of dharma through which all the worlds obtain a vision of the Supreme.'

abuddhyā nāgrahīryastvaṁ
tanme sumahadapriyaṁ
na ca sādya punar bhūyaḥ
smṛtirme saṁbhaviṣyati (XIV. 16.10)

Simple Meaning—'You are expressing regret that you forgot all that, and I too feel unhappy that you lost your mental concentration, particularly because a complete recollection of all that I told you on that occasion will not come to me now.'

nūnamaśraddadhāno'si
durmedhā hyasi pāṇḍava
na ca śakyaṁ punarvaktuṁ
aśeṣeṇa dhanañjaya (XIV. 16.11)

Simple Meaning—'It looks as if you are destitute of faith and your understanding too is faulty. The loss that you have suffered can not be undone, because I can not repeat, in full, all that I said on that occasion.'

sa hi dharmaḥ suparyāpto
brahmaṇaḥ padavedane
na śakyaṁ tanmayā bhūyas
tathā vaktumaśeṣataḥ (XIV. 16.12)

Simple Meaning—'The religion about which I discoursed to you then is sufficient in all respects for the attainment of brahman, but I can not go over the same ground again in detail.'

paraṁ hi brahma kathitaṁ
yogayuktena tanmayā (XIV. 16.13)

Simple Meaning—'The reason why my earlier discourse to you was so special is this—I was completely immersed in yoga when I explained the path leading to spiritual perfection.'

18.5. *itihāsaṁ tu vakṣyāmi*
tasminnarthe purātanaṁ
yathā tāṁ buddhimāsthāya
gatimagryām gamiṣyasi (XIV. 16.14)

Simple Meaning—Lord Kṛṣṇa continued, 'Since the situation now is different, I shall adopt a new approach, viz. the method of referring to ancient history, i.e. by whom was the subject of spiritual perfection discussed in the past? Through my new approach too, I shall clarify how you can equip yourself with the right understanding which leads to the highest state.'

18.6. Now, about the contents, i.e. the teachings of Anu-Gītā, which Lord Kṛṣṇa conveyed to Arjuna by narrating three ancient dialogues, viz. (i) between Kāśyapa (a spiritual aspirant) and a learned brahmin, (ii) between a brahmin couple, and (iii) between a teacher and his disciple. We give below selected verses from each of these three dialogues.

18.7. We start with dialogue no. one. Although the spiritual aspirant, Kāśyapa put several questions to the learned brahmin, we pick up only one question (specified below) because of its relevance to the subject-matter of this book :

kathaṁ śubhāśubhe cāyaṁ
karmaṇī svakṛte naraḥ
upabhuṅkte .... (XIV. 17.4)

Simple Meaning—Kāśyapa asked, 'O learned brahmin, how does a human being enjoy or suffer due to the good and bad acts done by him?'

18.8. From the long reply given by the learned brahmin, we omit verses dealing with heaven and hell, and concentrate our attention on the opportunity which a man gets in this world to get out of the vicious circle of bad acts and their effects :

karmabhūmiriyaṁ bhumir
yatra tiṣṭhanti jantavaḥ
tataḥ śubhāśubhaṁ kṛtvā
labhante sarvadehinaḥ
ihaivoccāvacān bhogān
prāpnuvanti svakarmabhiḥ (XIV. 17.34-35)

Simple Meaning—The learned brahmin said, 'This world where creatures dwell is called 'karmabhūmi' i.e. the field of action. Whatever acts—good or bad—are done, all embodied creatures get the fruits thereof. Good acts lead to enjoyments and bad acts lead to sufferings.'

tatastu kṣīyate caiva
punaścānyāt pracīyate
yāvat tanmokṣayogasthaṁ
dharmaṁ naivāvabudhyate (XIV. 18.13)

Simple Meaning—'Through a mixture of such experiences (i.e. enjoyments and sufferings), previous acts get exhausted. However, new acts keep on accumulating. This cycle persists till one understands (and performs) good acts as duty, leading to salvation.'

18.9. *tatra karma pravakṣyāmi*
sukhī bhavati yena vai

āvartamāno jātīṣu
yathānyonyāsu sattama (XIV. 18.14)

Simple Meaning—The learned brahmin continued, 'I shall now tell you about those acts, by doing which one can get out of the cycle of births and rebirths, and attain real happiness.'

dānaṁ vrataṁ brahmacaryaṁ
yathoktaṁ brahmadhāraṇaṁ
damaḥ praśāntatā caiva
bhūtānāṁ cānukampanaṁ (XIV. 18.15)

Simple Meaning—'Good acts include charity, austerity, self-discipline, study of scriptures, self-restraint, tranquillity, compassion for all creatures.'

saṁyamāścānṛśaṁsyaṁ ca
parasvādānavarjanaṁ
vyalīkānāmakaraṇaṁ
bhūtānāṁ manasā bhuvi (XIV. 18.16)

Simple Meaning—'Mental discipline, absence of cruelty, absence of desire to take what belongs to others, refraining from doing even mentally any act that might be injurious to living creatures on earth.'

mātāpitrośca śuśrūṣā
devatātithīpūjanaṁ
gurupūjā ghṛṇā śaucaṁ
nityamindriyasaṁyamaḥ (XIV. 18.17)

Simple Meaning—'Reverently serving mother and father, honoring deities and guests, worshipping teachers, dislike for bad deeds, maintaining purity, careful discipline of the senses.'

pravartanaṁ śubhānāṁ ca
tat satāṁ vṛttamucyate (XIV. 18.18)

Simple Meaning—'And finally, promotion of virtues and virtuous acts. Those who perform all these good acts are called good people.'

18.10. *vartamānasya dharmeṇa*
śubhaṁ yatra yathā tathā
saṁsāratāraṇaṁ hyasya
kālena mahatā bhavet (XIV. 18.22)

Simple Meaning—The learned brahmin went on, 'One who follows dharma by performing the above-mentioned good acts, experiences good effects of his actions, under all situations. In due course of time, he goes beyond the cycle of births and deaths.'

sarvamitraḥ sarvasahaḥ
śame rakto jitendriyaḥ
vyapetabhayamanyuśca
ātmavān mucyate naraḥ (XIV. 19.2)

Simple Meaning—'One who is friend of all, who can endure all, who has disciplined his mind and senses, who is free from fear and anger, and who sees the same ātman everywhere, succeeds in emancipating oneself from the cycle of births and deaths.'

ātmavat sarvabhūteṣu
yaścarenniyataḥ śuciḥ
amānī nirabhīmānaḥ
sarvato mukta eva saḥ (XIV. 19.3)

Simple Meaning—'One who behaves towards all creatures as towards oneself, who is disciplined, pure, free from vanity, and divested of egotism, is to be regarded as emancipated from all the ills of the world.'

jīvitaṁ maraṇaṁ cobhe
sukhaduḥkhe tathaiva ca
lābhālābhe priyadveṣe
yaḥ samaḥ sa ca mucyate (XIV. 19.4)

Simple Meaning—'One who looks with an equal eye upon life and death, pleasure and pain, gain and loss, and friend and foe, is to be regarded as emancipated.'

na kasyacit spṛhayate
nāvajānāti kincana
nirdvandvo vītarāgātmā
sarvathā mukta eva saḥ (XIV. 19.5)

Simple Meaning—'One who does not covet what belongs to others, who never disregards any body, who transcends all pairs of opposites, and who is free from attachment, is in every way emancipated.'

anamitraśca nirbandhur
anapatyaśca yaḥ kvacit
tyaktadharmārthakāmaśca
nirākāṅkṣī ca mucyate (XIV. 19.6)

Simple Meaning—'One who has no enemy, who makes no distinction between kinsmen and others, nor between one's own children and others, who does not look for selfish gain through dharma, wealth or pleasure, and who is free from desire, is to be regarded as emancipated.'

naiva dharmī na cādharmī
pūrvopacitahāyakaḥ
dhātukṣayapraśāntātmā
nirdvandvaḥ sa vimucyate (XIV. 19.7)

Simple Meaning—'One who has gone beyond any ritualistic approach towards dharma and adharma, who is not shaken by actions done in the past, who has attained tranquillity by achieving victory over past impressions, and who has transcended all pairs of opposites, is to be regarded as emancipated.'

18.11. After narrating the dialogue between Kāśyapa and the learned brahmin, Lord Kṛṣṇa addressed the following verse to Arjuna—and this verse has close resemblance to verse XVIII. 72 of Bhagavad-Gītā :

kaccidetat tvayā pārtha
śrutamekāgracetasā
tadāpi hi rathasthastvaṁ
śrutavānetadeva hi (XIV. 19.55)

Simple Meaning—Lord Kṛṣṇa said to Arjuna, 'Did you listen, with full attention, to the teachings contained in the dialogue between Kāśyapa and the learned brahmin? The same teachings were imparted to you by me, just before the war, when you were on your chariot (and I was your charioteer).'

18.12. Lord Kṛṣṇa referred to similarities between Bhagavad-Gītā and the words spoken by the learned brahmin to Kāśyapa. Obviously, para 18.9 reminds one of 'daivī sampat' (divine qualities) listed in verses XVI. 1-3 of Bhagavad-Gītā. Similarly, para 18.10 reminds one of characteristics of spiritually perfect persons given several times in Bhagavad-Gītā—and one of these descriptions (given in chapter five) uses (in verse V.28) the exact words 'mukta eva saḥ' that occur in para 18.10.

18.13. Before closing his narration of dialogue no. one (i.e. the one between Kāśyapa and the learned brahmin), Lord Kṛṣṇa uttered words (reproduced below) which remind one of verses IX.32-33 of Bhagavad-Gītā :

imaṁ dharmaṁ samāsthāya
ye'pi syuḥ pāpayonayaḥ
striyo vaiśyāstathā śūdrās
te'pi yānti parāṁ gatim
kiṁ punarbrāhmaṇāḥ pārtha
kṣatriyā vā bahuśrutāḥ
svadharmaratayo nityaṁ
brahmalokaparāyaṇāḥ (XIV. 19.61-62)

Simple Meaning—Lord Kṛṣṇa said, 'The dharma (taught by the learned brahmin to Kāśyapa) can be practiced by all, for example, women, and persons belonging to vaiśya and śūdra varṇas, and even those who are supposed to be of sinful birth—all can attain to the highest goal through this dharma. What need be said, then,of persons belonging to brahmin and kṣatriya varṇas, if they are learned, and devoted to their duties, and have spiritual perfection as their goal?'

18.14. We now move on to dialogue no. two, which took place between a brahmin and his wife. Although this dialogue is spread over fifteen chapters, we want to concentrate our attention to only two of its sections because they explain in detail the ideas of two important verses of Bhagavad-Gītā. More specifically, verse III.20 of Bhagavad-Gītā mentions Janaka as an ideal karmayogin, but no explanation of this statement is included therein. One of the sections of dialogue no. two of Anu-Gītā contains twenty-five verses about Janaka which clarify as to in what sense he was an ideal karmayogin. Another verse of Bhagavad-Gītā (relating to which an explanation is available in this dialogue of Anu-Gītā) is III. 11, which is important for glorifying 'paraspara-bhāva', i.e. an attitude of mutual cooperation and help. Before presenting selected verses from these two sections of dialogue no. two, we should point out that this dialogue by itself is also known as 'Brāhmaṇa-Gītā'.

18.15. In the light of the above, we look at the section dealing with

Janaka. The narration begins with an expulsion order, issued by Janaka as a king, to a brahmin who had committed some punishable offence :

brāhmaṇaṁ janako rājā
sannaṁ kaśmiṁścidāgasi
viṣaye me na vastavyaṁ
iti śiṣṭyarthamabravīt (XIV. 32.2)

Simple Meaning—The brahmin, the narrator, said to his wife, 'Once upon a time, King Janaka, finding that a brahmin was guilty of some offence, and taking a decision about the appropriate punishment, said to him (i.e. the guilty brahmin), 'I have to ask you not to stay within the boundary of my kingdom.'

ityuktaḥ pratyuvācātha
brāhmaṇo rājasattamaṁ
ācakṣva viṣayaṁ rājan
yāvāṁstava vaśe sthitaḥ (XIV. 32.3)

Simple Meaning—Thus addressed, the (guilty) brahmin spoke respectfully to the best of the kings, 'Please tell me, O king, where is the boundary of the territories that are under your control.'

so'nyasya viṣaye rājño
vastumicchāmyahaṁ vibho
vacaste kartumicchāmi
yathāśāstraṁ mahīpate (XIV. 32.4)

Simple Meaning—'O lord, as advised by the scriptures, I wish to obey your order. So, when I know where your territories end, I shall go out and dwell within the territory of another king.'

18.16. Janaka uvāca:
pitṛpaitāmahe rājye
vaśye janapade sati
viṣayaṁ nādhigacchāmi
vicinvan pṛthivīmaham (XIV. 32.8)

Simple Meaning—Janaka said to the (guilty) brahmin, 'You have raised a valid point. Although ancestral practice specified a certain boundary to the kingdom of Mithilā, yet, from a philosophical angle, I was unable to draw a line on earth, between what I could call my territory, and what I could not call my territory.'

nādhigacchaṁ yadā pṛthvyāṁ
mithilā mārgitā mayā
nādhyagacchaṁ yadā tasyāṁ
svaprajā mārgitā mayā
nādhyagacchaṁ tadā tasyāṁ
tadā me kaśmalo'bhavat (XIV. 32.9)

Simple Meaning—'To find a dividing line between 'mine' and 'not mine', I began the search on earth, but having failed to find it there, I searched in Mithilā, but having failed again, I searched among the people of Mithilā, but when I failed there too, a cloudedness of understanding came over me.'

18.17. *tato me kaśmalasyānte*
matiḥ punarupasthitā
tadā na viṣayaṁ manye
sarvo vā viṣayo mama
ātmāpi cāyaṁ na mama
sarvā vā pṛthivī mama (XIV. 32.10-11)

Simple Meaning—Janaka continued, 'After that cloudedness of understanding passed away, clear intelligence came back to me. Then I thought that either I have no dominion or that everything is in my dominion. Even this body is not mine, or the whole earth is mine.'

yathā mama tathānyeṣāṁ
iti manye dvijottama
uṣyatāṁ yāvadutsāho
bhujyatāṁ yāvaduṣyate (XIV. 32.12)

Simple Meaning—'O learned brahmin, according to my latest thinking, the territory (of Mithilā) is as much mine as it is of others. You may, therefore, stay here as long as you like, and wherever you want to stay, please feel free to enjoy your stay.'

18.18. Brāhmaṇa uvāca:
pitṛpaitāmahe rājye
vaśye janapade sati
brūhi kāṁ matimāsthāya
mamatvaṁ varjitaṁ tvayā (XIV. 32.13)

Simple Meaning—The brahmin said, 'I am happy to hear about your latest thinking, but I want to ask a question—since ancestral practice had specified a certain boundary to the kingdom of Mithilā, what is that new understanding which helped you give up the sense of mine-ness ?'

> *kāṁ vai buddhiṁ samāśritya*
> *sarvo vai viṣayastava*
> *nāvaiṣi viṣayaṁ yena*
> *sarvo vā viṣayastava* (XIV. 32.14)

Simple Meaning—'What is that new understanding which made you think that not only Mithilā but everything else too is in your dominion? How are you able to feel that either no territory is yours or the entire earth is your territory?'

18.19. Janaka uvāca:

> *antavanta ihāvasthā*
> *viditāḥ sarvakarmasu*
> *nādhyagacchamahaṁ tasmān*
> *mamedamiti yad bhavet* (XIV. 32.15)

Simple Meaning—Janaka said, 'All the situations and experiences in this world are the result of one's own actions, and they are all temporary—this is the knowledge which gave me the understanding that there is nothing which I can call mine for ever.'

> *kasyedamiti kasya svaṁ*
> *iti vedavacastathā*
> *nādhyagacchamahaṁ buddhyā*
> *mamedamiti yad bhavet* (XIV. 32.16)

Simple Meaning—'I recall the words of Īśā-upaniṣad which declare 'Do not covet anybody's property', and when I raise questions like 'Whose thing is this, whose wealth is this', I get a clear answer that 'No one is the real owner of anything because all belongs to God'. This is the knowledge which gave me the understanding that there is nothing which I can call mine.'

> *etāṁ buddhiṁ samāśritya*
> *mamatvaṁ varjitaṁ mayā*
> *śṛṇu buddhiṁ ca yāṁ jñātvā*
> *sarvatra viṣayo mama* (XIV. 32.17)

Simple Meaning—'I have told you about the knowledge which gave me the understanding that I can not call the territory of Mithilā as mine. Next I shall tell you how I got the understanding that the entire earth is my territory.'

18.20. *nāhamātmārthamicchāmi*
gandhān ghrāṇagatānapi
tasmānme nirjitā bhūmir
vaśe tiṣṭhati nityadā (XIV. 32.18)

Simple Meaning—Janaka continued, 'The technique that I have adopted for extending my vision to the entire earth is to control my desires. For example, I do not desire for my own enjoyment those smells that are in my nose. According to Sāṃkhya philosophy, the property of smell attaches to earth. Since I have transcended my sensation of smell, I can say that the earth is subjugated by me.'

nāhamātmārthamicchāmi
rasānāsye'pi vartataḥ
āpo me nirjitāstasmād
vaśe tiṣṭhanti nityadā (XIV. 32.19)

Simple Meaning—'I do not desire for my own enjoyment those tastes that are available to my tongue. Since the property of taste attaches to water, and since I have transcended my sensation of taste, I can say that water is subjugated by me.'

nāhamātmārthamicchāmi
rūpaṁ jyotiśca cakṣuṣaḥ
tasmān me nirjitaṁ jyotir
vaśe tiṣṭhati nityadā (XIV. 32.20)

Simple Meaning—'I do not desire for my own enjoyment the sights and the light that are visible to my eyes. Since the property of vision attaches to light, and since I have transcended my sensation of vision, I can say that light is subjugated by me.

nāhamātmārthamicchāmi
sparśāṁstvaci gatāśca ye
tasmān me nirjito vāyur
vaśe tiṣṭhati nityadā (XIV. 32.21)

Simple Meaning—'I do not desire for my own enjoyment those sensations of touch that occur with my skin. Since the property of touch attaches to wind, and since I have transcended my sensation of touch, I can say that wind is subjugated by me.'

nāhamātmārthamicchāmi
śabdāñśrotragatānapi
tasmānme nirjitāḥ śabdā
vaśe tiṣṭhanti nityadā (XIV. 32.22)

Simple Meaning—'I do not desire for my own enjoyment those sensations of sound which reach my ears. Since the property of sound attaches to ether, and since I have transcended my sensation of sound, I can say that ether and all sounds are subjugated by me.'

nāhamātmārthamicchāmi
mano nityaṁ mano'ntare
mano me nirjitaṁ tasmād
vaśe tiṣṭhati nityadā (XIV. 32.23)

Simple Meaning—'I do not desire for my own enjoyment those sensations of thought which occur in my mind. Since I have transcended my sensation of thought, I can say that mind is subjugated by me.'

18.21. *devebhyaśca pitṛbhyaśca*
bhūtebhyo'tithibhiḥ saha
ityarthaṁ sarva eveti
samārambhā bhavanti vai (XIV. 32.24)

Simple Meaning—'In conclusion, Janaka summarized in one verse the reason why he was still carrying on the activities of ruling as a king, although he had no selfish interest or advantage and had become perfectly non-attached to his kingdom, 'All activities of mine are for the benefit of the gods, the ancestors, all created beings, and my guests, but not for my own self.'

18.22. *tataḥ prahasya janakaṁ*
brāhmaṇaḥ punarabravīt
tvajjijñāsārthamadyeha
viddhi māṁ dharmamāgatam (XIV.32.25)

Simple Meaning—Through this verse (which is the closing verse of the Janaka-related narration of Anu-Gītā), the importance of the statements made by Janaka is firmly established because the (guilty) brahmin disclosed his identity as Dharma in disguise. This is how the narrator puts it, 'After listening to Janaka, the brahmin smiled and said, 'O righteous king, it is the right time now for me to tell you that I am Dharma (in disguise) and I came here to test you (and that you have passed the test)".

18.23. Next, we pick up the thread from para 18.14 and move on to the second important point that forms part of dialogue no. two (which took place between a brahmin and his wife). With a view to glorifying 'paraspara-bhāva', the brahmin narrated to his wife an ancient story which can be summarized as follows. Although life-breath is essentially a unified entity, experts have identified five variations of this entity and named them as prāṇa, apāna, udāna, samāna, and vyāna. These five, in stead of realizing their essential unity, adopted a competitive attitude, each one vying for superiority, but they left the decision (regarding who is superior) on the creator (Brahmā) :

te'pṛcchanta purā santaḥ
pūrvajātaṁ pitāmahaṁ
yo naḥ śreṣṭhastamācakṣva
sa naḥ śreṣṭho bhaviṣyati (XIV. 23.6)

Simple Meaning—They (i.e. the five variations of life-breath), long long ago, requested the creator (Brahmā) to decide who is superior (among those five), adding that they will all abide by that decision.

18.24. *tatastānabravīd brahmā*
samavetān prajāpatiḥ
sarve śreṣṭhā na vā śreṣṭhāḥ
sarve cānyonyadharmiṇaḥ (XIV. 23.21)

Simple Meaning—The creator (Brahmā) advised them that the spirit of competition and rivalry was not the right approach, 'My dicision is that you are all equally great, but none of you is greater than the others. Moreover, the greatness of each of you depends upon the support received from others.'

sarve svaviṣaye śreṣṭhāḥ
sarve cānyonyadharmiṇaḥ
iti tānabravīt sarvān
samavetān prajāpatiḥ (XIV. 23.22)

Simple Meaning—'Each of you is great in its own sphere, but the greatness of each depends also upon the support received from others.' The creator (Brahmā) repeated the words about interdependence.

ekaḥ sthiraścāsthiraśca
viśeṣāt pañca vāyavaḥ
eka eva mamaivātmā
bahudhāpyupacīyate (XIV. 23.23)

Simple Meaning—The creator (Brahmā) continued, 'The life-breath is essentially one, but there are variations of this, five in all—some of them moving and some still. The concept of 'One appearing as many' is commonly understood with reference to 'ātman'.'

18.25. *parasparasya suhṛdo*
bhāvayantaḥ parasparaṁ
svasti vrajata bhadraṁ vo
dhārayadhvaṁ parasparam (XIV. 23.24)

Simple Meaning—This is the closing verse of the section dealing with 'paraspara-bhāva' (reference para 18.23). Although nominally speaking to life-breath, the creator (Brahmā) really spoke to all mankind, 'Be friends of one another and foster one another. I bless you and wish you well. You will certainly prosper if you uphold one another.'

18.26. Finally, we come to dialogue no. three which took place between a teacher and his disciple. Although this dialogue is spread over seventeen chapters, we want to concentrate our attention to only four of its sections, because of their resemblance to Bhagavad-Gītā. More specifically, the four topics picked up by us are :

(i) Viewing the world as a tree (as in chapter XV of Bhagavad-Gītā)
(ii) Importance of seeing unity in diversity (comparable to verse XVIII.20 of Bhagavad-Gītā).
(iii) Technique of self-discipline (resembling verse II.58 of Bhagavad-Gītā).
(iv) Glorification of sattva-guṇa and condemnation of rajas and tamas guṇas (as in chapter XIV of Bhagavad-Gītā).

Selected verses from dialogue no. three (of Anu-Gītā), covering these four topics are presented below.

18.27. *ājīvyaḥ sarvabhūtānāṁ*
brahmavṛkṣaḥ sanātanaḥ
enaṁ chittvā ca bhittvā ca

tattvajñānāsinā budhaḥ
hitvā saṅgamayān pāśān
mucyate nātra saṁśayaḥ (XIV. 47.14-15)

Simple Meaning—The eternal tree of brahman forms the support of all creatures. Cutting and piercing that tree, using knowledge of truth as sword, the man of wisdom, abandoning bonds made of attachment, can become emancipated—and there is no doubt in this matter.

There are obvious similarities between these verses, and verses XV.1-3 of Bhagavad-Gītā, for example, the words 'chittvā' and 'saṅga' are common to both (apart from the overall similarity of the concept of the world-tree).

18.28. *sarvabhūtasthamātmānaṁ*
yaḥ paśyati na sa mṛtaḥ ...
paśyanekatvaṁ nānātve
sa duḥkhāt pratimucyate (XIV. 46.49, 47.7)

Simple Meaning—One who sees the same ātman in all beings, becomes immortal .... By seeing unity in (apparent) diversity, he finds a sure way out of all sorrow.

We want to draw attention to comparable verses of Bhagavad-Gītā, for example, verses XIII. 30 and XVIII.20.

18.29. *vidvān kūrma ivāṅgāni*
kāmān saṁhṛtya sarvaśaḥ
virajāḥ sarvato mukto
yo naraḥ sa sukhī sadā (XIV. 42.46)

Simple Meaning—The learned man who absorbs all desires into himself from all sides like the tortoise withdrawing all its limbs, succeeds in self-discipline. Devoid of passion and released from all bonds, he is always happy.

The expression 'tortoise withdrawing all its limbs' occurs in verse II.58 of Bhagavad-Gītā.

18.30. *ūrdhvaṁ gacchanti sattvasthā*
madhye tiṣṭhanti rājasāḥ
jaghanyaguṇasaṁyuktā
yāntyadhastāmasā janāḥ (XIV. 39.10)

Simple Meaning—Those who are established in sattva guṇa rise upwards; those who act according to rajas-guṇa remain in the middle; but those who are victims of tamas-guṇa (which leads them to deplorable acts) sink low.

This verse is practically the same as verse XIV. 18 of Bhagavad-Gītā.

18.31. Before closing this chapter, we want to present two of the concluding verses of Anu-Gītā, one of which shows similarity with verse XVIII. 66 of Bhagavad-Gītā, and the other makes a general reference to overall similarity with Bhagavad-Gītā :

tatastvaṁ samyagācīrṇe
dharme'sminnarikarṣaṇa
sarvapāpavinirmukto
mokṣaṁ prāpsyasi kevalam (XIV. 51.48)

Simple Meaning—Lord Kṛṣṇa said to Arjuna, 'If you put into practice this dharma (taught to you in Anu-Gītā), you will become free from all sins and attain to absolute emancipation.'

pūrvamapyetadevoktaṁ
yuddhakāla upasthite
mayā tava mahābāho
tasmādatra manaḥ kuru (XIV. 51.49)

Simple Meaning—Lord Kṛṣṇa concluded the teaching contained in Anu-Gītā, by these words, 'O Arjuna, I taught the same dharma to you earlier, when the battle was about to start. Now that you have heard it twice from me, I advise that you commit yourself to it whole-heartedly'.[1]

CHAPTER 19

Yudhiṣṭhira's Refusal to Enter Heaven Without the Dog who had Walked behind Him

19.1. The Mahābhārata contains several stories in which Dharmarāja (the Lord of Dharma) declares a person great after testing him—and for conducting such a test, Dharmarāja disguises himself in different forms. Yudhiṣṭhira is the person who faced such tests more than anyone else. We described in chapter six how Dharmarāja tested him by assuming the form of Yakṣa. That narration formed part of Vana-Parva (i.e. Parva no. 3). The topic of the present chapter is the second test of Yudhiṣṭhira by Dharmarāja, which occurred in Mahāprasthānika Parva (i.e. Parva no. 17). The occasion (for this test) was 'The great departure', i.e. the final journey on foot, to high mountains and heaven, by the five Pāṇḍava brothers and Draupadī (i.e. six in all). This time, Dharmarāja assumed the form of a dog who became the seventh member of the walking team. We follow Vaiśampāyana's narration, starting from his depiction of the order in which they walked, the final destination being heaven.

19.2. *yudhiṣṭhiro yayāvagre*
bhīmastu tadanantaraṁ
arjunastasya cānveva
yamau cāpi yathākramam (XVII. 1.31)

Simple Meaning—Yudhiṣṭhira proceeded first. Behind him was Bhīma; next walked Arjuna; after him were the twins (Nakula and Sahadeva).

pṛṣṭhatastu varārohā
śyāmā padmadalekṣaṇā
draupadī yoṣitāṁ śreṣṭhā
yayau bharatasattama (XVII. 1.32)

Simple Meaning—Behind these five, proceeded Draupadī, a great woman, possessed of genuine beauty, of dark complexion, and endued with eyes resembling lotus petals.

śvā caivānuyayāvekaḥ
prasthitān pāṇḍavān vanaṁ
krameṇa te yayurvīrā
lauhityaṁ salilārṇavam (XVII. 1.33)

Simple Meaning—While the Pāṇḍavas set out for the forest (en route to heaven), a dog followed them. Proceeding on, these heroes reached the sea of red waters.

tataste tūttareṇaiva
tīreṇa lavaṇāmbhasaḥ
jagmurbharataśārdūla
diśaṁ dakṣiṇapaścimām (XVII. 1.44)

Simple Meaning—Walking on and on, they passed by the northern coast of the salt sea, and then proceeded to the south-west.

tataḥ punaḥ samāvṛttāḥ
paścimāṁ diśameva te
dadṛśurdvārakāṁ cāpi
sāgareṇa pariplutām (XVII. 1.45)

Simple Meaning—Thereafter they turned towards the west. They beheld (from a distance) the city of Dvārakā which was at that time covered by the ocean.

udīcīṁ punarāvṛtya
yayur bharatasattamāḥ
prādakṣiṇyaṁ cikīrṣantaḥ
pṛthivyā yogadharmiṇaḥ (XVII. 1.46)

Simple Meaning—Next, they turned to the north and walked on. All the time, they practiced yoga, and they thought of making a round of the whole earth (before proceeding to the final destination, i.e. heaven).

19.3. *tataste niyatātmāna*
udīcīṁ diśamāsthitāḥ
dadṛśuryogayuktāśca
himavantaṁ mahāgirim (XVII. 2.1)

Simple Meaning—Observing self-discipline and practicing yoga, the Pāṇḍavas walked north-ward till they saw the Himalaya mountains.

taṁ cāpyatikramantaste
dadṛśurvālukārṇavaṁ
avaikṣanta mahāśailaṁ
meruṁ śikhariṇāṁ varam (XVII. 2.2)

Simple Meaning—After crossing the Himalaya mountains, they beheld a vast desert of sand. Then they saw the mighty mountain Meru.

19.4. *teṣāṁ tu gacchatāṁ śīghraṁ*
sarveṣāṁ yogadharmiṇāṁ
yājñasenī bhraṣṭayogā
nipapāta mahītale (XVII. 2.3)

Simple Meaning—Because of concentration in yoga, all of them were proceeding quickly. However, suddenly Draupadī lost her concentration and dropped down on earth.

tāṁ tu prapatitāṁ dṛṣṭvā
bhīmaseno mahābalaḥ
uvāca dharmarājānaṁ
yājñasenīmavekṣya ha (XVII. 2.4)

Simple Meaning—Beholding Draupadī fallen down, Bhīma of great strength put a question to Yudhiṣṭhira (in whose practice of dharma Bhīma had great faith).

nādharmaścaritaḥ kaścid
rājaputryā parantapa
kāraṇaṁ kiṁ nu tad brūhi
yat kṛṣṇā patitā bhuvi (XVII. 2.5)

Simple Meaning—Bhīma asked Yudhiṣṭhira, 'O learned brother, as far as I know, this princess (Draupadī) never did any sinful act. Can you please tell me the reason why such a pious soul has fallen down on earth'.

Yudhiṣṭhira uvāca:
pakṣapāto mahānasyā
viśeṣeṇa dhananjaye
tasyaitat phalamadyaiṣā
bhuṅkte puruṣasattama (XVII. 2.6)

Simple Meaning—Yudhiṣṭhira replied, 'My dear brother, a delicate psychological point is involved here. You know that we five brothers were Draupadī's husbands. Although she loved each one of us, yet she had a lot of partiality for Arjuna. She has fallen today because of that fault of hers'.

19.5. Vaiśampāyana uvāca:
evamuktvānavekṣyaināṁ
yayau bharatasattamaḥ
samādhāya mano dhīmān
dharmātmā puruṣarṣabhaḥ (XVII. 2.7)

Simple Meaning—Vaiśampāyana (the narrator) said, 'Having answered Bhīma's question, and having reconciled himself to Draupadī's fall, the righteous-souled Yudhiṣṭhira walked on. He maintained his concentration in yoga, and (as a sign of non-attachment), he did not look back towards Draupadī'.

19.6. *sahadevastato vidvān*
nipapāta mahītale
taṁ cāpi patitaṁ dṛṣṭvā
bhīmo rājānamabravīt (XVII. 2.8)

Simple Meaning—After some time, Sahadeva, the youngest brother who was very learned, fell down on earth. Beholding him fallen down, Bhīma put a question to Yudhiṣṭhira (as he had done after Draupadī's fall).

yo'yamasmāsu sarveṣu
śuśrūṣuranahaṁkṛtaḥ
so'yaṁ mādravatīputraḥ
kasmān nipatito bhuvi (XVII. 2.9)

Simple Meaning—Bhīma asked Yudhiṣṭhira, 'O learned brother, as far as I know, this youngest brother of ours (i.e. Sahadeva, son of Mādrī who was the second wife of Pāṇḍu) served all of us with great humility. Can you please tell me the reason why such a fine soul has fallen down on earth!'

Yudhiṣṭhira uvāca:

ātmanaḥ sadṛśaṁ prājñaṁ
naiṣo'manyata kancana
tena doṣeṇa patitas
tasmādeṣa nṛpātmajaḥ (XVII. 2.10)

Simple Meaning—Yudhiṣṭhira replied, 'My dear brother, I agree that our youngest brother Sahadeva served us well but he never thought of anybody as his equal in wisdom. It is because of that fault of his that today he has fallen down.'

19.7. Vaiśampāyana uvāca:

ityuktvā taṁ samutsṛjya
sahadevaṁ yayau tadā
bhrātṛbhiḥ saha kaunteyaḥ
śunā caiva yudhiṣṭhiraḥ (XVII. 2.11)

Simple Meaning—Vaiśampāyana said, 'Having answered Bhīma's question, and having reconciled himself to Sahadeva's fall, the righteous-souled Yudhiṣṭhira walked on, followed by three (surviving) brothers and the dog.'

19.8. *kṛṣṇāṁ nipatītāṁ dṛṣṭvā*
sahadevaṁ ca pāṇḍavaṁ
ārto bandhupriyaḥ śūro
nakulo nipapāta ha (XVII. 2.12)

Simple Meaning—Nakula, the youngest of the three surviving brothers, suddenly lost his concentration and fell down, because (although he was very brave) he was struck with grief at the loss of Draupadī and Sahadeva whom he loved dearly.

tasmin nipatite vīre
nakule cārudarśane
punareva tadā bhīmo
rājānamidamabravīt (XVII. 2.13)

Simple Meaning—Upon the falling down of the heroic Nakula of great personal beauty, Bhīma once more put a question to Yudhiṣṭhira (as he had done after the fall of Draupadī and Sahadeva).

yo'yamakṣatadharmātmā
bhrātā vacanakārakaḥ

rūpeṇāpratimo loke
nakulaḥ patito bhuvi (XVII. 2.14)

Simple Meaning—Bhīma asked Yudhiṣṭhira, 'O learned brother, as far as I know, this brother of ours (i.e. Nakula), in spite of having unrivalled beauty, practiced dharma faultlessly and always carried out our wishes. Can you please tell me the reason why such a fine soul has fallen down on earth!'

ityukto bhīmasenena
pratyuvāca yudhiṣṭhiraḥ
nakulaṁ prati dharmātmā
sarvabuddhimatāṁ varaḥ (XVII. 2.15)

Simple Meaning—After listening to Bhīma's question, the righteous-souled Yudhiṣṭhira, endowed with the highest wisdom, pondered over the cause of Nakula's fall and conveyed it to Bhīma in the following words.

rūpeṇa mạtsamo nāsti
kaścidityasya darśanaṁ
adhikaścāhamevaika
ityasya manasi sthitam (XVII. 2.16)

Simple Meaning—Yudhiṣṭhira replied to Bhīma, 'My dear brother, I agree with what you said about Nakula, but I have to point out one fault of his, viz. that he thought there was no one that equalled him in beauty, so much so that he regarded himself as far superior to all in that respect.'

nakulaḥ patitastasmād
āgaccha tvaṁ vṛkodara
yasya yad vihitaṁ vīra
so'vaśyaṁ tadupāśnute (XVII. 2.17)

Simple Meaning—Yudhiṣṭhira concluded by adding, 'It is because of this fault of his that today Nakula has fallen down. My advice to you, my dear brother, is that we must reconcile with these losses and walk on, because everyone has to endure the consequences of faults committed in the past'.

19.9. *tāṁstu prapatitān dṛṣṭvā*
pāṇḍavaḥ śvetavāhanaḥ
papāta śokasantaptas
tato nu paravīrahā (XVII. 2.18)

Simple Meaning—After some time, Arjuna, who had earned so much fame as a warrior (and whose chariot used to be pulled by white steeds), suddenly lost his concentration and fell down, because he was struck with grief at the loss of Draupadī, Sahadeva and Nakula.

tasmiṁstu puruṣavyāghre
patite śakratejasi
mriyamāṇe durādharṣe
bhīmo rājānamabravīt (XVII. 2.19)

Simple Meaning—Seeing that Arjuna, who was like a lion among men and who had the energy of Indra, has fallen down and was on the point of death, Bhīma once more put a question to Yudhiṣṭhira (as he had done after the fall of Draupadī, Sahadeva and Nakula).

anṛtaṁ na smarāmyasya
svaireṣvapi mahātmanaḥ
atha kasya vikāro'yaṁ
yenāyaṁ patito bhuvi (XVII. 2.20)

Simple Meaning—Bhīma asked Yudhiṣṭhira, 'O learned brother, as far as I know, this brother of ours (i.e. Arjuna) was a high-souled man; in fact, I do not recollect any untruth uttered by him, even in jest. Can you please tell me what wrong he could have committed, because of which he has fallen down on earth!'

19.10. Yudhiṣṭhira uvāca:

ekānhā nirdaheyaṁ vai
śatrūnityarjuno'bravīt
na ca tat kṛtavāneṣa
śūramānī tato'patat (XVII. 2.21)

Simple Meaning—Yudhiṣṭhira replied, 'My dear brother, I agree with what you said about Arjuna, but I have to point out one fault of his, viz. that he overestimated his capacity; he declared that he would destroy all our enemies in a single day, but he was not able to do that. Hence he has fallen down.'

avamene dhanurgrāhān
eṣa sarvāṁśca phālgunaḥ
tathā caitanna tu tathā
kartavyaṁ bhūtimicchatā (XVII. 2.22)

Simple Meaning—Yudhiṣṭhira concluded by adding, 'But we can learn a lesson from Arjuna's experience. He did not show proper regard to other wielders of bows. The lesson to be learnt is that no one seeking one's own welfare should disregard others.'

19.11. Vaiśampāyana uvāca:

ityuktvā prasthito rājā
bhīmo'tha nipapāta ha
patitaścābravīd bhīmo
dharmarājaṁ yudhiṣṭhiram (XVII. 2.23)

Simple Meaning—Vaiśampāyana said, 'Having said so, Yudhiṣṭhira walked on. Then suddenly Bhīma fell down. Realizing that he too has fallen like others, Bhīma put his final question to Yudhiṣṭhira (as he had done after the fall of Draupadī, Sahadeva, Nakula, and Arjuna).'

bho bho rājannavekṣasva
patito'haṁ priyastava
kiṁ nimittaṁ ca patanaṁ
brūhi me yadi vettha ha (XVII. 2.24)

Simple Meaning—Bhīma asked Yudhiṣṭhira, 'O learned brother, please look towards me. Although I am so dear to you, I too have fallen down. If you know the reason for my fall, please let me know.'

19.12. Yudhiṣṭhira uvāca:

atibhuktaṁ ca bhavatā
prāṇena ca vikatthase
anavekṣya paraṁ pārtha
tenāsi patitaḥ kṣitau (XVII. 2.25)

Simple Meaning—Yudhiṣṭhira replied, 'My dear brother, you are so dear to me, but I have to point out the reason for your fall. You were a great eater so much so that you did not leave enough for others. Also you used to boast of your strength.'

19.13. Vaiśampāyana uvāca:

ityuktvā taṁ mahābāhur
jagāmānavalokayan
śvāpyeko'nuyayau yaste
bahuśaḥ kīrtito mayā (XVII. 2.26)

Simple Meaning—Vaiśampāyana said, 'Having replied to Bhīma's last question, Yudhiṣṭhira walked on, without looking back. At this point he had only one companion, viz. the dog that walked behind him. Because of the special role of this dog, I have drawn attention to him several times.'

tataḥ sannādayañśakro
divaṁ bhūmiṁ ca sarvaśaḥ
rathenopayayau pārthaṁ
ārohetyabravīcca tam (XVII. 3.1)

Simple Meaning—'Suddenly Indra's chariot arrived there, the sound of which filled the skies and the worlds. Indra greeted Yudhiṣṭhira and said, "Welcome, O Pārtha, please ascend this chariot so that I can take you to heaven." '

svabhrātṛn patitān dṛṣṭvā
dharmarājo yudhiṣṭhiraḥ
abravīcchokasantaptaḥ
sahasrākṣamidaṁ vacaḥ (XVII. 3.2)

Simple Meaning—'The righteous-souled Yudhiṣṭhira was, at that time, filled with grief because his wife and brothers were no longer with him since they had fallen on the way. With a heavy heart, Yudhiṣṭhira spoke to Indra.'

19.14. Yudhiṣṭhira uvāca:

bhrātaraḥ patitā me'tra
gaccheyuste mayā saha
na vinā bhrātṛbhiḥ svargaṁ
icche gantuṁ sureśvara (XVII. 3.3)

Simple Meaning—Yudhiṣṭhira said, 'O chief of heaven, I do not want to go to heaven alone. So, if you want to take me to heaven, please arrange that my brothers and wife, who have fallen on the way, may accompany me.'

sukumarī sukhārhā ca
rājaputrī purandara
sāsmābhiḥ saha gaccheta
tad bhavānanumanyatām (XVII. 3.4)

Simple Meaning—Yudhiṣṭhira concluded, 'Among those who fell on the way, Draupadī was the first one. Having been an excellent princess, she deserves heavenly comforts. Please allow that she may accompany me and my brothers to heaven.'

19.15. Śakra uvāca:

bhrātan drakṣyasi svarge tvaṁ
agratastridivaṁ gatān
kṛṣṇayā sahitān sarvān
mā śuco bharatarṣabha (XVII. 3.5)

Simple Meaning—Indra said, 'O chief of the Bharatas, your brothers and Draupadī have already arrived in heaven, and you will see them there. You need not grieve on their account.'

19.16. Yudhiṣṭhira uvāca:

ayaṁ śvā bhūtabhavyeśa
bhakto māṁ nityameva ha
sa gaccheta mayā sārdhaṁ
ānṛśaṁsyā hi me matiḥ (XVII. 3.7)

Simple Meaning—Yudhiṣṭhira said, 'O Lord of the past and the present, this dog is a great devotee of mine. He has been walking with me, so please allow that he may accompany me to heaven. In my opinion, absence of cruelty is most important.'

19.17. Śakra uvāca:

amartyatvaṁ matsamatvaṁ ca rājan
śriyaṁ kṛtsnāṁ mahatīṁ caiva siddhiṁ
samprāpto'dya svargasukhāni ca tvaṁ
tyaj śvānaṁ nātra nṛśaṁsamasti (XVII. 3.8)

Simple Meaning—Indra said, 'O king, today you have achieved so many great things, viz. immortality, a condition equal to mine, vast prosperity, high success, and all the joys of heaven. So leave this dog. There is no cruelty in that.'

19.18. Yudhiṣṭhira uvāca:

anāryamāryeṇa sahasranetra
śakyaṁ kartuṁ duṣkarametadārya
mā me śriyā sangamanaṁ tayāstu
yasyāḥ kṛte bhaktajanaṁ tyajeyam (XVII. 3.9)

Simple Meaning—Yudhiṣṭhira said, 'O righteous-souled chief having a vision of thousand eyes, you know how difficult it is for a person of righteous behavior to do something which is unrighteous. On my part, I would never wish to have that prosperity for which I shall have to cast off one that is devoted to me.'

19.19. Indra uvāca:

svarge loke śvavatāṁ nāsti dhiṣṇyaṁ ...
tato vicārya kriyatāṁ dharmarāja
tyaja śvānaṁ nātra nṛśaṁsamasti (XVII. 3.10)

Simple Meaning—Indra said, 'O righteous-souled king, I appreciate your wish to avoid cruelty, but I also have to observe a rule that persons with dogs are not allowed entry into heaven. Therefore, please take a decision after careful consideration. My advice to you again is to leave this dog, because there is no cruelty in that'.

19.20. Yudhiṣṭhira uvāca:

bhaktatyāgaṁ prāhuratyantapāpaṁ ...
tasmānnāhaṁ jātu kathancanādya
tyakṣyāmyenaṁ svasukhārthī mahendra (XVII. 3.11)

Simple Meaning—Yudhiṣṭhira said, 'O great Indra, it has been said that the sin caused by abandonment of a devotee will haunt one for ever. Hence, my decision is that, for the sake of my happiness, I shall not abandon this dog today, under any circumstances.'

bhītaṁ bhaktaṁ nānyadastīti cārtaṁ ...
prāṇatyāgādapyahaṁ naiva moktuṁ
yateyaṁ vai nityametad vrataṁ me (XVII. 3.12)

Simple Meaning—Yudhiṣṭhira concluded , 'Not only today, for I have always firmly stood by this principle, viz. that, even at the cost of my own life, I shall not abandon one who is terrified, or one who is devoted to me, or one who is in distress, or one who seeks my protection, saying that I have no other person to help me.'

19.21. Indra uvāca:

tyaktvā bhrātṛn dayitāṁ cāpi kṛṣṇāṁ
prāpto lokaḥ karmaṇā svena vira
śvānaṁ cainaṁ na tyajase kathaṁ nu
tyāgaṁ kṛtsnaṁ cāsthito muhyase'dya (XVII. 3.14)

Simple Meaning—Indra said, 'O brave and kind soul, please look at the situation dispassionately. You abandoned your brothers and Draupadī, but that did not keep you away from heaven which you earned by your own good deeds. So why can't you abandon this dog? In fact, it seems as if you gave up everything and now got stuck with this dog in attachment caused due to ignorance.'

19.22. Yudhiṣṭhira uvāca:

na vidyate sandhirathāpi vigraho
mṛtairmartyairiti lokeṣu niṣṭhā
na te mayā jīvayituṁ hi śakyās
tatastyāgasteṣu kṛto na jīvātām (XVII. 3.15)

Simple Meaning—Yudhiṣṭhira said, 'O kind soul, please look at my situation sympathetically. It is well-known in all the worlds that there is neither friendship nor enmity with those that are dead. When my brothers and Draupadī died, I was unable to revive them. Hence it was at that point that I abandoned them. I did not, however, abandon them as long as they were alive.'

bhītipradānaṁ śaraṇāgatasya
striyā vadho brāhmaṇasvāpahāraḥ
mitradrohastāni catvāri śakra
bhaktatyāgaścaiva samo mato me (XVII. 3.16)

Simple Meaning—Yudhiṣṭhira concluded, 'O Indra, in my opinion, the abandonment of a devotee (who is still alive) is the worst sin, because this by itself is as bad as the following four sinful acts put together—to frighten one who has sought protection, to slay a woman, to steal what belongs to a brahmin, and to do harm to a friend.'

19.23. Vaiśampāyana uvāca:

tad dharmarājasya vaco niśamya
dharmasvarūpī bhagavānuvāca
yudhiṣṭhiraṁ prītiyukto narendraṁ
ślakṣṇairvākyaiḥ saṁstavasamprayuktaiḥ
(XVII. 3.17)

Simple Meaning—Vaiśampāyana said, 'Upon hearing these words of King Yudhiṣṭhira (who was himself the son of Dharmarāja), the dog became transformed into his real form (i.e. Dharmarāja). The Lord of Dharma felt great joy at Yudhiṣṭhira's success in the test (which was conducted jointly by Indra and Dharmarāja). With a view to clarifying the whole thing, Dharmarāja spoke to (his son) Yudhiṣṭhira, in sweet words (which were full of praise for the latter).'

19.24. Dharmarāja uvāca:

abhijāto'si rājendra
piturvṛttena medhayā

anukrośena cānena
sarvabhūteṣu bhārata (XVII. 3.18)

Simple Meaning—The Lord of Dharma said to Yudhiṣṭhira, 'O descendent of Bharata, I am very happy to see that, through your good conduct, intelligence, and compassion towards all beings, you have proved to be a worthy son of a worthy father.'

purā dvaitavane cāsi
mayā putra parīkṣitaḥ ....
ayaṁ śvā bhakta ityevaṁ
tyakto devarathastvayā
tasmāt svarge na te tulyaḥ
kaścidasti narādhipaḥ (XVII. 3.19,22)

Simple Meaning—The Lord of Dharma concluded, 'My son, I tested you on an earlier occasion also when you were in the woods (and I was pleased when you passed that test)... On the present occasion, thinking that the dog was a devotee of yours, you renounced Indra's chariot, but not the dog. Hence there is no one in heaven that is equal to thee.'[1]

Part Three

GĪTĀ'S CALL FOR THE GOOD OF ALL AND MAHĀBHĀRATA'S SUPPORT TO IT

CHAPTER 20

Ten Points of Gītā's Call for the Good of All

20.1. The purpose of this chapter is to provide a framework which helps summarize the socio-spiritual message of Bhagavad-Gītā (or Gītā for short) in such a way as to facilitate the linkage between the Gītā and the rest of the Mahābhārata. We have developed such a framework in the earlier studies on the Gītā that we have made[1], so here we shall present the main conclusions of those studies (and omit many of the explanatory details). The foundation of the framework is the commonly accepted statement that "the good of all" is the single most important criterion of excellence of any socio-spiritual approach to life's problems, particularly in the context of the conflict-ridden society of today. We take the view that, to draw such a message from the Gītā, and to consider it as the main message of this scripture for modern times, is in the best interest of mankind. Another way of expressing this idea is to say that the message of the Gītā is universal and that Arjuna is only an instrument through whom the message has been delivered.

20.2. The underlying basis of the Gītā's call for the good of all is the faith that, in reality, God is looking after the whole universe, and therefore, human beings too can best worship God by putting in their best in the work that God does. Unity of mankind is the essence of dharma, because the Gītā calls God as 'śāsvatadharmagoptā' (XI. 18), i.e. the protector of dharma that is free from man-made narrowmindedness. A follower of such broad-based dharma views the whole world as one family—this being a translation of the ancient

Indian ideal 'vasudhaiva kuṭumbakam'. To see unity in the midst of diversity is referred to in the Gītā as 'avibhaktaṁ vibhakteṣu' (XVIII. 20). We identify this as the first of the ten key points that together constitute the framework, to provide which was indicated to be the purpose of this chapter in the preceding paragraph.

20.3. In the process of identifying the concept of unifying dharma, our attention was drawn to the basis thereof viz. God's work as the sustainer of the world. Another expression for God's work in the Gītā is 'suhṛdaṁ sarvabhūtānām' (V. 29) i.e. the friend who does good to all without expecting any return. And connected therewith is the call of Lord Kṛṣṇa to participate in God's work, i.e. 'mat-karma' (XI. 55). We identify this as the second point, or key expression that conveys the message of the good of all.

20.4. In broad-based dharma, although the primary example-setter is God, the Gītā has listed several others also whose conduct can inspire mankind to work for the good of all. Such a list includes the sun, Manu, Ikṣvāku and Janaka—but these should be viewed only as illustrative because the Gītā has used the expression 'Janaka and others' (IV. 1 and III. 20). In another context (IV. 15), the Gītā has stated that all those who have worked hard for the welfare of mankind have shown the way for others to follow. An appropriate expression for such commendable conduct is 'yogārūḍha-vṛtti', i.e. the spontaneous social work of those who have achieved spiritual perfection through any of the yogas like karma, bhakti or jñāna (i.e. action, devotion or knowledge). The word 'yogārūḍha' occurs twice in the Gītā (VI. 3,4). We identify this as the third of the ten points of the framework. To complete the description of such persons, the Gītā talks about them under six different categories in chapters II, V, VI, XII, XIV and XVIII. The expression 'santa' (meaning saint) also occurs once in the Gītā (III. 13). All these references tell us about yogārūḍha-vṛtti.

20.5. Although the way shown by God or perfect persons is mentioned as example-setting, the Gītā has clarified that it is neither necessary nor advisable to stick to their path blindly, i.e. without changes or adjustments. The favourite expression of the Gītā to convey this message is 'deśe kāle ca pātre ca' (XVII. 20) which means that dharma has to be relevant to the particular place, time and social needs. We identify this as the fourth point.

20.6. Since example-setting persons are usually of a high status, a doubt could arise in the minds of ordinary people whether acts of social service are supposed to be undertaken only by a selected few. The Gītā removes this doubt in two ways. First, it says that whatever a person does, it should be in accordance with one's 'pauruṣam' or capacity because otherwise the act becomes tāmasika or harmful (XVIII.25). Secondly, the Gītā says that acts of social service do not become great by virtue of quantitative measures, because what counts is the motivation or genuine desire to help—in fact, even a small amount of work done in accordance with dharma achieves a lot (II. 40)

20.7. A consideration of pauruṣam or capacity provides an indication of a limited role that an individual can play. A similar indication is given by using the prefix 'sva'—meaning one's own—to karma or dharma. In other words, Gītā-expressions like svakarma or svadharma indirectly convey the idea that individuals have limited capacities. In spite of such limitation, the Gītā speaks of the ideal of śarvabhūtahitam', i.e. the good of all beings. We identify this word (which occurs twice in the Gītā, V. 25 and XII. 4) as the fifth key expression (or point of the framework). Only by understanding the process of harmonization between 'sva' and 'sarva', can we hope to grasp the Gītā's message of trying one's best to achieve the good of all.

20.8. Although śarvabhūtahitam' is the most explicit word for the good of all beings, the Gītā also uses one more expression, viz. 'lokasaṁgraha' to convey the message of the good of the world. In this context, the Gītā classifies human desires into two categories, viz. desires for selfish gains and desires for the good of the world. Those who entertain desires only for selfish gains are condemned by the Gītā as 'kāmakāmī'. On the other hand, the expression 'niṣkāma karmayogins' is used to glorify those who perform their duties (including social service) without entertaining the desire for selfish gains, i.e. their desires are for the good of the world. Verse III. 25 establishes a strong link between 'niṣkāma karma' and 'lokasaṁgraha'—the former representing the technique of work, and the latter representing its purpose. Because of the conceptual importance of this link—and also for other reasons—the word 'lokasaṁgraha' has occupied a prominent place, among all the expressions that are used in the Gītā for the message of the good of all. We identify this as the sixth key expression (or point of the framework).

20.9. The Gītā says that svadharma, aimed at sarvabhūtahitam (i.e. the good of all), will bring about svahitam (one's own good) also, because all members of the society are inter-related. This follows from verse III. 11(which will be presented in para 20.17), and which summarizes the social philosophy of the Gītā. In terms of practical behaviour, this philosophy calls for a big change in ordinary people's priorities as well as attitudes. This can be stated in two steps. First, considering 'me' as the doer, a higher priority needs to be given to the social good rather than to 'my' good—and this is what the Gītā calls 'nirmama' or giving up the sense of mine. Secondly, priority needs to be shifted from a self-centered approach to a non-egotistic approach—and this is what the Gītā calls 'nirahaṁkāra' or giving up egotism. Putting both of these ideas together, we get the expression 'nirmamo nirahaṁkāraḥ' which occurs twice in the Gītā (II. 71 and XII. 13). We identify this as the seventh key expression (or point of the framework).

20.10. The Gītā has raised the question, 'Why should we have the desire to do good to all?', and reminded us that the most effective answer to this is provided by the Vedāntic philosophy according to which the same 'ātman' is in all of the beings. However, since merely academic knowledge of the philosophy is not enough by itself, the Gītā wants that it should be put into practice too. A follower of such an approach can be characterized as practising even-minded social behaviour or equal vision or 'samadṛṣṭi' in the language of the Gītā. We identify this as the eighth key expression (or point of the framework).

20.11. Although the Gītā wants that its message of the good of all should spread far and wide, it warns us against harbouring an unrealistic hope that anti-social elements will disappear from the face of the earth. In the terminology of the Gītā, the society will remain a mixture of sattva-rajas-tamas, i.e. good, average, and bad components. Among tāmasika or bad components, the most harmful from the viewpoint of universal welfare are—violence, hatred, injustice, etc. Of the various expressions that the Gītā uses for anti-social elements, 'āsurī sampat' can be considered special because it suggests that forces of evil try to entrap people by their dangerous practice of forming a chain. We identify this as the ninth key expression (or point of the framework). By warning us of the damage that such forces can cause, the Gītā has indirectly strengthened its call for the good of all.

20.12. We now come to the last of the key words or phrases, viz. 'daivī sampat' which is the opposite of what we described in the preceding paragraph. We identify this as the tenth key expression (or point of the framework). Glorification of virtues is a favourite topic of the Gītā. In fact, repeated descriptions of 'yogārūḍha-vṛtti', already referred to in para 20.4, can also be included in this topic. The inclusion of 'daivī sampat' in the selected list of ten is considered necessary for purposes of indicating the way of overpowering 'āsurī sampat'. The most important virtues are obviously those that can remedy the ills listed in the preceding paragraph. The promotion of virtues like non-violence, compassion, equitable sharing, etc. is an important way of supporting the message of the good of all.

20.13. In the light of the above, the ten key words or phrases (or points of the framework), that play an important role in conveying the Gītā's message of the good of all, are listed below, using the Sanskrit expressions of the Gītā (but preceded by a simple English rendering thereof) :

(1) Dharma that unites—Avibhaktaṁ vibhakteṣu ;
(2) God's work—Mat-karma ;
(3) Service spontaneously rendered by saints—Yogārūḍha-vṛtti ;
(4) Adapting religious practices to changing needs—deśa-kāla-pātra ;
(5) Doing good to all beings—sarvabhūtahitam ;
(6) Good of the world—lokasaṁgraha ;
(7) Going beyond mineness and egotism—nirmamo nirahaṁkāraḥ ;
(8) Even-minded vision—samadṛṣṭi ;
(9) Not to succumb to forces of evil—āsurī sampat ; and
(10) Promote virtues—daivī sampat

It should be clarified that no in-built order of importance is associated with the sequence of presentation of expressions in the above list. For example, the most prominent word 'lokasaṁgraha' has been listed in the sixth place.

20.14. Following the same practice as we adopted in Part Two of this book, we shall now present selected verses from the Gītā which help us understand some of the basic elements that are contained in each of the ten key points listed in the preceding paragraph. We begin with the first point, viz. 'avibhaktaṁ vibhakteṣu'.

sarvabhūteṣu yenaikaṁ
bhāvamavyayamīkṣate
avibhaktaṁ vibhakteṣu
tajjñānaṁ viddhi sāttvikam (XVIII. 20)

Simple Meaning—That knowledge is sāttvika (good) by which the One Imperishable Being is seen in all existences, undivided in the divided, giving the message of unity in diversity (or of joining those who are divided).

yadā bhūtapṛthagbhāvaṁ
ekasthamanupaśyati
tata eva ca vistāraṁ
brahma sampadyate tadā (XIII. 30)

Simple Meaning—One attains brahman (spiritual perfection) when the idea of separateness of beings is realized as essentially unreal, because the underlying Reality is one, of which all the manifestations are varying forms.

20.15. The Gītā's expression 'avibhaktaṁ vibhakteṣu' reminds us that the basic concept of dharma is to hold people together, voluntarily and not by force. The Gītā's approach to dharma can be characterized as 'harmonization', which implies integration and not conflict. Some of the issues causing religious conflicts are—by what name to call God, whose prayers does God accept, and so on. The Gītā declares that devotees of God may choose any name that appeals to them, and similarly that God accepts all prayers that come from the devotees' hearts. Verse IV.11 contains a summary of such declaration :

ye yathā māṁ prapadyante
tāṁstathaiva bhajāmyahaṁ
mama vartmā'nuvartante
manuṣyāḥ pārtha sarvaśah (IV. 11)

Simple Meaning—Lord Kṛṣṇa says, as men approach me, so do I accept them ; whatever path they follow, they come to me.

This is one of the verses which Swami Vivekananda used in his address to the Parliament of World's Religions in Chicago (USA) in 1893, to plead for equal respect to all faiths and beliefs.

20.16. Unequal and unjust distribution of prosperity is another cause of social conflict. Verse XVIII. 78 highlights the importance of ensuring justice along with prosperity :

> *yatra yogeśvaraḥ kṛṣṇo*
> *yatra pārtho dhanurdharaḥ*
> *tatra śrirvijayo bhūtir*
> *dhruvā nītirmatirmama* (XVIII. 78)

Simple Meaning—Wherever there is Kṛṣṇa, the lord of yoga (showing the way), and Arjuna, ready to use energy (for implementing that yoga), then there will surely be prosperity, victory, welfare and perfect justice.

20.17. The process of joining together the divided elements of the society is facilitated by what the Gītā calls 'paraspara-bhāva' , i.e. an attitude of mutual co-operation and help. Although verse III. 11, which contains this idea, can be used in connection with several points of the framework, (and to which we referred in para 20.9), we present it here to supplement the idea of 'avibhaktaṁ vibhakteṣu' :

> *parasparaṁ bhāvayantaḥ*
> *śreyaḥ paramavāpsyatha* (III. 11)

Simple Meaning—In reply to Arjuna's question asked in verse III. 2 (viz. Please tell me one sure way by which I may attain śreyas i.e. good), Lord Kṛṣṇa said, 'You will attain 'paraṁ śreyas' i.e. supreme good, by means of an attitude of mutual co-operation and help.'

20.18. Next we take up the second point, viz. 'mat-karma'. This expression (meaning 'My work', i.e. God's work) represents a harmonious combination of karma-yoga and bhakti-yoga. Although God is the creator, preserver and destroyer of the universe, we believe it is reasonable to limit the scope of 'mat-karma' to acts of preservation and sustenance only. Really speaking, it is not a serious limitation because so many useful things can be done by observing this yardstick. We may also clarify that our discussion is mainly related to non-governmental actions.

20.19. The following two verses of the Gītā can help us in identifying the general nature of God's work that is suitable for human participation. The first one is verse XV. 17 which speaks of sustenance of the universe :

uttamaḥ puruṣastvanyaḥ
paramātme'tyudāhṛtaḥ
yo lokatrayamāviśya
vibhartyavyaya īśvaraḥ (XV. 17)

Simple Meaning—God as Puruṣottama or Paramātmā or the supreme self is beyond the kṣara and the akṣara (i.e. the perishable and the imperishable). Paramātma enters the three worlds and sustains them.

The second verse is from chapter V, but rather than quote the entire verse V.29, we only write here a part thereof which is enough for our present purpose :

suhṛdaṁ sarvabhūtānām (V. 29)

Simple Meaning—God is 'suhṛd' of all beings, i.e. the friend who does good to them without expecting any return. (This is the complete meaning of the word 'suhṛd' as explained by Śaṁkarācārya).

20.20. In the light of the above, it can be said that the Gītā wants us to be a 'suhṛd' of all beings, and that would be a component of 'mat-karma' because God himself is the 'suhṛd' of all beings. Furthermore, since persons in distress (or ārta as mentioned in verse VII.16) receive priority attention when they pray to God for help, to be a 'suhṛd' of 'ārta' would be the most important, practical component of 'mat-karma'. Following this approach, Swami Vivekananda coined the famous phrase 'Daridra-Nārāyaṇa' which meant that the service of the poor was the service of God.

20.21. Verse XI.55 of the Gītā, which, in Śaṃkarācārya's opinion, is the substance of the whole teaching of this scripture, lists four practical components of 'mat-karma' :

matkarmakṛnmatparamo
madbhaktaḥ sangavarjitaḥ
nirvairaḥ sarvabhūteṣu
yaḥ sa māmeti pāṇḍava (XI. 55)

Simple Meaning—Lord Kṛṣṇa says—one who does 'mat-karma' looks upon Me as his or her goal, he or she is a bhakta or devotee of God, is also free from attachment and from enmity to all creatures—such a person attains Me.

Śaṃkarācārya explains in his commentary that this person is bereft of the idea of enmity even towards those who might be engaged in doing harm to him or her.[2] In other words, doing 'mat-karma' means doing good to all.

20.22. The mental attitude which can convert 'sva-dharma' into 'mat-karma' can be expressed by the words : 'dedicate all acts to God'. This technique of 'karma-samarpaṇam' is contained in the following verse :

yat karoṣi yadaśnāsi
yajjuhoṣi dadāsi yat
yattapasyasi kaunteya
tat kuruṣva madarpaṇam (IX. 27)

Simple Meaning—Lord Kṛṣṇa says—Whatever you do, whatever you eat, whatever you sacrifice, whatever you give away, whatever austerities you practise, do that as an offering to me.

The technique of 'karma-samarpaṇam' implies several things. First, it is a safeguard against egotism. Secondly, an attitude of 'samarpaṇam' makes it easier to give up the desire for selfish gains. Thirdly, such a person would feel the urge to do only sāttvika (good) deeds, because how can impure deeds be dedicated to God ?

20.23. As a guide to one who would like to develop the mental attitude of 'samarpaṇam', the Gītā's message is :

nimittamātraṁ bhava (XI. 33)

Simple Meaning—Be thou merely an instrument in the hands of God, i.e. be free from the egotistic thought as if you are the doer.

The main practical implication of becoming merely an instrument is that we act like a soldier in God's army—not for destructive purposes, but only for the good of the world. Since we are God's instrument, our ultimate victory is certain. This gives us courage and confidence, but no arrogance.

20.24. Next we take up the third point, viz. yogārūḍha-vṛtti, i.e. the spontaneous social work of those who have achieved spiritual perfection. Six of the eighteen chapters of the Gītā (viz. II, V, VI, XII, XIV, XVIII) contain an account of the characteristics of such persons. One of the reasons why this topic has appeared so many times is, that perfection can be achieved in many ways and the state of perfection has therefore been given many names. But there is an underlying unity in all these descriptions, viz. the sameness of their goal (which is good of the world). Dr. Radhakrishnan has expressed this by a simile :

> "We do not proceed on the same lines but that which we seek is the same. We may climb the mountain by different paths but the view from the summit is identical for all. The liberated souls take upon themselves the burden of the redemption of the whole world."[3]

20.25. The six descriptions of spiritually perfect persons, referred to in the preceding paragraph, contain statements, (explicit as well as implicit), to the effect that they are engaged in selfless service of mankind. But the Gītā also makes a related point that the journey to spiritual perfection is facilitated by acts of social service. This point has been emphasized by the modern interpreters of the Gītā, and one of the verses which they quote in this connection is the following :

na hi kalyāṇakṛt kaścid
durgatiṁ tāta gacchati (VI. 40)

Simple Meaning—One who does 'kalyāṇa', i.e. good to others, can never go down spiritually.

An interesting question arising from this is the following—if doing good to others helps one become spiritually perfect (and in that perfection you also do good to others), then what is the difference between the perfect state and the one prior to perfection? A simple answer to this question is that, prior to achieving perfection, one does good to others by convincing oneself that this is a part of one's duty, whereas the perfect person does the same thing spontaneously. Dr. Radhakrishnan has derived this idea from the following verse :

ārurukṣormuneryogaṁ karma kāraṇamucyate
yogārūḍhasya tasyaiva śamaḥ kāraṇamucyate (VI. 3)

Simple Meaning—An aspirant views acts of social service as a means to perfection. A spiritually perfect person performs such acts as if inspired by serenity i.e. spontaneously.

Further clarification of the meaning of this verse is provided by Dr. Radhakrishnan in a long commentary, a part of which is reproduced below :

"Through work we struggle to obtain self-control; when self-control is attained, we obtain peace. It does not follow that we then abandon all action .... The yogin attains complete tranquillity by abandoning the fruit of action. He performs actions with perfect equanimity. He overflows with a spontaneous vitality and works with a generosity which arises from his own inexhaustible strength."[4]

20.26. Next we take up the fourth point, viz. deśa-kāla-pātra, i.e. adapting religious practices to changing needs. This message of the Gītā is effective because it actually changed the Vedic form of yajña, and modified the upaniṣadic concept of saṁnyāsa (i.e. renunciation). In relation to yajña, first, the main change that the Gītā introduced was to remove the element of selfish desire. For example, through a Vedic yajña householders wanted to obtain children, grandchildren, cows, horses or other wealth in this life and a happy state after death. According to the Gītā, selfish desires lead to attachment, i.e. āsakti or saṅga, which in turn causes bondage. This new idea was given through several verses, one of which is the following :

tadarthaṁ karma kaunteya muktasangaḥ samācara

(III. 9)

Simple Meaning—Lord Kṛṣṇa tells Arjuna, working for yajña is good provided that the doer of the yajña is free from attachment.

Although it may look like a simple change suggested by the Gītā, it transforms the entire concept of Vedic yajña. As Dr. Radhakrishnan says, "The religious duty to the Vedic gods here becomes service of creation in the name of the supreme."[5]

20.27. Verses IV.23-33 give the message that yajña can be performed in many ways, none of which includes animal sacrifice. The revolt against animal sacrifice was thus strengthened by the Gītā. Furthermore, although 'dravya' or sacrificial matter was an important component of a Vedic yajña, the Gītā did not attach much value thereto :

śreyān dravyamayādyajñāj
jñānayajñaḥ parantapa (IV.33)

Simple Meaning—Lord Kṛṣṇa says, in comparison to a yajña based on 'dravya' (material), a yajña based on jñāna (knowledge) is superior.

20.28. Secondly, in relation to saṁnyāsa, the main change that the

Gītā introduced was to limit it to mental renunciation only, which meant that external appearances of saṁnyāsa were not important at all. Since the main teaching of the Gītā is 'karmayoga', it does not envisage the giving up of one's duties and social obligations, by any person at any stage. Bondage, according to the Gītā, is not caused by karma, but by attachment to the fruits of one's action. There are many verses which convey these ideas but we present below only three :

samaḥ siddhāvasiddhau ca
kṛtvā'pi na nibadhyate ...
asakto hyācarankarma
paramāpnoti pūruṣaḥ ...
na ca sannyasanādeva
siddhiṁ samadhigacchati (IV. 22, III. 19,4)

Simple Meaning—Actions do not cause any bondage to a karmayogin because he or she performs them without attachment, staying even-minded in success or failure .... Such a person attains the highest state, i.e. becomes liberated while still alive .... On the other hand, it is inadvisable to think that physical renunciation will lead to liberation.

D.S. Sarma is of opinion that the emphasis on jñāna in the upaniṣads had encouraged karma-saṁnyāsa (i.e. giving up of karma), but the problem was set right by the Gītā :

"The Gītā supplied a much needed corrective to the over-emphasis on jñāna and renunciation, which had led to mere quietism. It may be said that the whole Gītā is a long and sustained protest against the dangers of quietism."[6]

20.29. After having looked at the changes or new meanings introduced by the Gītā in relation to yajña and saṁnyāsa, we consider a similar message in the context of 'dānam'. In fact, the actual words 'deśa-kāla-pātra' occur in the dānam-related verses (XVII. 20-22). Since this chapter is only like a summary of Gītā's message, we give below only one of these three verses :

adeśakāle yaddānaṁ
apātrebhyaśca dīyate
asatkṛtamavajñātam
tattāmasamudāhṛtam (XVII. 22)

Simple Meaning—That gift which is made at a wrong place or time or to an unworthy person, without proper respect, or with contempt, that is declared to be tāmasika or bad.

'Not to help an unworthy cause'—this message has great social significance. Closely related to this is the technique of civil disobedience which Mahatma Gandhi used to disobey unjust laws (like the Salt Tax law).

20.30. About the impact of kāla (time), the Gītā says :

sa kāleneha mahatā
yogo naṣṭaḥ parantapa (IV. 2)

Simple Meaning—Owing to a long lapse of time, some elements of the yoga taught in the past became irrelevant.

In general we can say that some of the dharmic practices need to be reviewed from time to time, in the light of new reasoning (buddhiyoga) and scientific knowledge (vijñana), because the Gītā attaches great value to both of these (II. 49 and IX. 1). No wonder that Mahatma Gandhi suggested the abandonment of the old practice of burning wood for a yajña :

"There were big forests in old days, and it may have been regarded as every one's duty to help in clearing these forests .... why should we at all pollute the air?.... In burning wood in this age, we misuse the capital of our forefathers, or we show ourselves witless pedants by understanding the thing in a literal sense."[7]

20.31. Next we take up the fifth point, viz. sarvabhūtahitam (i.e. doing good to all beings). This word occurs as such in the following two verses :

labhante brahmanirvāṇaṁ
ṛṣayaḥ kṣīṇakalmaṣāḥ
chinnadvaidhā yatātmānaḥ
sarvabhūtahite ratāḥ (V. 25)

Simple Meaning—Ṛṣis whose sins are destroyed, whose doubts or dualities are cut asunder, whose minds are disciplined and who rejoice in doing good to all beings—they attain brahmanirvāṇa.

saṁniyamye'ndriyagrāmaṁ
sarvatra samabuddhayaḥ
te prāpnuvanti māmeva
sarvabhūtahite ratāh (XII. 4)

Simple Meaning—Lord Kṛṣṇa says, those who restrain and discipline all the senses, who are even-minded in all situations, and who rejoice in doing good to all beings—they attain Me.

20.32. To ensure that the big goal of sarvabaūtahitam is brought within feasible limits, the Gītā's advice to every person is 'do what is within your capacity, because otherwise your action will be tāmasika i.e. bad'. This is the purpose of the following verse :

anubandhaṁ kṣayaṁ hiṁsāṁ
anavekṣya ca pauruṣaṁ
mohādārabhyate karma
yattattāmasamucyate (XVIII. 25)

Simple Meaning—Lord Kṛṣṇa says, a tāmasika karma is that which is undertaken through ignorance, without taking into account four things, viz. consequence, loss, violence, and the capacity of the doer.

In day-to-day life, we can avoid being tāmasika by doing only those things which are socially useful and which promote non-violence. But these are external considerations. In addition to these, the last item in the above verse draws attention to an internal factor, viz. the capacity of the doer. In other words, the Gītā wants everyone to try to do only that much of sarvabhūtahitam which is within the doer's capacity, and so can be done efficiently, because otherwise it will not come up to the desired standard of 'yogaḥ karmasu kauśalam' (II.50)—which means that yoga is skill in action.

20.33. Next we take up the sixth point, viz. lokasaṁgraha (i.e. good of the world). This word occurs twice in the Gītā (III. 20,25), but the complete message based thereon is contained in seven verses (III. 20-26). B.G. Tilak was the first Gītā-commentator who highlighted the importance of these seven verses.[8] Thereafter Śrī Aurobindo also declared :

"There are few more important passages in the Gītā than these seven striking couplets."[9]

20.34. Since this chapter has to adopt a selective approach, we shall present here only two of the seven verses :

utsīdeyurime lokā
na kuryāṁ karma cedahaṁ

saṁkarasya ca kartā syāṁ
upahanyāmimāḥ prajāḥ (III. 24)

Simple Meaning—Lord Kṛṣṇa says, if I do not work for lokasaṁgraha, all these worlds would perish, and I would be held responsible for creating confusion and for destroying the people.

saktāḥ karmaṇyavidvāṁso
yathā kurvanti bhārata
kuryādvidvāṁstathāsaktas
cikīrṣurlokasaṁgraham (III. 25)

Simple Meaning—Those who act from attachment (which is a sign of their selfish desires) are devoid of learning. On the other hand, learned people are those who act with the desire for lokasaṁgraha, and without attachment.

20.35. The first verse (III. 24) gives a practical definition of lokasaṁgraha as any work that prevents world's destruction and social confusion, or contributes to world's protection and social development. The scope of lokasaṁgraha-activities can thus be widened to include environmental protection. The second verse (III.25) helps classify human desires into two categories, viz. desires for selfish gains (which are condemned), and desires for the good of the world (which are glorified).

20.36. Next we take up the seventh point, viz. nirmamo nirahaṁkāraḥ (i.e. going beyond mineness and egotism). This is a favorite expression of the Gītā, directly used in the context of karma-yoga and bhakti-yoga, and indirectly used in the context of jñāna-yoga too. However, before we come to the relevant verses of these three yogas, we want to draw attention to the first part of this expression, viz. the word 'nirmamo' by itself. The Gītā summarized through this word the essence of the yajña-related mantras of the Vedas which included the words 'idaṁ na mama' (meaning, this is not mine). The Gītā then supplemented this idea with the realization that 'this wealth or capability is God-given and made available by society' and so should be used for social purposes :

yadyadvibhūtimatsattvaṁ
śrīmadūrjitameva vā
tattadevāvagaccha tvam
mama tejo'ṁśasambhavam (X. 41)

Simple Meaning—Whatsoever being there is, endowed with glory, grace and vigour, know that to have sprung from a fragment of God's splendour.

tairdattānapradāyaibhyo
yo bhunkte stena eva saḥ (III. 12)

Simple Meaning—If one takes (from God and society) and consumes it oneself, without giving (to God and society), then one can be called a 'thief'.

20.37. Having summarized the Gītā's call for social service based on the word 'nirmamo', we now present the verses which use the expression 'nirmamo nirahaṁkāraḥ', both directly and indirectly :

vihāya kāmān yaḥ sarvān
pumāṁścarati niḥspṛhaḥ
nirmamo nirahaṁkāraḥ
sa śāntimadhigacchati (II. 71)

Simple Meaning—A spiritually perfect karmayogin does not have selfish desires—since he is free from longing, his actions are spontaneous—he has gone beyond the sense of I and mine, and he attains peace, i.e. he is liberated while still living.

adveṣṭā sarvabhūtānāṁ
maitraḥ karuṇa eva ca
nirmamo nirahaṁkāraḥ
samaduḥkhasukhaḥ kṣamī (XII. 13)

Simple Meaning—A spiritually perfect bhakta has no ill will towards any being i.e. even towards those who have ill will towards him (or her). Such a bhakta is also compassionate and friendly. Furthermore, this bhakta, being beyond the sense of I and mine, gives priority to social service, and tries to make others happy, remaining even-minded towards one's own sorrows and pleasures. Besides all this, such a bhakta has the quality of forgiveness.

ahaṁkāraṁ balaṁ darpaṁ
kāmaṁ krodhaṁ parigrahaṁ
virmucya nirmamaḥ śānto
brahmabhūyāya kalpate (XVIII. 53)

Simple Meaning—A spiritually perfect jñānin, who is worthy of becoming one with brahman is tranquil in mind, 'nirmamaḥ', and he or she casts aside 'ahaṁkāra', force, arrogance, desire, anger and possessiveness.

It is clear that this verse indirectly uses the expression 'nirmamo nirahaṁkāraḥ'. Taking the three verses of this paragraph together, this expression is used in the Gītā for all spiritually perfect persons, irrespective of the yoga (karma, bhakti, jñāna) which made them perfect.

20.38. Next we take up the eighth point, viz. samadṛṣṭi (i.e. even-minded vision). This subject is of great importance because social workers all over the world are battling against discriminatory practices based on race, colour, creed, sex, socio-economic status and so on. The fragmentation of the society on the basis of the caste, and the attitude of neglect of the poorer sections in the minds of the rich, have been particularly alarming in India. The Gītā wanted 'paṇḍits' (i.e. scholars) to take the lead in overcoming all discriminatory practices :

vidyāvinayasampanne
brāhmaṇe gavi hastini
śuni caiva śvapāke ca
paṇḍitāḥ samadarśinaḥ (V. 18)

Simple Meaning—Paṇḍits are those who have equal vision towards all, for example, towards a learned and humble brahmin, a cow, an elephant, a dog or a dog-eater.

20.39. The word 'sāmya' is also used in the Gītā (V. 19) to denote even-minded vision, so a yogin having such a vision can be called 'sāmya-yogin'. He not only knows the Vedānta philosophy but also puts it into practice :

ātmaupamyena sarvatra
samaṁ paśyati yo'rjuna
sukhaṁ vā yadi vā duḥkhaṁ
sa yogī paramo mataḥ (VI. 32)

Simple Meaning—A sāmya-yogin is guided by the philosophy of 'ātmaupamya' which sees the same ātman in all the beings. Furthermore, his sympathetic behaviour towards all reflects this philosophy fully, in the sense that he is happy when others are happy, and he is unhappy when others are unhappy.

20.40. Almost parallel to samadṛṣṭi (i.e. even-minded vision towards people), we have in the Gītā 'even-mindedness towards situations' which has been expressed in various ways, e.g. samaduḥkhasukham (II.15) or samaḥ siddhāvasiddhau (IV.22), which mean, respectively, same in pain and pleasure, or same in success or failure. Another way to clarify this is to recognize two variants of 'samattva' (sameness)—the first variant being towards situations, and the second variant being towards people. The subtle difference between these two variants can be explained by linking them, one at a time, to two important goals, for example, 'samattva towards situations' leads one to the individual goal of 'śreyas' (i.e. good) (referred to in para 20.17), while 'samattva towards people' leads its practitioners to the social goal of 'lokasaṁgraha' (good of the world). Verses VI.8-9 refer to these two variants of 'samattva', one after the other, in two consecutive verses, which although admiring both, glorify the second variant as 'excellent'.

yukta ityucyate yogī
samaloṣṭāśmakāñcanaḥ (VI. 8)

Simple Meaning—One to whom a clod, a stone, and piece of gold are the same (i.e. samattva variant one, towards situations), is said to be firm in yoga.

sādhuṣvapi ca pāpeṣu
samabuddhirviśiṣyate (VI. 9)

Simple Meaning—One who is even-minded towards saints and sinners (i.e. samattva variant two, towards people), he excels.

20.41. Next we take up the ninth point, viz. āsurī sampat (i.e. not to succumb to forces of evil). The worst of the evil forces are those who want to destroy the world :

prabhavantyugrakarmāṇaḥ
kṣayāya jagato'hitāh (XVI. 9)

Simple Meaning—Persons with demoniac mentality are enemies of the world—they use their power to commit cruel deeds and for destructive purposes.

But to classify individuals as "good" or "bad" is only a part of the story. The other side of the story was told by Mahatma Gandhi who took the view that the real struggle between the good and the bad goes on in the heart of each individual. Explaining this, Mahadev

Desai wrote—"Let no one misunderstand these labels (of good and bad) and misapply them. We may only say that when particular characteristics predominate us, we are of God, and when the opposite ones do so, we are of the devil."[10]

Verse VI. 5 supports this approach :

ātmaiva ripurātmanaḥ (VI. 5)

Simple Meaning—Oneself is verily one's own enemy.

20.42. There are sixteen verses in chapter XVI of the Gītā which describe the demoniac forces that reside within us as well as outside. These forces are particularly dangerous when they form a chain. We shall present here only two chains. The first chain consists of kāma-lobha-anyāya, i.e. lust-greed-injustice :

kāmamāśritya duṣpūraṁ ....
bhaviṣyati punardhanaṁ ....
anyāyenārthasaṁcayān (XVI. 10,12-13)

Simple Meaning—Desires of the demoniac persons are insatiable, so they become greedy, anxious to increase their wealth, even if they have to employ unjust means for that purpose.

The second chain can be called 'chain of hatred rooted in egotism'.

ahaṁkāraṁ balaṁ darpaṁ
kāmaṁ krodhaṁ ca saṁśritāḥ
māmātmaparadeheṣu
pradviṣanto'bhyasūyakāḥ (XVI. 18)

Simple Meaning—Demoniac persons suffer from the vice of egotism, then they take recourse to force, arrogance, lust, anger, and malice, and then they despise God dwelling in the bodies of themselves and others, i.e. they spread hatred in the society.

20.43. The Gītā's purpose behind the description of evil forces is to sound a note of caution so as not to succumb to them. The root of the whole trouble really exists in the minds of men and is called 'tāmasika-buddhi' :

adharmaṁ dharmamiti yā
manyate tamasāvṛtā
sarvārthānviparītāṁśca
buddhiḥ sā pārtha tāmasī (XVIII. 32)

Simple Meaning—That way of thinking is harmful which is perverted, i.e. which considers good as bad, and bad as good, thus prompting one to act contrary to social norms and values.

The Gītā warns that although 'tapas' generally has the meaning of self-discipline, yet under the influence of tāmasika-buddhi, it becomes tāmasika too :

mūḍhagrāheṇātmano
yatpīḍayā kriyate tapaḥ
parasyotsādanārthaṁ vā
tattāmasamudāhṛtam (XVII. 19)

Simple Meaning—That tapas is tāmasika (bad) which is performed with a foolish obstinacy by means of self-torture or for causing injury to others.

20.44. Finally, we come to the tenth point, viz. daivī sampat (i.e. promote virtues). This is a favorite topic of the Gītā :

daivo vistarśaḥ proktaḥ (XVI. 6)

Simple Meaning—Divine persons and their virtues have been described (in the Gītā) at length.

For our present purposes we need to take a selective approach and identify virtues that help overpower 'āsurī sampat' (evil forces) and contribute to the good of all. Our task is facilitated by the work already done by modern interpreters of the Gītā. For example, Swami Vivekananda exphasized the importance of 'unselfishness', 'fearlessness', and 'spirit of dedicated service to the needy'.[11] Lokamānya Tilak and Śri Aurobindo, fully recognizing the supreme value of these three virtues, added thereto two more, viz. 'respect for the values which have held the society together' and 'willingness to sacrifice for a just cause'—the latter assuming particular significance in the light of their confrontation with the British empire. Mahatma Gandhi did not deny the importance of the virtues identified by his predecessors, but added 'truth' and 'non-violence' to the list—almost placing non-violence on the top.

20.45. Apart from linking divine virtues with spiritually perfect or sāttvika persons, the Gītā has given two long lists of such virtues, in verses XIII. 7-11 and XVI. 1-3. We reproduce here the latter, as the concluding part of this chapter :

abhayaṁ sattvasaṁśuddhir
jñānayogavyavasthitiḥ
dānaṁ damaśca yajñaśca
svādhyāyastapa ārjavam (XVI. 1)

Simple Meaning—Nine virtues are listed in this verse—fearlessness, purity of mind, wise apportionment of knowledge and concentration, sharing, self-control, yajña, study of the scriptures, tapas (austerity), and uprightness.

ahiṁsā satyamakrodhas
tyāgaḥ śāntirapaiśunaṁ
dayā bhūteṣvaloluptvaṁ
mārdavaṁ hrīracāpalam (XVI. 2)

Simple Meaning—Eleven virtues are listed in this verse—non-violence, truth, freedom from anger, non-possessiveness, tranquillity, aversion to fault-finding, compassion to living beings, freedom from covetousness, gentleness, modesty, and absence of fickleness.

tejaḥ kṣamā dhṛtiḥ śaucaṁ
adroho nātimānitā
bhavanti sampadaṁ daivīṁ
abhijātasya bhārata (XVI. 3)

Simple Meaning—Six virtues are listed in this verse (bringing the total to twenty-six)—vigour, forgiveness, fortitude, purity, freedom from ill-will, and absence of excessive pride—all these virtues constitute divine nature.

CHAPTER 21

How Mahābhārata supports Gītā's Call for the Good of All

21.1. The Mahābhārata declared, about its own ocean-like, comprehensive coverage, just before concluding Svargārohaṇa-Parva (i.e. Parva No.18) :

dharme cārthe ca kāme ca
mokṣe ca bharatarṣabha
yadihāsti tadanyatra
yannehāsti na kutracit (XVIII. 5.50)

Simple Meaning—On the topics of dharma, artha, kāma and mokṣa (i.e. the four goals of life), what you find in the Mahābhārata may be found elsewhere, but whatever is not found here you will not be able to find anywhere else.

Keeping this in mind and desiring to accomplish the goal that we set before ourselves, we have adopted the technique of a three-stage selection. Accordingly, in the earlier chapters, we have (by going through two stages) made a preliminary selection of the Mahābhārata-narrations, to obtain a fairly large pool of material broadly relevant to the purpose of this book. What we are now attempting to do in this chapter is to apply the third (and final) stage of selection—which is like picking up drops of a particular nectar from a large pool of nectars. The task of locating these invigorating drops has been made manageable for us because we are using Bhagavad-Gītā as the reference-provider. More specifically, we use the Gītā's call for the good of all as a ten-point framework (summarized in the preceding chapter) and concentrate our attention on those of the Mahābhārata-verses which express the same or similar ideas. We find that our approach is fully justified because we are able to identify several verses in the Mahābhārata for each of the ten points of the Gītā-based framework. However, with a view to keeping the size of this chapter within reasonable limits, we restrict our final selection to only a small number of the eligible verses of the Mahābhārata for each point.

A point-by-point presentation of the selected verses of the Mahābhārata follows.

21.2. The first point of the framework (reference para 20.13) is 'avibhaktaṁ vibhakteṣu'. The same idea of unifying dharma occurs in the Anu-Gītā section of the Mahābhārata (reference para 18.28) :

paśyanekatvaṁ nānātve
sa duḥkhāt pratimucyate (XIV. 47.7)

Simple Meaning—One who sees unity in (apparent) diversity, finds a sure way out of all sorrow.

For elaborating the same (first) point, we quoted verse XIII.30 of the Gītā (reference para 20.14), and that verse occurs as such in Śānti-Parva too :

yadā bhūtapṛthagbhāvaṁ
ekasthamanupaśyati
tata eva ca vistāraṁ
brahma sampadyate tadā (XII. 17.23)

Simple Meaning—One attains brahman (spiritual perfection) when the idea of separateness of beings is realized as essentially unreal, because the underlying Reality is one, of which all the manifestations are varying forms.

21.3. As a practical way of achieving the ideal of unity, the Gītā calls for 'paraspara-bhāva', i.e. an attitude of mutual co-operation and help (ref. para 20.17). The Anu-Gītā section of the Mahābhārata not only repeats the key words of the Gītā but also adds other words that reinforce the Gītā's call (ref. para 18.25) :

parasparasya suhṛdo
bhāvayantaḥ parasparaṁ
svasti vrajata bhadraṁ vo
dhārayadhvaṁ parasparam (XIV. 23.24)

Simple Meaning—Be friends of one another and foster one another. I bless you and wish you well. You will certainly prosper if you uphold one another.

21.4. A variant of 'paraspara-bhāva' is 'paraspara-prīti' (i.e. to love one another)—and this is the expression used in Vidura-Nīti (reference para 7.6) :

sambhojanaṁ saṁkathanaṁ
samprītiśca parasparaṁ
jñātibhiḥ saha kāryāṇi (V.39.24)

Simple Meaning—To eat with one another, to talk with one another, and to love one another—these are the things that relatives should do.

21.5. An important factor which, according to the Gītā, can help bring about unity is 'justice' (ref. para 20.16). A similar approach was suggested by Lord Kṛṣṇa in Udyoga-Parva of the Mahābhārata when he addressed the Kaurava Assembly (ref. Chapter nine, para 9.16) :

ye dharmamanupaśyantas
tūṣṇīṁ dhyāyanta āsate
te satyamāhurdharmyaṁ ca
nyāyyaṁ ca bharatarṣabha (V. 95.51)

Simple Meaning—Lord Kṛṣṇa said to Dhṛtarāṣṭra, 'O King, please appreciate that the Pāṇḍavas are sticking to the path of dharma. They are waiting patiently to receive their share of the kingdom—and their demand is in conformity with dharma, truth and justice.'

21.6. A plea for equal respect for all faiths, as a basis of unity or harmony, was put forward by Swami Vivekananda, utilizing verse IV.11 of the Gītā (ref. para 20.15). A similar plea can be made by using the following words from Śānti-Parva :

bahudvārasya dharmasya (XII. 174.2)

Simple Meaning—Religion has many doors.

21.7. The second point of the framework (reference para 20.13) is 'mat-karma' (i.e. God's work). It was explained in para 20.22 that the mental attitude which can convert 'sva-dharma' into 'mat-karma' can be expressed by the words : 'dedicate all acts to God'. Such was the attitude of King Uparicara, as described in the Nārāyaṇīya-dharma section of Śānti-Parva (reference para 13.6) :

ātmarājyaṁ dhanaṁ caiva
kalatraṁ vāhanaṁ tathā
yattadbhāgavataṁ sarvaṁ
iti tat prokṣitaṁ sadā (XII.335.23)

Simple Meaning—All that he (i.e. King Uparicara) had, e.g. kingdom, wealth, family and glory, he viewed them as God-given, and so he dedicated all his actions to Nārāyaṇa.

21.8. As a guide to one who would like to develop the mental attitude of 'dedication', the Gītā's message is 'Don't regard yourself as the doer' (reference para 20.23). A similar advice was given by Tulādhāra to Jājali in Śānti-Parva (reference chapter twelve) :

kartavyamiti kartavyaṁ ...
naiva kartavyatāṁ punaḥ (XII. 263.16)

Simple Meaning—Be guided by the principle, 'duty for duty's sake', and don't regard yourself as the doer.

21.9. When 'sva-dharma' becomes 'mat-karma', one becomes a friend (i.e. suhṛd) of all beings (ref. para 20.19). Śānti-Parva highlights this idea through several dialogues, but we give below parts of only two verses from the dialogue between Vyāsa and Śuka :

sarvabhūtasuhṛdbhāvaḥ ...
tulyapriyāpriyo dhīraḥ ...
kuryādanyanna vā kuryān
maitro brāhmaṇa ucyate (XII. 237.38, 238.13)

Simple Meaning—A spiritually perfect person is filled with spontaneous feelings of friendship towards all beings, making no distinction between friend or foe ... In fact, such friendship is the main criterion of perfection, and it does not matter whether other religious practices are undertaken or not.

21.10. The third point of the framework (reference para 20.13) is 'yogārūḍha-vṛtti' (i.e. service spontaneously rendered by spiritually perfect persons). The Gītā contains six detailed descriptions of the characteristics of such persons. Their number, according to the Mahābhārata, is very large, but we present below selected verses which throw light on the socially useful activities of only ten of them.

21.11. We begin with Janaka whose name is mentioned in the Gītā (III.20) as an ideal karmayogin, but about whose greatness no details are given there. The Anu-Gītā section of Aśvamedha-Parva (ref. chapter 18) contains twenty-five verses about Janaka which clarify as to in what sense he was an ideal karmayogin. Out of the verses already presented in chapter 18, we give below only one :

devebhyaśca pitṛbhyaśca
bhūtebhyo'tithibhiḥ saha
ityarthaṁ sarva eveti
samārambhā bhavanti vai (XIV. 32.24)

Simple Meaning—In this verse, Janaka summarized the reason why he was still carrying on the activities of ruling as a king, although he had no selfish interest or advantage and had become perfectly non-attached to his kingdom, 'All activities of mine are for the benefit of the gods, the ancestors, all created beings, and my guests, but not for my own self.'

21.12. The second person selected by us for inclusion in this list of ten spiritually perfect entities is Janaka's wife (reference chapter 14). Śānti-Parva refers to a critical juncture in Janaka's life when his understanding of karma-yoga failed him—he shaved off his head and assumed the garb of a mendicant. It was due to the effective advice of his wife that Janaka realized his error. Out of the verses (attributed to Janaka's wife), already presented in chapter 14, we give below only two :

tyāgānna bhikṣukaṁ vidyān
na mauḍhyānna ca yācanāt
ṛjustu yo'rthaṁ tyajati
nasukhaṁ viddhi bhikṣukam (XII. 18.30)

Simple Meaning—In this verse, the queen drew Janaka's attention to the very concept of renunciation, 'I want to say that real renunciation is a state of mind. To leave the home and to take a begging bowl do not mean renunciation—they only denote ignorance. On the other hand, by giving up attachment, crookedness and selfishness (while staying at home), one is entitled to be regarded as a true mendicant.'

samaḥ śatrau ca mitre ca
sa vai mukto mahīpate (XII. 18.31)

Simple Meaning—The queen added, 'O my husband, you are a great king, and even staying as a king, you will attain salvation if you become even-minded towards all and have an equal vision towards friends and foes.'

21.13. The third person selected by us for inclusion in this list of ten great entities is Vyādha, i.e. a butcher who taught a brahmin (ref. chapter four). The erring disciple of Vyādha was Kauśika who had left home without the permission of his parents, for the purpose of learning the Vedas and for practising austerities. Although Vyādha was a śūdra (belonging to a lower caste), he succeeded in bringing Kauśika back to a life of righteousness, devoted to the performance of his normal duties, towards his parents as well as others, and free from arrogance, selfishness and anger. This interesting narration occurs in Vana-Parva.

21.14. In his teaching (considered so great as to be called a 'Gītā'), Vyādha explained to Kauśika that his own hereditary occupation was to sell meat—and that he performed it with honesty and efficiency, himself being a vegetarian. He adhered to sāttvika (i.e. good) values, in which service of parents had a high place :

prayatnācca gurū vṛddhau
śuśrūṣe'haṁ dvijottama (III. 207.21)

Simple Meaning—'O learned brahmin, I devote a good deal of my time to look after my parents who are quite old now.'

ahiṁsā satyavacanaṁ
sarvabhūtahitaṁ paraṁ ....
yad bhūtahitamatyantaṁ
tat satyamiti dhāraṇā (III. 207.74 and 209.4)

Simple Meaning—'Ahiṁsā (non-violence) and Satya (truth) are the two main pillars of dharma through which the highest good of all can be achieved .... In fact, a decision on what is true (under difficult circumstances) should be made by sticking to that course of action which leads to the highest good of beings.'

sarvabhūtadayāvanto
ahiṁsāniratāḥ sadā ....
nyāyopetā guṇopetāḥ
sarvalokahitaiṣiṇaḥ (III. 207.84, 86)

Simple Meaning—'A visible characteristic of those who are devoted to ahiṁsā is that they have compassion towards all beings and their conduct is lawful and just. Moreover, the essence of all the virtues that these people have, is the desire to do good to all.'

21.15. The fourth person selected by us for inclusion in this list of ten is Tulādhāra (a person engaged in trade), from whom religious advice was sought by Jājali, a brahmin (ref. chapter 12). Śānti-Parva describes how Jājali was engaged in severe austerities (standing still for a long time and giving shelter to birds in his hair). When feelings of arrogance arose in him, he heard a heavenly voice, 'Don't think too much of yourself. Go and see Tulādhāra who is a more genuine follower of dharma.' Tulādhāra's teachings helped Jājali attain salvation by going along a new spiritual path.

21.16. Since the dialogue between Tulādhāra and Jājali is already given in chapter 12, we present below only two verses which contain the essence of Tulādhāra's teachings :

sarveṣāṁ yaḥ suhṛnnityaṁ
sarveṣāṁ ca hite rataḥ
karmaṇā manasā vācā
sa dharmaṁ veda jājale (XII. 262.9)

Simple Meaning—'O Jājali, in the field of dharma, theoretical knowledge is not enough. A real knower of dharma is one who is friendly to all and who is always engaged in doing good to all, in thought, word and deed.'

samo'haṁ sarvabhūteṣu
paśya me jājale vrataṁ
tulā me sarvabhūteṣu
samā tiṣṭhati sarvadā (XII. 262.10)

Simple Meaning—'O Jājali, in my behavior towards fellow beings, I practice equal vision. The same is true about my trading practice—all my customers are guaranteed equal treatment.'

21.17. The fifth person selected by us for inclusion in this list of ten is Subhadrā whose young son Abhimanyu was killed treacherously by the Kauravas (ref. para 1.14). Our recognition of Subhadrā's greatness is not confined to her alone, rather it is a tribute to both Subhadrā and Abhimanyu. The son's untimely death naturally shocked Subhadrā, but she faced the calamity with heroic spirit and prayed for peace to the departed soul. Droṇa-Parva (i.e. Parva no.7) describes Subhadrā's emotional outburst in the course of which she said, 'O son, let that end be thine which is theirs who give up their life for a righteous cause'. Subhadrā's words are a testimony to her greatness, because they make us understand the characteristics of those who, according to her, are spiritually perfect. We reproduce below only one verse, to give a glimpse of Subhadrā's views :

dīnānukampināṁ yā ca
satataṁ saṁvibhāginām
paiśunyācca nivṛttānāṁ
tāṁ gatiṁ vraja putraka (VII. 78.28)

Simple Meaning—'O son, let that end be thine which is theirs who are compassionate towards the poor, who believe in sharing their prosperity with others, and who never speak harshly of others.'

21.18. The sixth person selected by us for inclusion in this list of ten is Aśvapati, father of Sāvitrī (who is often depicted as an ideal wife in Indian literature). In recognizing Aśvapati's greatness, we pay tribute, not only to him but to Sāvitrī also (ref. chapter 5). Vana-Parva (i.e. Parva no.3) describes the qualities of King Aśvapati, and our present purpose will be served by reproducing only one verse below :

āsīnmadreṣu dharmātmā
satyasandho jitendriyaḥ
pārthivo'śvapatirnāma
sarvabhūtahite rataḥ (III. 293.5)

Simple Meaning—Once upon a time, long ago, Aśvapati was the king of Madra-deśa. His devotion to dharma was perfect, he adhered to truth, and was self-disciplined. He was always engaged in doing good to all the people.

21.19. The seventh person selected by us for inclusion in this list of ten is Jaigīṣavya Muni who is depicted in Śānti-Parva as a wise man whom people approached for advice in religious matters, and who has been identified by B.G. Tilak as an ideal karmayogin. From the description of spiritually perfect persons that Jaigīṣavya gives in Śānti-Parva, we reproduce below only two verses :

pakkavidyā mahāprājñā
jitakrodhā jitendriyāḥ

manasā karmaṇā vācā
nāparādhyanti karhicit (XII. 229.12)

Simple Meaning—Of mature knowledge, of great wisdom, with wrath under complete control, and with their passions kept under sway, they never cause injury to anyone in thought, and word or deed.

sarvataśca praśāntā ye
sarvabhūtahite ratāḥ (XII. 229.15)

Simple Meaning—They are tranquil in all respects, and are engaged in doing good to all the people.

21.20. The eighth person selected by us for inclusion in this list of ten is Ṛṣi Nārada, about whom Lord Kṛṣṇa himself tells in Śānti-Parva as to why he (i.e. Nārada) is revered everywhere. We present below two of the verses which highlight the virtues of Nārada :

na cāritranimitto'syā
'haṁkāro dehatāpanaḥ
abhinnaśrutacāritras
tasmāt sarvatra pūjitaḥ (XII. 230.5)

Simple Meaning—Nārada is not only learned in all the scriptures, he is also great in his conduct, and because of this greatness, he is free from egotism (which makes ordinary people restless). Due to these qualities, Nārada is revered everywhere.

kalyāṇaṁ kurute bāḍhaṁ
pāpamasminna vidyate
na prīyate parānarthais
tasmāt sarvatra pūjitaḥ (XII. 230.11)

Simple Meaning—Nārada is free from sins. He rejoices in doing good to all people—he never rejoices at other people's misfortunes. Due to these qualities, he is revered everywhere.

21.21. The ninth person selected by us for inclusion in this list of ten is Ṛṣi Dadhīci who is depicted in Vana-Parva as well as Śānti-Parva as a spiritually perfect person who willingly gave up his life for a great cause (Reference chapter 3). The narration of Dadhīci's sacrifice begins with a description of the atrocities committed by a demon named Vṛtrāsura. Feeling helpless against the might of this demon, the gods made a deep search as to what special weapon could overpower him. They discovered that only a weapon made from the bones of Ṛṣi Dadhīci can kill Vṛtrāsura. So all the gods assembled and went to the Ṛṣi, praying for help—and although this meant a great sacrifice on the part of the Ṛṣi, he replied.

karomi yad vo hitamadya devāḥ
svaṁ cāpi dehaṁ svayamutsṛjāmi (III. 100.21)

Simple Meaning—'O gods, what is to the good of all of you will be done by me immediately, i.e. I shall give up my body voluntarily.'

Ṛṣi Dadhīci thus bacame instrumental in saving the world from horrors caused by Vṛtrāsura.

21.22. The tenth (and the last) person (or persons) selected by us for inclusion in the present list is (or are) a Nāga couple, viz. Padmanābha and his wife, who are described in Śānti-Parva as both spiritually perfect, and who acted together with complete co-ordination. When a brahmin guest visited this couple, to obtain advice in religious matters, the wife of the Nāga summarized the duty of a household by saying :

gṛhasthadharmaḥ sarvadā
sarvabhūtahitaiṣitā (XII. 359.7)

Simple Meaning—The desire to do good to all, under all circumstances, constitutes the basis of a householder's dharma (i.e. duty).

And Padmanābha concluded his conversation with the brahmin guest with the following words which contained high philosophy as well as full assurance of help :

tvayi cāhaṁ dvijaśreṣṭha
bhavān mayi na saṁśayaḥ
loko'yaṁ bhavataḥ sarvaḥ
kā cintā mayi te'nagha (XII. 364.6)

Simple Meaning—'O learned brahmin, you and I have the same ātman, therefore we can say that I am in you and you are in me. Since you are pure, I can say that this whole world is yours. Due to mutual love between you and me, I feel that you need not have any worries.'

21.23. The fourth point of the framework (reference para 20.13) is 'deśa-kāla-pātra' (i.e. adapting religious practices to changing needs). The Mahābhārata gave strong support to Gītā's call on this point, both on the particular issue of 'yajña', and also on the general question of change over time. Considering yajña, first, the main thrust of the Mahābhārata's revolt against the orthodox method of performing a yajña was to denounce animal sacrifice. We have presented five stories on this topic in chapters 11,12,13 and 15. Our immediate objective will be served by recalling and giving below, one verse from each of these five stories :

avyavasthitamaryādair
vimūdhairnāstikairnaraiḥ
saṁśayātmabhiravyaktair
hiṁsā samanuvarṇitā (XII. 265.4)

Simple Meaning—King Vicakhnu said (ref. para 11.6), 'Only those who violate norms of righteous conduct, and who are ignorant or atheists or sceptics, want to acquire fame through rituals and take recourse to animal sacrifice.'

vakṣyāmi jājale vṛttiṁ
nāsmi brāhmaṇa nāstikaḥ
na yajñaṁ ca vinindāmi
yajñavit tu sudurlabhaḥ (XII. 263.4)

Simple Meaning—Tulādhāra said (ref. para 12.11), 'O Jājali, please do not think that I am an atheist. I am not against yajña itself. I am only against animal sacrifice. My view may not be supported by many people, but those who know the real meaning of yajña (and such persons are rare) are in agreement with me.'

tasya yajño mahānāsīd
aśvamedho mahātmanaḥ ....
na tatra paśughāto'bhūt
sa rājaivaṁ sthito'bhavat (XII. 336.5,10)

Simple Meaning—As a follower of Nārāyaṇīya dharma (ref. para 13.6), King Uparicara performed a grand yajña. Although this yajña was called 'aśvamedha' (literally meaning horse sacrifice), no animal was killed because the king believed in ahiṁsā (non-violence).

sa tu dharmo mṛgo bhūtvā
bahuvarṣoṣito vane
tasya niṣkṛtimādhatta
na tvasau yajñasaṁvidhiḥ (XII. 272.17)

Simple Meaning—(Ref. para 15.8)—It was the Lord Dharma himself who (had assumed the form of Parṇāda and who in turn) became a deer that lived in those woods for many years. Seeing that Satya (the brahmin) was tempted by the heavenly prospect, Dharma provided for his salvation and counselled him, saying, 'This (i.e. even the thought of animal sacrifice) is a violation of the right method of performing yajña.'

anālambhe hyadoṣaḥ syād
ālambhe doṣa uttamaḥ ....
yadyatra kincit pratyakṣaṁ
ahiṁsāyāḥ paraṁ mataṁ
ṛte tvāgamaśāstrebhyo
brūhi tad yadi paśyasi (XII. 268.16-17)

Simple Meaning—(Ref. para 15.14)—Ṛṣi Kapila said to Syūmaraśmi, 'You asked me about the basic criterion, and my answer is 'non-violence'. I believe that animal sacrifice is unrighteous, and to abstain from it is righteous .... If you know of any principle as being superior to non-violence, which is supported by direct experience rather than by a wrong interpretation of scriptures, then you please tell me about it.'

21.24. Considering, next, the general question of change over time, there are repeated statements in the Mahābhārata to the effect that a religious practice does not become doable simply because ancient people did it. We present here two verses attributed to Tulādhāra (ref. para 12.12) :

īdṛśānaśivān ghorān
ācārāniha jājale
kevalācaritatvāt tu
nipuṇo nāvabuddhyase
kāraṇād dharmamanvicchen
na lokacaritaṁ caret (XII. 262.52-53)

Simple Meaning—Tulādhāra said, 'O Jājali, I am pained to see that some of the unrighteous and violent practices keep going in the world, only because people like you, in spite of being scholars, ignore their anti-social drawbacks. My advice in such cases is this—do not follow old practices blindly, and examine whether they can stand to reason.'

21.25. We already quoted two verses from Ādi-Parva (ref. para 1.30) which say that Bhīṣma taught Yudhiṣṭhira in Anuśāsana-Parva about the importance of time and place. It will be useful to reproduce here a part of one of these two verses :

rahasyaṁ caiva dharmāṇāṁ
deśakālopasaṁhitam (I. 2.335)

Simple Meaning—Bhīṣma's advice on practical aspects of dharma included the need to take into account both place and time.

As a follow-up of this advice of Bhīṣma, Yudhiṣṭhira himself suggested in Anuśāsana-Parva that the traditional definition of yajña should be modified in the light of the new awareness of the needs of the poor (reference para 1.31) :

na te śakyā daridreṇa
yajñāḥ prāptuṁ pitāmaha
bahūpakaraṇā yajñā
nānāsambhāravistarāḥ (XIII. 107.2)

Simple Meaning—Yudhiṣṭhira said to Bhiṣma, 'O grandfather, (traditional) yajña requires so many costly commodities, etc. and is thus beyond the reach of poor people.

21.26. We conclude this summarization of Mahābhārata's support to 'deśa-kāla-pātra' by reproducing the following verse from Śānti-Parva :

sa eva dharmaḥ so'dharmas
taṁ taṁ prati naraṁ bhavet
pātrakarmaviśeṣeṇa
deśakālāvaveksya ca (XII. 309.16)

Simple Meaning—The same act may be dharma (righteous) for some persons and adharma (unrighteous) for other persons, depending on considerations of place, time, and appropriateness of what was done and for whom.

21.27. The fifth point of the framework (reference para 20.13) is 'sarvabhūtahitam' (i.e. doing good to all beings). This is a favorite word of the Mahābhārata too, which provides strong support to all the important ideas of the Gītā connected with this point. For example, Gītā-verse XII. 4 glorifies those who do good to all, by saying that such actions lead them to God (ref. para 20.31). The same idea is expressed by Vyāsa to his son Śuka in Śānti Parva :

> *taṁ paśyanti mahātmāno*
> *brāhmaṇā ye manīṣiṇaḥ*
> *dhṛtimanto mahāprājñāḥ*
> *sarvabhūtahite ratāḥ* (XII. 240.21)

Simple Meaning—Paramātman is seen by those who have knowledge of brahman and are called high-souled, who are wise and firm in their knowledge, and who are engaged in doing good to all the beings.

A related idea of the Gītā is (ref. para 20.25) that spiritually perfect persons do good to all spontaneously. Apart from stating this in a general way in verse VI.3, the Gītā also provides six illustrations which show that it does not matter as to by which yoga these persons attained spiritual perfection (ref. para 20.24). The number of such illustrations in the Mahābhārata is very large, but we have presented ten of them in paragraphs 21.10—22. Corresponding to the general statement of verse VI.3 of the Gītā, we give below Bhīṣma's statement made to Yudhiṣṭhira in Śānti-Parva :

> *suvratāḥ sthiramaryādāḥ* ....
> *dayāvantastathaiva ca* ....
> *sarvopakāriṇo vīrāḥ* ....
> *nityodyuktāstathaiva ca* ....
> *sarvabhūtahitāścaiva*
> *sarvadeyāśca bhārata* (XII. 158, 25-26,29)

Simple Meaning—When spiritual perfection, achieved through strong determination, becomes firmly established in such persons, compassion towards others becomes spontaneous to them .... Strong desire and will to do good to all also become spontaneous to them .... In this process of doing good to all, they are willing to give whatever they have.

21.28. Another important idea of the Gītā connected with 'sarvabhūtahitam' is : 'Take into account your capacity' (reference para 20.32). The favorite expression of the Mahābhārata to convey the same idea is 'yathā śakti' (which means 'according to your capacity). Out of the numerous instances of this that the epic provides, we present here only two. The first one is from

Vidura-Nīti (reference para 7.13) :

yathāśakti cikīrṣanti
yathāśakti ca kurvate
na kincidavamanyante
narāḥ paṇḍitabuddhayaḥ (V. 33.21)

Simple Meaning—Wise people adjust their goals and actions according to their capacity—they do not ignore anything.

21.29. For the second instance of 'yathāśakti' from the Mahābhārata, we turn to an interesting story of a mongoose given in Aśvamedha-Parva (ref. para 1.35). We first state the message of the story :

sahasraśaktiśca śataṁ
śataśaktirdaśāpi ca
dadyādapaśca yaḥ śaktyā
sarve tulyaphalāḥ smṛtāḥ (XIV. 90.96)

Simple Meaning—A person who owns a thousand giving a hundred, or a person who owns a hundred giving ten, or a person giving only a drink of water according to one's capacity—all these acts are equally praiseworthy.

Now the mongoose story in brief. When Yudhiṣṭhira ascended the throne after the defeat of the Kauravas, food was served to thousands of people who, in turn, admired his generosity. But a half-golden mongoose expressed disagreement with such admiration, and he explained this in the following words—A poor brahmin, with his wife and children, who had not eaten for many days, finally got some food. However, just then a hungry mendicant came. The poor family made a sacrifice by giving all the food to the hungry visitor. When I rolled about in the remnants of food in that house, half of my body became golden. Now, although I rolled about in the remnants of food in this vast canopy of Yudhiṣṭhira, the remaining half of my body has not become golden.

21.30. The sixth point of the framework (ref. para 20.13) is 'loksaṁgraha' (i.e. good of the world). This word occurs several times in the Mahābhārata. In fact, the prominence of this word is partly due to the support received from the Mahābhārata, and an indicator of that support is the following verse from Śānti-Parva :

lokasaṁgrahasaṁyuktaṁ
vidhātrā vihitaṁ purā

sūkṣmadharmārthaniyataṁ
satāṁ caritamuttamam (XII. 259.26)

Simple Meaning—Brahmā created the excellent lives of saints in order to explain which path of duty should be followed on critical occasions, so as to promote lokasaṁgraha.

21.31. The favorite expression of the Mahābhārata in the context of lokasaṁgraha is 'lokānāṁ hitakāmyayā' which refers to action done with a desire to contribute to the good of the worlds. It is interesting to note the similarity in meaning, between this Mahābhārata-expression and the corresponding Gītā-expression (ref. para 20.34) :

cikīrṣurlokasaṁgraham (III. 25)

The above Mahābhārata-expression or its equivalent occurs more than ten times in the epic, but we reproduce here only two of the relevant verses, one from Vana-Parva and the other from Śānti-Parva. The story from Vana-Parva is related to atrocities committed by the monster 'Dhundhu', without overpowering whom the good of the people could not be achieved. A plea to this effect was made to the King by Uttanka, a learned brahmin :

lokāḥ svasthā bhaviṣyanti
tasmin vinihite'sure
taṁ vināśaya rājendra
lokānāṁ hitakāmyayā (III. 202.26)

Simple Meaning—Uttanka said, 'O King, people will feel safe and happy only when this monster is destroyed. Therefore, please act with the desire to contribute to the good of the worlds and destroy this monster.'

21.32. The story from Śānti-Parva is related to Nārāyaṇīya dharma (reference chapter 13). The narrator of the story (Vaiśampāyana) said to Janamejaya (son of Parīkṣita, ref. para 1.14) how the creator Brahmā set in motion the process of spreading the dharma :

dharmapratiṣṭhāhetośca
manuṁ svārociṣaṁ tataḥ
adhyāpayāmāsa tadā
lokānāṁ hitakāmyayā (XII. 348.36)

Simple Meaning—Brahmā was desirous of ensuring the good of the worlds, and he knew that this was possible only through the spread of dharma ; so he taught dharma to Svārociṣa Manu.

21.33. Some aspects of environmental protection, which form a part of lokasaṁgraha (ref. para 20.35), find support in the Mahābhārata. We give below verses from three different Parvans in which the need to protect trees and wild animals, and for other socially useful measures, has been stressed. For example, we begin with Bhīṣma's advice to Yudhiṣṭhira, given in the rāja-dharma section of Śānti-Parva, concerning plants and trees :

vanaspatīn bhakṣyaphalān
na cchindyurviṣaye tava (XII. 89.1)

Simple Meaning—As a king you should ensure that plants and trees which yield edible fruits should not be cut down in your kingdom.

In Anuśāsana-Parva, Bhīṣma tells Yudhiṣṭhira how meritorious it is to dig tanks and plant trees :

evametat taḍāgasya
kīrtitaṁ phalamuttamaṁ
ata ūrdhvaṁ pravakṣyāmi
vṛkṣāṇāmavaropaṇam (XIII. 58.22)

Simple Meaning—So far I told you about the merit that one acquires by digging tanks. Now I shall tell you about the merit that one acquires by planting trees.

Vana-Parva describes how the Pāṇḍavas spent twelve years in exile, moving from one forest to another. In the following verses from that Parva, Vyāsa tells Yudhiṣṭhira that since he (i.e. Yudhiṣṭhira) is accompanied with a large number of persons, their prolonged stay in any one forest could adversely affect the plant life as well as the animals that roam in that forest :

ekatra ciravāso hi
na prītijanano bhavet ....
mṛgāṇāmupayogaśca
vīrudoṣadhisaṁkṣayaḥ
bibharṣi ca bahūn viprān (III. 36.36-37)

Simple Meaning—It will not be proper for you to stay in any one forest for a long time. Because of your needs and the food that you offer to so many other persons, animal life as well as plant life gets depleted.

21.34. The seventh point of the framework (reference para 20.13) is 'nirmamo nirahaṁkāraḥ' (i.e. going beyond mineness and egotism). The expression is used in the Gītā as a characteristic of spiritually perfect persons (ref. para 20.37). The same is done in the Mahābhārata too, on many occasions, out of which we refer to only two below. The first one occurs in the dialogue between Prahlāda and Indra narrated in Śānti-Parva. Indra is amazed at the perfection achieved by Prahlāda, who in turn explains what enabled him to become what he is :

nordhvaṁ nāvānna tiryak ca
na kvacicchakra kāmaye ....
nirmamo nirahaṁkāro
nirāśīrmuktabandhanaḥ (XII. 222.29,32)

Simple Meaning—Prahlāda said, 'O Indra, I have given up all selfish desires, be they for heaven or hell or for this world .... I have gone beyond the sense of mineness and egotism. In fact, by getting rid of desires, I have liberated myself from bondage.'

For the second instance, we recall the description of spiritually perfect persons aheady presented in para 21.27. As a continuation of that description, we have :

kāmakrodhavyapetā ye
nirmamā nirahaṁkṛtāḥ (XII. 158.29)

Simple Meaning—Bhīṣma said to Yudhiṣṭhira, 'When spiritual perfection is firmly established, a person becomes free from selfish desires and anger, and goes beyond the sense of mineness and egotism.'

21.35. The Gītā enlarged the meaning of 'nirmamo' to give the message that all capabilities are God-given and made available to an individual by society, and therefore these should be used for social purposes (ref. para 20.36). The same message is given by the Mahābhārata by means of the following words :

ṛṇavantaḥ sadā martyāḥ (XII. 269.16)

Simple Meaning—All human beings should realize that they are always indebted to society.

As to how such debt should be repaid, the Mahābhārata suggests :

trastaṁ ca vyādhitaṁ kṛśam ....
nityamāśvāsayanti te (XII. 228.41)

Simple Meaning—Those who are oppressed, weak and disabled, always need to receive sympathy and support.

21.36. The eighth point of the framework (reference para 20.13) is 'samadṛṣṭi' (i.e. even-minded vision). Through verse V. 18, the Gītā called on 'paṇḍits' (i.e. scholars) to take the lead in overcoming all discriminatory practices (ref. para 20.38). Full support to this call by the Mahābhārata is obvious because the same verse (i.e. V. 18) occurs in Śānti-Parva with just a small change (of only one word), as will be clear by looking at the following verse of the Mahābhārata :

vidyābhijanasampanne
brāhmaṇe gavi hastini
śuni caiva śvapāke ca
paṇḍitāḥ samadarśinaḥ (XII. 239.19)

Simple Meaning—Paṇḍits are those who have equal vision towards all, for example, towards a learned and high-class brahmin, a cow, an elephant, a dog or a dog-eater.

21.37. The Gītā's concept of equal vision in practice is summarized in verse VI. 32 (ref. para 20.39). The corresponding verse of the Mahābhārata occurs in Anuśāsana-Parva and is given below :

pratyākhyāne ca dāne ca
sukhaduḥkhe priyāpriye
ātmaupamyena puruṣaḥ
pramāṇamadhigacchati (XIII. 113.9)

Simple Meaning—'ātmaupamya' means seeing the same ātman in all the beings. Putting this into practice gives the following yardstick for behavior—just as I feel happy to receive a pleasant thing of my choice, and I feel unhappy in the opposite situation, everyone else will feel the same way.

Another variant of this yardstick is available in Vidura-Nīti (reference para 7.6) :

na tat parasya sandadhyāt
pratikūlaṁ yadātmanaḥ (V. 39.71)

Simple Meaning—That behavior, which is disagreeable to one's own self, should never be applied to others.

21.38. Almost parallel to samadṛṣṭi (i.e. even-minded vision towards people), the Gītā speaks of 'even-mindedness towards situations' (ref. para 20.40). An interesting expression for this variant of sameness in the Gītā is :

> *samaloṣṭāśmakāñcanaḥ* (VI.8)

i.e. one to whom a clod, a stone, and piece of gold are the same.

This expression occurs repeatedly in the Mahābhārata, in Udyoga-Parva as well as Śānti-Parva, but we give below only one verse from each of these two Parvans :

> *aroṣaṇo yaḥ samaloṣṭāśmakāñcanaḥ*
> *prahīṇaśoko gatasandhivigrahaḥ* (V. 38.6)

Simple Meaning—Characteristics of a state of perfection are : to be free from anger, to view a clod, a stone, and piece of gold as the same, to be above grief, and to rise above the concept of friendship and enmity.

> *na prahṛṣyeta lābheṣu*
> *nālābheṣu ca cintayet ....*
> *samaloṣṭāśmakāñcanaḥ* (XII. 240.31,33)

Simple Meaning—An aspirant for perfection needs to cultivate even-mindedness, e.g. not to rejoice at an acquisition, and similarly not to be down with anxiety at a loss, and to view a clod, a stone, and piece of gold as the same.

21.39. The ninth point of the framework (reference para 20.13) is 'āsurī sampat' (i.e. not to succumb to forces of evil). The Gītā warns that demoniac forces are particularly dangerous when they form a chain (reference para 20.42). The Mahābhārata has depicted the characters of Duryodhana, Śakuni, Duḥśāsana, and Karṇa as personification of four of the most dangerous vices (reference para 1.8). Pandit Ram Kinkar Upadhyay has suggested that the first three (out of these four) may be considered as forming a chain of vices, and that the fourth one (i.e. Karṇa) may be viewed separately as a bundle of four unrighteous elements packed into one. We agree with Upadhyay's suggestion and give below a summary of what he has written in Hindi, supplementing it with quotations from the Mahābhārata.

21.40. We recall from para 9.8 how Lord Kṛṣṇa warned Dhṛtarāṣṭra of the vices of Duryodhana and his associates :

aśiṣṭā gatamaryādā
lobhena hṛtacetasaḥ ....
dharmārthau pṛṣṭhataḥ kṛtvā
pracaranti nṛśaṁsavat (V. 95.9-10)

Simple Meaning—Their thinking is vitiated by excessive greed (lobha), and they have disregarded all norms of civilized conduct (gatamaryādā).... They have set aside dharma (righteousness) and artha (legitimate acquisition of wealth), and are behaving like cruel people (nṛśaṁsa).

And this is how Upadhyay describes the chain of vices formed by the gang of three :

"Duryodhana is an embodiment of lobha (greed) because he refused to give even an inch of land to the Pāṇḍavas. Duḥśāsana is an embodiment of cruelty (nṛśaṁsa) because he tried to drag Draupadī's dress off her person. Śakuni is an embodiment of dishonesty and unrighteousness (aśiṣṭā gatamaryādā) because he won the game of dice by foul means. Thus this wicked trio constituted a clearly visible chain or gang of demoniac forces who were responsible for the Mahābhārata war."[1]

21.41. A brief reference to Karṇa's evil deeds has already been made by us in para 1.8. Bhīṣma warned Duryodhana in Udyoga-Parva :

paruṣaḥ katthano nīcaḥ
karṇo vaikartanastava
mantrī netā ca bandhuśca
mānī cātyantamucchritaḥ (V. 168.4)

Simple Meaning—Bhīṣma said to Duryodhana, 'O king, this cruel, mean and vile braggart, Karṇa, who is your counsellor, guide and friend, is full of arrogance because you have given him too high a position of which he is not worthy.'

Upadhyay explains how Karṇa should be viewed as a bundle of four unrighteous elements packed into one :

"Ignorance was the first problem with Karṇa. For a long time, he did not even know that he was the son of Kuntī. Lord Kṛṣṇa removed this ignorance of Karṇa, but the latter said that he had already joined hands with Duryodhana, the enemy of the Pāṇḍavas.

"Karṇa's second problem was arrogance. Because of that he

picked up a quarrel with Bhīṣma and declared that, so long as Bhīṣma was fighting, he (i.e. Karṇa) would not participate in the war.

The third problem with Karṇa was falsehood. He went to Paraśurāma and became his disciple by telling him a lie (that he i.e. Karṇa was a brahmin). But Karṇa's lie was ultimately detected. Paraśurāma in his anger pronounced this curse on Karṇa, 'Since you deceived your guru, the weapon you have learnt shall fail you at the fated moment. You will be unable to recall the mantra when your hour comes.'

"The fourth problem with Karṇa was impropriety. He joined the Kauravas in conspiracies, but during his last battle, he appealed to Arjuna to observe dharma. Lord Kṛṣṇa told him that an appeal to dharma can be made only by one who had himself observed it."[2]

21.42. The Mahābhārata's condemnation of vices is not confined to Kauravas. There are strong words against gambling (dyūta) too, the vice from which Yudhiṣṭhira suffered. Lord Kṛṣṇa himself told Yudhiṣṭhira in Vana-Parva :

> *āgaccheyamahaṁ dyūtaṁ ....*
> *bahūn doṣān pradarśayan ....*
> *vīrasenasuto yaistu*
> *rājyāt prabhraṁśitaḥ purā* (III. 13.2, 5)

> ***Simple Meaning***—Kṛṣṇa said, 'I wish I had come to the hall where gambling took place .... Then I would have told everyone about the great destruction that gambling causes .... giving the example of King Nala who lost his kingdom due to gambling.'

We should mention that the story of Nala was later told to Yudhiṣṭhira by Bṛhadaśva in Vana-Parva itself. We would have liked to include a summary of that story in this book, but had to decide against it, in the interest of not exceeding the planned size of the book.[3]

21.43. In para 21.41, we referred to 'arrogance' as a serious problem in the context of Karṇa. The Mahābhārata contains many stories condemning this vice, which show that an attitude of arrogance could arise out of prosperity or learning or beauty or bravery or even tapas (austerity). We have included summaries of five of these stories in different chapters of Part II of this book, the specific references being as follows :

(a) For arrogance arising out of prosperity (para 2.10)
(b) For arrogance arising out of learning (para 4.4)
(c) For arrogance arising out of beauty (para 19.8)
(d) For arrogance arising out of bravery (para 19.10)
(e) For arrogance arising out of tapas (para 12.3)

21.44. In para 21.40, we referred to 'nṛśaṁsa' (i.e. cruel behavior) of Duḥśāsana. This vice is repeatedly condemned in the Mahābhārata, irrespective of the question as to who behaves in a cruel manner. Perhaps the most detailed analysis of this vice was made by Ṛṣi Sanat-Sujāta who said to Dhṛtarāṣṭra (reference para 8.10)—

nṛśāṁsāni daśatri rājan (V. 43.15)

Simple Meaning—O king, cruel behavior includes as many as thirteen vices.

Lack of compassion (i.e. nirdayatā) is one of these thirteen, which is highlighted by Yudhiṣṭhira in his dialogue with Yakṣa (ref. para 6.28) :

asādhurnirdayaḥ smṛtaḥ (III. 313.92)

Simple Meaning—Lack of compassion is the main characteristic of a bad man.

The Mahābhārata condemns lack of compassion, not only towards human beings but also towards animals (ref. chapter 17).

Our final observation on the topic of vices relates to Gītā verse XVI. 21, which warns against kāma (selfish desire), krodha (anger) and lobha (greed), and which appears as such in Vidura-Nīti (ref. chapter 7) :

trividhaṁ narakasyedaṁ
dvāraṁ naśanamātmanaḥ
kāmaḥ krodhastathā lobhas
tasmādetat trayaṁ tyajet (V. 33.66)

Simple Meaning—The gateway of the hell leading to the ruin of the soul is threefold—kāma, krodha, lobha—so one should abandon these three vices in particular.[4]

21.45. The tenth (and the final) point of the framework (ref.

para 20.13) is 'daivī sampat' (i.e. promote virtues). This is a favorite topic of the Gītā (ref. para 20.44) and of the Mahābhārata too. However, since a selective approach constitutes the basis of this book, we shall concentrate our attention on five virtues, viz. abhaya (fearlessness), ahiṁsā (non-violence), ānṛśaṁsya (absence of cruelty), adroha (absence of ill-will), and satya (truth).

21.46. According to the Gītā (ref. para 20.45), abhaya (fearlessness) occupies the first place in 'daivī sampat'. The Mahābhārata has explained that a practitioner of this virtue not only becomes free from fear himself (or herself), but also makes others free from fear. In fact, Tulādhāra (ref. chapter 12) says :

loke yaḥ sarvabhūtebhyo
dadātyabhayadakṣiṇāṁ
sa sarvayajñairījānaḥ
prāpnotyabhayadakṣiṇām (XII. 262.29)

Simple Meaning—A person who makes all others free from fear earns merit as if he has performed all the yajñas, and in return, all other people make him free from fear too.

21.47. The second virtue in our list of five is ahiṁsā (non-violence). Although the great war between the Pāṇḍavas and the Kauravas is the basic story of the Mahābhārata, the virtue that is glorified in its dialogues is ahiṁsā. This apparent inconsistency between the subject-matter and the message of the epic prompted Mahatma Gandhi to make the following observations (ref. para 1.17):

"The author of the Mahābhārata has not established the necessity of physical warfare; on the contrary he has proved its futility. He has made the victors shed tears of sorrow and repentance, and has left them nothing but a legacy of miseries ....

"It may be freely admitted that the Gītā (which is the crown of the Mahābhārata) was not written to establish ahiṁsā. It was an accepted and primary duty even before the Gītā age ....

"But if the Gītā believed in ahiṁsā or it was included in desirelessness, why did the author take a war-like illustration? When the Gītā was written, although people believed in ahiṁsā, wars were not only not taboo, but nobody observed the contradiction between them and ahiṁsā."[5]

21.48. Out of a large number of verses that glorify ahiṁsā in the Mahābhārata, we present here only two. The first one from Anuśāsana-Parva is quoted most frequently :

ahiṁsā paramo dharmas
tathāhiṁsā paraṁ tapaḥ
ahiṁsā paramaṁ satyaṁ
yato dharmaḥ pravartate (XIII. 115.23)

Simple Meaning—Ahiṁsā is the greatest dharma (virtue), ahiṁsā is the greatest tapas (austerity), ahiṁsā is the greatest satya (truth), ahiṁsā is the basic support of all dharma.

The second verse is from Sānti-Parva; it declares ahiṁsā as that element of dharma which can be called self-sufficient in terms of achieving what is good :

ahiṁsā sakalo dharmo
hiṁsādharmastathāhitaḥ (XII. 272.20)

Simple Meaning—Ahiṁsā can be considered as a complete and self-sufficient dharma. On the other hand, hiṁsā (violence) is the negation of dharma and is sure to be an obstacle in the path of 'good'.

21.49. The third virtue in our list of five is 'ānṛśaṁsya' (absence of cruelty). In our opinion, this expression is a useful addition, introduced by the Mahābhārata, to the terminology of the Gītā in the field of virtues. Glorification of 'ānṛśaṁsya' occurs repeatedly in the Mahābhārata, spread over several Parvans, but the most effective instances of the use of this expression are to be found in the context of the tests of Yudhiṣṭhira conducted by Dharmarāja (ref. chapters 6 and 19). We recall here relevant parts of only three verses already quoted in these two chapters :

ānṛśaṁsyaṁ paro dharmaḥ (III. 313.76)

Simple Meaning—Yudhiṣṭhira (replying to Yakṣa) said, 'ānṛśaṁsya (absence of cruelty) is the highest dharma.

tasya te'rthācca kāmācca
ānṛśaṁsyaṁ paraṁ mataṁ
tasmāt te bhrātaraḥ sarve
jīvantu bharatarṣabha (III. 313.133)

Simple Meaning—Yakṣa said to Yudhiṣṭhira, 'You have demonstrated your highest devotion to 'ānṛśaṁsya'—even higher than to wealth and to psychological value. Therefore, I grant you a boon, viz. may all your brothers come back to life.'

ayaṁ śvā bhūtabhavyeśa
bhakto māṁ nityameva ha
sa gaccheta mayā sārdhaṁ
ānṛśaṁsyā hi me matiḥ (XVII. 3.7)

Simple Meaning—Yudhiṣṭhira said to Indra, 'O Lord of the past and the present, this dog is a great devotee of mine. He has been walking with me, so please allow that he may accompany me to heaven. In my opinion, ānṛśaṁsya (absence of cruelty) is most important.'

21.50. The fourth virtue in our list of five is 'adroha' (absence of ill-will). The importance attached to 'adroha' in the Mahābhārata has been highlighted by B.A. van Nooten.[6] Out of the many verses of the epic that glorify 'adroha', we present here only two, one from the story of Sāvitrī (reference chapter 5) and the other from Tulādhāra-Jājali dialogue (ref. chapter 12) :

adrohaḥ sarvabhūteṣu
karmaṇā manasā girā
anugrahaśca dānaṁ ca
satāṁ dharmaḥ sanātanaḥ (III. 297.35)

Simple Meaning—Savitrī said to Yama, 'Absence of ill-will in thought, word or deed, supplemented with goodwill and charity is the eternal dharma of the righteous.'

adroheṇaiva bhūtānāṁ
alpadroheṇa vā punaḥ
yā vṛttiḥ sa paro dharmas
tena jīvāmi jājale (XII. 262.6)

Simple Meaning—Tulādhāra said to Jājali, 'I not only have knowledge of dharma, but I also try to live according to it. For example, my goal is to have no ill-will towards any being, but if I am unable to achieve that goal, then minimization of ill-will becomes my objective. I believe that such an approach leads me to the highest level of practicable dharma.'

21.51. The fifth (and the final) virtue in our list is 'satya' (truth). There is extensive coverage of this virtue in the Mahābhārata, and the selected verses that we present will reveal not only the epic's support to the practice of 'satya' but also an attempt to introduce a new definition thereof. To begin with, we have a verse from Śānti-Parva which glorifies satya :

nāsti satyāt paro dharmo
nānṛtāt pātakaṁ paraṁ
sthitirhi satyaṁ dharmasya
tasmāt satyaṁ na lopayet (XII. 162.24)

Simple Meaning—There is no dharma higher than satya. There is no sin lower than untruth. Satya constitutes the foundation of dharma. Therefore there should be no turning away from satya.

21.52. Verse XVII. 15 of the Gītā says that right speech should not only be truthful, but should have other desirable characteristics too :

anudvegakaraṁ vākyaṁ
satyaṁ priyahitaṁ ca yat (XVII. 15)

Simple Meaning—Right speech gives no offence, is truthful, pleasant and beneficial.

Vidura-Nīti (ref. chapter 7) attempts to provide a graded value-system associated with these characteristics of speech (ref. para 7.8) :

avyāhṛtaṁ vyāhṛtācchreya āhuḥ
satyaṁ vaded vyāhṛtaṁ tad dvitīyaṁ
priyaṁ vaded vyāhṛtaṁ tat tṛtīyaṁ
dharmaṁ vaded vyāhṛtaṁ taccaturtham (V. 36.12)

Simple Meaning—There are occasions when 'not to speak at all' is better than speaking ; if speak you must, then it is better to say what is true; going further, it is better to say what is pleasant; going still further, it is better to say what is in accordance with dharma (i.e. righteousness).

21.53. Leaving aside the consideration of 'priyaṁ' (i.e. pleasant), what do the Gītā and the Mahābhārata say about the (relative) importance of 'hitaṁ' (i.e. good or beneficial)? First, we have parts of two verses from the Gītā :

vakṣyāmi hitakāmyayā (X. 1)

(i.e. I shall speak with the desire to do 'hitaṁ').

vakṣyāmi te hitaṁ (XVIII. 64)

(i.e. I shall speak what is 'hitaṁ' for you).

Next, we have the following verse from Śānti-Parva :

satyasya vacanaṁ śreyaḥ
satyādapi hitaṁ vadet
yad bhūtahitamatyantaṁ
etat satyaṁ mataṁ mama (XII. 329.13)

Simple Meaning—It is good to say what is true, but it is even better to say what will do 'hitaṁ' (good). In my opinion, a decision on what is true (under difficult circumstances) should be made by sticking to that course of action (or speech) which leads to the highest good of beings.

We should mention that the words :

'yad bhūtahitamatyantaṁ'

which occur in this verse, are repeated several times in the Mahābhārata (e.g. in Vyādha-Gītā—ref. para 4.9). This can be viewed as the Mahābhārata's attempt to introduce a new definition of 'satya', or rather a new priority scale in which 'sarva-hitaṁ' (good of all) is at the top and even 'satya' comes next (if there is a conflict between the two).

21.54. In conclusion we can say that all the ten points of the framework (ref. para 20.13), which summarize the Gītā's call for the good of all, are strongly supported by the Mahābhārata. Even on the last point (raised in the preceding para), the epic demonstrates its willingness to dilute the definition of satya (truth) rather than weaken its support to the cause of 'sarvabhūtahitaṁ' (i.e. the good of all).

21.55. A similar conclusion has been arrived at by Arvind Sharma on the basis of his analysis of the story of Kauśika from Karṇa-Parva :

"The Mahābhārata mentions an ascetic, Kauśika by name, who was known for his veracity, but finally had to go to hell under the following circumstances. While he was engaged in penance in the forest, some robbers came upon him in hot pursuit of their would-be victims.

Kauśika, when asked, truthfully pointed out the direction in which they had gone. The robbers caught up with their intended victims and killed them and the bad karma of the killing fell to Kauśika's share. So in the end Kauśika was thrown into hell. This story was narrated to Arjuna by Kṛṣṇa as a warning against a purely formal approach to ethics. I would like to use it here to illustrate the point how general good (lokasaṁgraha) may require the sacrifice of personal morality, narrowly conceived."[7]

Notes

PART ONE

Chapter 1

1. Mahadev Desai, *The Gospel of Selfless Action or The Gita according to Gandhi.* Navajivan Publishing House, Ahmedabad, 1977, p.128.
2. Kisari Mohan Ganguli, *The Mahabharata of Krishna-Dwaipayana Vyasa* (four volumes). Munshiram Manoharlal, New Delhi, 2000, Vol.I, Ādi-Parva, pp.282-3.
3. *Ibid.*, Vol.II, Droṇa Parva, p.446.
4. *Ibid.*, Vol.II, Droṇa Parva, p.104.
5. Mahadev Desai, *The Gospel of Selfless Action or The Gita according to Gandhi,* op.cit., pp. 128-133.
6. Barend A.van Nooten, *The Mahābhārata attributed to Kṛṣṇa Dvaipāyana Vyāsa.* Twayne Publishers, New York, 1971, p.40.
7. V.S. Sukthankar et al (eds.), *Mahābhārata* (Critical Edition), nineteen volumes. Bhandarkar Oriental Research Institute, Poona, 1933-1959.

PART TWO

Chapter 2

1. Barend A.van Nooten, *The Mahābhārata attributed to Kṛṣṇa Dvaipāyana Vyāsa,* op.cit., p.7
2. For more details, please see Amal Bhakta, *Mystical stories from the Mahābhārata: Twenty Timeless Lessons in Wisdom and Virtue.* Torchlight Publishing, 2000, pp. 55-61.
3. For more details, please see A.Ryder (tr.), *Shakuntala and other Writings of Kalidasa.* Evaryman, London, 1912.
4. For more details, please see C. Rajagopalachari, *Mahābhārata,* Bharatiya Vidya Bhavan, Bombay, 1970, pp. 180-183.

5. For more details, please see C. Rajagopalachari, *Mahābhārata, Ibid.*, pp. 36-38.

Chapter 3

1. For more details, please see Klaus K. Klostermaier, *Hinduism: A Short History*. One World, Oxford, 2000, pp.58-68.

Chapter 4

1. Swami Vivekananda, *Complete Works* (eight volumes). Advaita Ashrama, Calcutta, fourteenth edition, 1972, vol.I, pp.25-118.

Chapter 5

1. Vidyut Aklujkar, "*Savitri: Old and New*", in Arvind Sharma (ed.), *Essays on the Mahābhārata*, E.J. Brill, Laiden, 1991, pp. 324-333.
2. For more details, please see William Buck, *Mahābhārata*, Meridian and University of California, Berkeley, 1987, pp. 112-117.
3. Vidyut Aklujkar, "*Savitri: Old and New*", in Arvind Sharma (ed.), *Essays on the Mahābhārata*, op.cit., p.326

Chapter 6

1. Barend A.van Nooten, *The Mahābhārata attributed to Kṛṣṇa Dvaipāyana Vyāsa*, op.cit., p.62.
2. Arvind Sharma expresses "*unhesitating choice*" for the second meaning. Please see his book *Hinduism for Our Times*, Oxford University Press, Delhi, 1996, p.20.

Chapter 7

1. For more details, please see C. Rajagopalachari, *Mahābhārata*, op.cit. pp. 38-40.

Chapter 8

1. For more details, please see Nicholas Sutton, *Religious Doctrines in the Mahābhārata*, Motilal Banarsidass, Delhi, 2000, pp. 99 and 109.

Chapter 9

1. For more details, please see *Vanamali, The Play of God: Visions of*

the Life of Krishna, Blue Dove Press, San Diago, 1996, pp.221-236.

Chapter 10

1. Barend A.van Nooten traces the journey of the Mahābhārata story of Man in the Well, from the middle Ages to Leo Tolstoy. Please see his book, *The Mahābhārata attributed to Kṛṣṇa Dvaipāyana Vyāsa*, op.cit., p.133.
2. *Ibid.*, pp. 110-111.

Chapter 11

1. B.G. Tilak, *Gita Rahasya*. Tilak Brothers, Poona, sixth edition, 1986, p.4.
2. *Ibid.*, p.4.
3. Kisari Mohan Ganguli, *The Mahabharata of Krishna-Dvaipayana Vyasa*, op.cit., Vol.III, Śānti Parva (Part II), p.14.

Chapter 12

1. Nicholas Sutton, *Religious Doctrines in the Mahābhārata*, op.cit., p.322.
2. For comments on the special significance of this story, please see Vinoba (Bhave), *Talks on the Gita*, Sarva Seva Sangh Prakashan, Varanasi, 1978, p.93.

Chapter 13

1. For more details, please see K.N. Upadhyaya, *Early Buddhism and the Bhagavad-Gita*, Motilal Banarsidass, Delhi, 1971, pp.138-145.

Chapter 14

1. For comments on the special significance of this dialogue, please see Vinoba (Bhave), *Talks on the Gita*, op. cit., p.93.

Chapter 15

1. Nicholas Sutton, *Religious Doctrines in the Mahābhārata*, op.cit., p.322.

Chapter 16

1. For more details, please see Vinoba (Bhave), *Talks on the Gita*, op.cit., pp. 192-196.

Chapter 17

1. For more details, please see Vinoba (Bhave), *Talks on the Gita*, op.cit., pp. 192-196.

Chapter 18

1. For more details, please see Arvind Sharma, *The Hindu Gita: Ancient and Classical Interpretations of the Bhagavad-Gita*. Open Court, La Salle, Illinois, 1986, pp. 1-11.

Chapter 19

1. For more details, please see Elizabeth Seeger, *The Five Sons of King Pandu: The Story of the Mahābhārata*. William R. Scott, Inc., New York, 1967, pp.326-340.

PART THREE

Chapter 20

1. Satya P. Agarwal, *The Gita and Tulasi-Ramayana: Their Common Call for the Good of All*, Motilal Banarsidass, Delhi, 2000, pp. 23-30. For more details, please see earlier publications of the same author, particularly. *The Social Role of the Gita: How & Why*, 1993, and *The Social Message of the Gita: Symbolized as Lokasaṁgraha*, 1995.
2. Swami Gambhirananda (translator), *Bhagavad-Gita* (with the commentary of Shankaracharya), Advaita Ashram, Calcutta, 1984, p.472.
3. S. Radhakrishnan, *The Bhagavad-Gita*, Harper and Row, New York, 1973, pp. 75-76.
4. *Ibid.*, p.188.
5. *Ibid.* p.135.
6. D.S. Sarma, *"The Path of Yoga in the Gita"*, in the Cultural Heritage of India, Vol.III, H. Bhattacharya, ed., The Ramakrishna Mission Institute of Culture, Calcutta, 1983, p.403.

7. M.K. Gandhi, *The Bhagavad-Gita,* Orient Paperbacks, New Delhi, no date, pp. 79-80.
8. B.G. Tilak, *Gita Rahasya,* op.cit., pp. 456-466.
9. Sri Aurobindo, *Essays on the Gita,* Sri Aurobindo Ashram, Pondicherry, 1989, p.128.
10. Mahadev Desai, *The Gospel of Selfless Action,* op.cit., p.94.
11. Swami Vivekananda, *Complete Works,* op.cit., Vol.I, pp.110-118.

Chapter 21

1. Ram Kinkar Upadhyay, *A comparative Study of Manas and Gita* (in Hindi), Tulsi Tattvanusandhan Kendra, Kanpur, 1987, pp.82-83.
2. *Ibid.* pp. 143-152.
3. For the story of Nala, please see Amal Bhakta, *Mystical stories from the Mahābhārata,* op.cit., pp. 81-117.
4. For more details, please see Georg Feuerstein, *Sacred Paths: Essays on Wisdom, Love and Mystical Realization,* Larson Publications, Burdett N.Y., 1991, pp. 248-249.
5. Mahadev Desai, *The Gospel of Selfless Action or The Gita according to Gandhi,* op.cit., pp.128-133.
6. Barend A.van Nooten, *The Mahābhārata attributed to Kṛṣṇa - Dvaipāyana Vyāsa,* op.cit., p.117.
7. Arvind Sharma, *Hinduism for our Times,* op.cit., p.28.

Index

References are to paragraph numbers, not to pages.